THE PRACTITIONER'S HANDBOOK

RELATED BOOKS PUBLISHED BY SAGE

A Beginner's Guide to Training in Counselling & Psychotherapy
Edited by Robert Bor and Stephen Palmer

The Trainee Handbook, second edition
Edited by Robert Bor and Mary Watts

THE PRACTITIONER'S HANDBOOK

A Guide for Counsellors, Psychotherapists and Counselling Psychologists

EDITED BY

Stephen Palmer and Robert Bor

Los Angeles • London • New Delhi • Singapore

To my mother and father.
To my colleagues who have made this book possible.

Stephen Palmer

To all the professional colleagues with whom I have had the privilege to work who have enriched my practice, and to my family.

Robert Bor

CONTENTS

THE EDITORS

PROFESSOR STEPHEN PALMER PhD CPsychol CSci FBACP FRSA
Professor Stephen Palmer PhD is Founder Director of the Centre for Stress Management and the Centre for Coaching London. He is an honorary professor of psychology at City University and director of their Coaching Psychology Unit and Visiting Professor of Work Based Learning and Stress Management at NCWBLP, Middlesex University. He is a Chartered Psychologist and Chartered Scientist, a UKCP registered psychotherapist and a certified supervisor of Rational Emotional Behaviour Therapy.

Currently he is President of the Association for Coaching, Honorary Vice President of the Institute of Health Promotion and Education, Honorary Vice President of the International Stress Management Association (UK). He was the first Chair of the British Psychological Society Special Group in Coaching Psychology and former Chair of the Scientific Awards Committee of the British Psychological Society's Division of Counselling Psychology. He was an academic consultant for the Surrey Police Deepcut Investigation Final Report and was a specialist advisor to the House of Commons Defence Select Committee on the Duty of Care Inquiry 2004–2005.

He is the UK Coordinating Editor of *International Coaching Psychology Review*, Editor of *International Journal of Health Promotion and Education*, Co-editor of *Rational Emotive Behaviour Therapist*, Consultant Editor of *Counselling Psychology Review* and *The Coaching Psychologist* and former Co-editor of the Counselling Psychology Section of *Psychology and Psychotherapy: Theory, Research and Practice*. He has authored or edited over 30 books, including *Introduction to Counselling and Psychotherapy: The Essential Guide* (Sage, 2000). The book series he edits includes *Stress Counselling* (Sage) and *Brief Therapies* (Sage).

He received the Annual Counselling Psychology Award for outstanding professional and scientific contribution to counselling psychology in Britain for 2000 from the British Psychological Society, Division of Counselling Psychology. In 2004, he received an achievement award from the Association for Rational Emotive Behaviour Therapy. His interests include jazz, astronomy, walking, writing and art.

PROFESSOR ROBERT BOR DPhil CPsychol CSci FBPsS UKCP Reg FRAeS
Professor Robert Bor is Consultant Lead Clinical Psychologist in the Medical Specialities Directorate (Infectious Diseases) at the Royal Free

Hospital, London. He is a Chartered Clinical, Counselling and Health Psychologist, a Chartered Scientist, as well as a Fellow of the British Psychological Society. He is also a UKCP Registered Family Therapist.

He completed his specialist systemic training at the Tavistock Clinic, London, and is a clinical member of the Institute of Family Therapy, London, and a member of the UK Association for Family Therapy, The American Association for Marital & Family Therapy, American Psychological Association and American Family Therapy Academy.

He is extensively involved in the training and supervision of practitioner psychologists and psychotherapists, and has previously developed and also co-directed the postgraduate counselling psychology training programmes at City University and London Metropolitan University. He has published more than 20 books and 130 academic papers in peer-reviewed journals. He serves on the editorial board of numerous academic journals. He also serves on the Fellowships Committee of the British Psychological Society and is past Lead Assessor for Continuing Professional Development within the Division of Counselling Psychology.

In his NHS and private practice, he works with individuals, couples and families using cognitive behavioural and systemic therapies within a time-limited framework. One of his specialisms is in helping people to cope with acute or chronic illness. In addition to his work with adults, he is a specialist in child, adolescent and family psychology and is the consultant psychologist to three schools, St. Paul's School, the Royal Ballet School and JFS. He also consults to the London Oncology Clinic as well as the London Clinic, both in Harley Street.

He is an aviation clinical psychologist with expertise in passenger and crew behaviour. Robert provides a specialist consultation and assessment service to leading airlines for aircrew who suffer emotional problems at the Royal Free Travel Health Clinic in London. He is a Fellow of the Royal Aeronautical Society, holds the Freedom of the City of London and is a Liveryman of the Guild of Air Pilots and Air Navigators, and is also a Member of the Aerospace Medical Society.

He is a past recipient of the BPS Division of Counselling Psychology Award for Outstanding Scientific Achievement. Robert is a Churchill Fellow. His interests include flying (he has a pilot's licence), collecting Ndebele tribal art and travel.

THE CONTRIBUTORS

Sarah Corrie is an Associate of the Professional Development Foundation and the University of London. She trained as a clinical psychologist and, in addition to running her own practice, is a member of British Actors Equity and the Imperial Society of Teachers of Dancing. She is also a freelance writer, trainer and lecturer.

Berni Curwen works at the Primary Care Counselling and Psychology Department, Dartford, Kent, as a UKCP Registered and BABCP Accredited Psychotherapist (CBT). She is co-author of *Brief Cognitive Behaviour Therapy* (with Palmer and Ruddell).

Alan Frankland is a Consultant Counselling Psychologist in independent practice (APSI in Nottingham), and with North East London Mental Health Trust. As part of his current work he contributes to the Counselling Psychology programmes at the Universities of Surrey, Wolverhampton and East London. He has been engaged in the world of counselling and psychotherapy for over 30 years having originally trained in marriage guidance in the 1970s at the beginning of an academic career in which he taught psychology to a wide variety of undergraduate and professional students before moving on to teach counselling and psychotherapy and heading up the Division of Counselling and Psychotherapy at Nottingham Trent University, developing with colleagues there a suite of courses from Foundation to Masters level when he was also accredited by BACP as a counsellor and trainer.

Nicola Hurton (BSc, MSc) is an Occupational Psychologist who specialises in supporting individuals' career development. She has also worked on a large number of consultancy and research projects in areas such as organisation and management development, recruitment and leadership coaching. She is a project assessor for Professional Development Foundation/Middlesex University Masters Programmes, and also currently holds a part-time research post at Goldsmiths, University of London.

Peter Jenkins is a Senior Lecturer in Counselling at Salford University, a BACP accredited counsellor trainer and member of the UKCP Ethics Committee. He has written widely on legal aspects of counselling and psychotherapy, including *Therapy with Children*, as co-author with Debbie

Daniels (Sage, 2000), *Legal Issues in Counselling and Psychotherapy*, as editor (Sage, 2002), and *Counselling, Psychotherapy and the Law* (Second edition, Sage, 2007).

Colin Lago was Director of the Counselling Service at the University of Sheffield from 1987 to 2003. He now works as an independent counsellor, trainer, supervisor and consultant. Trained initially as an engineer, Colin went on to become a full-time youth worker in London and then a teacher in Jamaica. He is a Fellow of BACP, an accredited counsellor and trainer and UKRC registered practitioner. Deeply committed to 'transcultural concerns' he has had articles, videos and books published on the subject.

Professor David A. Lane (PhD, C.Psychol, FBPsS, FCIPD) is Research Director of the International Centre for the Study of Coaching at Middlesex University and contributes to leading edge research in coaching as well as supervising leading coaches undertaking doctoral research with the centre. He is Chair of the British Psychological Society Register of Psychologists Specialising in Psychotherapy and convenes the Psychotherapy Group of the European Federation of Psychologists Associations. His work with the European Mentoring and Coaching Council has been concerned with codes of conduct and standards and kite marking of coach training. Working with the Worldwide Association of Business Coaches he has researched and developed the standards for the Certified Master Business Coach award. He is a member of the steering group for the Global Convention on Coaching. His contributions to counselling psychology led to the senior award of the BPS for 'outstanding scientific contribution'.

Del Loewenthal is Professor of Psychotherapy and Counselling and Director of the Centre for Therapeutic Education at Roehampton University, UK, where he also convenes the Psych Ds in counselling psychology and psychotherapy. He is an existential-analytic psychotherapist and chartered counselling psychologist. He is editor of the *European Journal of Psychotherapy and Counselling* (Routledge).

Dina B. Lubin is a therapist in the Department of Family and Community Medicine at St. Michael's Hospital in Toronto, Canada. She specialises in working with addicted populations. Ms. Lubin holds an MA in Counselling Psychology from Boston College and a BA in Psychology from McGill University.

Gladeana McMahon is Fellow and Vice President of the Association for Coaching, Fellow of the British Association for Counselling and

Psychotherapy, Institute of Management Studies and Royal Society of Arts. She is an Accredited Counsellor and cognitive-behavioural psychotherapist.

Riva Miller is a UKCP Registered Systemic Family Therapist with a background in medical social work. She has worked for many years with people with a range of chronic and acute medical conditions. She trained as a family therapist at the Tavistock Clinic, the Institute of Family Therapy and with the Milan Associates in Italy. She has held positions as manager, practitioner, supervisor, teacher and consultant within several organisations. She currently works as a family therapist in the Haemophilia Centre at the Royal Free Hospital, London. She is Honorary Senior Lecturer at the Royal Free and University College School of Medicine and has taught at the Metropolitan University. Since 1985 she has been a consultant to the National Blood and Tissue Service and has acted as an advisor for the World Health Organisation. She currently has a private practice dealing with a range of issues for individuals, couples and families. Supervision for others and herself has been integral to her practice over the years.

Roy Moodley (PhD) is an Associate Professor in Counselling Psychology at the Ontario Institute for Studies in Education at the University of Toronto. Research and publication interests include traditional and cultural healing; multicultural and diversity counselling; race, culture and ethnicity in psychotherapy; and masculinities. Roy co-edited *Transforming Managers: Gendering Change in the Public Sector* (UCL Press/Taylor and Francis, 1999), *Carl Rogers Counsels a Black Client: Race and Culture in Person-Centred Counselling* (PCCS Books, 2004), *Integrating Traditional Healing Practices into Counseling and Psychotherapy* (Sage: California, 2005) and *Race, Culture and Psychotherapy: Critical Perspectives in Multicultural Practice* (Routledge, 2006).

Dr. David G. Purves is a Principal Lecturer in Counselling Psychology at London Metropolitan University. He is also a Consultant Psychologist in the Berkshire Traumatic Stress Service. Originally trained as a professional diver he spent many years in that industry before returning to Oxford University to receive a doctorate in experimental psychology followed by qualifications in counselling psychology and psychotherapy. He now divides his time between work in the NHS, private practice and lecturing and research. He has recently authored the electronic self-help programme *Blues Begone* for the treatment of depression and anxiety. Dr. Purves has spoken and run workshops on the treatment of PTSD both nationally and internationally.

Dr. Neha Pandit (C.Psychol) is a Principal Lecturer in Psychology at London Metropolitan University, with a special interest in cognitive-behavioural theory and multicultural issues in psychotherapy. She is currently the Course Leader for the MSc CBT programme, and is also in private practice. She holds a PhD in Counselling Psychology, and completed her clinical training in the Department of Psychiatry at the University of Pennsylvania in Philadelphia, Pennsylvania.

Peter Ruddell is the Clinical Director of the Centre for Stress Management and Training Director of the Centre for Coaching, London, UK. He is a UKCP Registered Psychotherapist (CBT and REBT) and a Director of the Association for Rational Emotive Behaviour Therapy. He is co-author of *Brief Cognitive Behaviour Therapy* (with Curwen and Palmer) and Commissioning Editor of *Stress News*.

Kasia Szymanska is a Chartered Psychologist, an Associate Fellow of the British Psychological Society and BABCP accredited psychotherapist. She is an Associate Director of the Centre for Stress Management where she runs training programmes in Post Traumatic Stress Disorder and is the Director of Distance Learning at the Centre for Coaching. Kasia also has a private practice in central and west London as a psychologist and a trainer.

Annette Fillery-Travis is a coach, researcher and academic. After authoring a substantial number of research publications in the natural sciences she became fascinated by how such knowledge was then used by professionals in the development of their expertise. She has since supervised professional masters and doctorate students from a range of backgrounds and has a passion for practitioner research and enquiry.

Yvonne Walsh is a Chartered Counselling Psychologist and works as a Consultant Counselling Psychologist in a large NHS mental health trust as Professional Lead for Counselling Psychology and providing a Clinical Lead for Complex Needs: Mental Health and Substance Misuse for the Trust. She has had the role of Lead for Practice on the Executive Committee of the Division of Counselling Psychology and is an examiner on the division's independent route for qualification as a counselling psychologist. Yvonne worked as a visiting lecturer at City University for over five years where she taught both psychology undergraduates and postgraduate students working towards their accreditation as Chartered Counselling Psychologists. She has written and co-authored a number of papers and has guest edited two issues of *Counselling Psychology Review*.

Christine Wilding is a Chartered MCIPD human resource practitioner and a BACP accredited psychotherapist. She works as a CBT therapist and also as a professional coach and inter-personal skills trainer. She is co-author with Stephen Palmer of *Moody to Mellow* and *Zero to Hero* from Hodder's Get a Life! self-help series as well as *Teach Yourself Emotional Intelligence*, to be published in November 2007.

David Winter is Professor of Clinical Psychology and Programme Director of the Doctorate in Clinical Psychology at the University of Hertfordshire. He is Head of Clinical Psychology Services for Barnet in Barnet, Enfield and Haringey Mental Health NHS Trust. His extensive publications on personal construct psychology and psychotherapy research include *Personal Construct Psychology in Clinical Practice* (Routledge, 1992), *Personal Construct Psychotherapy* (with Linda Viney, Whurr/Wiley, 2005), and *What is Psychotherapeutic Research?* (with Del Loewenthal, Karnac, 2006).

FOREWORD

Although professional training in counselling and psychotherapy have developed enormously over the past couple of decades, arming those in the psychological and talking therapies with outstanding professional skills, there is still a need for practitioners to develop the skills of running a business.

This handbook for practitioners systematically helps to explore most of the issues confronted in the 'business' of working with clients. It highlights the importance of continued professional development (which in any case is now a requirement of many professional bodies), of understanding the variety of assessment measures and tools in the marketplace, of managing a client base, of dealing with issues in private practice, of being able to minimise the communication problems which can occur between professionals, of understanding the importance of research and how to conceptualise it and of being able to communicate through lectures and other media as part of your overall business. This is a practical guide which enables practitioners in the psychological therapies to access relevant skills from leading experts in their field.

This book is a valuable supplement to our professional library, in our quest to help support and manage our professional practice in providing the best service to our clients.

Cary L. Cooper, CBE, is Professor of Organisational Psychology and Health at Lancaster University, and President of the British Association of Counselling and Psychotherapy.

Professor Cary L. Cooper, CBE

PREFACE

The Practitioner's Handbook addresses issues and themes that relate to counsellors, psychotherapists and counselling psychologists once they have qualified and gained some experience. The handbook has 13 chapters in total and includes appendices of useful books and organisations. Major topics that are relevant to modern therapeutic practice are included, such as writing client reports, developing a private practice, working with multi-cultural and diversity clients, developing research interests and dealing with stress. This book will provide continuing professional development (CPD).

This handbook forms part of a set of three books published by Sage Publications which are for aspiring beginners, those in training and experienced practitioners (Bor and Palmer, 2002; Bor and Watts, 2006; Palmer and Bor, 2008). We hope they provide a comprehensive collection of relevant topics focusing on the fields of counselling, psychotherapy and counselling psychology in the twenty-first century.

REFERENCES

Bor, R. and Palmer, S. (2002) *A Beginner's Guide to Training in Counselling and Psychotherapy*, London: Sage.
Bor, R. and Watts, M (2006) *The Trainee Handbook*, London: Sage.
Palmer, S. and Bor, R. (2008) *The Practitioner's Handbook: A Guide for Counsellors, Psychotherapists and Counselling Psychologists*, London: Sage.

Stephen Palmer and Robert Bor

ACKNOWLEDGEMENTS

As editors, we were privileged to work with such an enthusiastic and supportive range of contributors. All of them willingly accepted the invitation to contribute to this book, recognising the importance and value of sharing their own skills and experience with a broader audience of qualified practitioners. In addition, we thank all of our colleagues who discussed with us their ideas about what should be included in *The Practitioner's Handbook*.

We appreciate the support and encouragement provided by Sage staff on this project, in particular, Alison Poyner, Rachel Burrows and Alice Oven. They are a great team to work with. Final thanks go to Jais K. Alphonse for project managing this book.

Stephen Palmer and Robert Bor, London, 2007.

INTRODUCTION

Stephen Palmer and Robert Bor

If you have just picked up this book and are glancing through it now, it is likely that you are an experienced therapeutic practitioner wondering how this handbook may help you, your practice and your career. There is a finite range of skills that can be taught on postgraduate counselling, psychotherapy and counselling psychology courses and trainees can only expect to acquire a limited proficiency in key theoretical models and approaches to guide them in their practice. Whilst these respective professional trainings equip graduates to start out as independent practitioners, they cannot teach all the skills necessary to develop one's career nor can they help us to prepare for every eventuality that may come to challenge us in the course of our careers.

Increasing professionalisation in the practice of psychological therapies is characterised by the numerous requirements and obligations placed on both trainees and more so on qualified practitioners. It is no longer sufficient to complete a basic or intermediate training in counselling, psychotherapy or counselling psychology and hope to succeed as a practitioner without giving thought to how to develop one's career and broaden and hone one's skills. Indeed, the requirement for continued professional development (CPD) to maintain one's registration is shared by all of the three main professional bodies: the British Association for Counselling and Psychotherapy, the United Kingdom Council for Psychotherapy and the British Psychological Society. The proposed Health Professions Council therapist registration will also have CPD requirements.

In selecting the range of chapters for this handbook, we were mindful of current issues and challenges in the practice of psychological therapies as much as we sought to respond to what our professional colleagues have told us would be of value to learn more about. Therefore the chapters in this book reflect both the editors' and our experienced colleagues' ideas on what should be included in a practitioner's handbook: from developing your career and giving lectures, to writing client reports and going into private practice.

In Chapter 1, Sarah Corrie, Nicola Hurton and David Lane discuss how to develop your career and organise your CPD. This chapter introduces the reader to the demands placed on the recent graduate and seasoned practitioner alike. It sets the tone for the remainder of the book by pointing out the limitations of one's training in preparing one to readily manage many different aspects of one's professional career. This is a very practical chapter which has a significant focus on continuing professional development and how best to organise this. Despite the fact that all practitioners will have sat through hours of lectures through the course of their training and beyond, very few (including lecturers) have undergone a formal training in how to teach. Chapter 2, written by David G. Purves and Neha Pandit, describes how to prepare a lecture, how to teach and deliver material, as well as how to run a training workshop. They stress that lecturing can be enjoyable and enhance your professional reputation, as well as provide a source of additional income. Their own experience as seasoned trainers and lecturers shines out in this chapter and will hopefully inspire those who are keen to teach but perhaps baulk at the challenge to do so.

What are medical and psychiatric assessments? How are they under-taken? What are the major categories of psychiatric disorder? What is the benefit of assessments to the client and mental health practitioner? These important issues are covered in Chapter 3, by Berni Curwen and Peter Ruddell. Although some of these issues are covered in one's professional training, most practitioners recognise upon qualifying that they may be inadequately prepared for the range of medical and psychiatric problems that they may confront in practice and this chapter, presented at a more advanced level, may help to fill some important gaps and improve the confidence of the practitioner. This chapter also prepares the reader for Chapter 4, written by Robert Bor, on how to prepare a report on a client. Whether for legal purposes or as part of one's clinical practice, client reports should be written and presented in a particular format. Again this is seldom formally taught on professional training courses and yet we cannot stress enough the importance of getting this right, both for the client's sake and for the reputation of the practitioner. This chapter describes how to prepare a client report and offers practical hints and suggestions for improving the style and presentation of a report which can be used as evidence in a court of law.

Chapter 5 discusses the important issue of communication with pro-fessional colleagues. Yvonne Walsh and Alan Frankland explore some of the difficulties that may arise in communication between professional colleagues, whether this is between therapists or between therapists and related professionals such as medically qualified practitioners. Both verbal and written communication is addressed in this chapter. There is also a strong emphasis on practical application of communication skills and to this end it is very much a skills-based chapter. In Chapter 6, Riva Miller discusses how to supervise other practitioners and trainees. She recognises that it is a requirement for professional registration to ensure that adequate levels of supervision are arranged for one's clinical practice. Therefore there is an increasing demand on qualified practitioners to supervise and mentor more junior colleagues, including trainees. This chapter describes how to develop your skills as a supervisor and how to negotiate a supervisory relationship.

Few counsellors or psychotherapists receive training in service management. Given the complexities of even small organisations, negotiating purchaser-provider agreements and managing colleagues, even the most resilient and competent practitioner will find themself challenged by some managerial tasks. The reader is given a helpful overview of service management guidelines and concepts in Chapter 7, which is written by Colin Lago. Chapter 8, written by Peter Jenkins, highlights the essential steps that need to be taken to reduce the risk of complaints and litigation against the practitioner. In an era in which there are increased levels of litigation against professionals, few practising counsellors and psychotherapists can ignore the potentially ruinous risks of a complaint or disciplinary hearing against them. Thankfully, as Peter points out, these risks are significantly reduced if care is taken to ensure high standards of practice and by following clear procedures, many of which are described in this chapter.

With experience as a practitioner comes the increased possibility for private practice. In Chapter 9, Christine Wilding, Gladeana McMahon and Stephen Palmer describe how to develop your private practice. This is especially relevant now that there are restricted or even reduced services available to clients in the state health services. For this reason, practitioners increasingly find that they will be challenged to find other contexts in which to work and develop their practice. Private practice may be an attractive alternative or sideline to one's main job, but it is not without its pitfalls. Careful planning, sound financial management and focused marketing may not themselves ensure success, but they certainly may prevent failure which can be costly both financially and to one's professional image. The experience of the three authors in this chapter is invaluable. Chapter 10 concerns how to develop your career in working with multicultural and diverse clients. Roy Moodley and Dina B. Lubin discuss this important area of work which is often overlooked by textbooks in counselling and psychotherapy. This chapter focuses on how to undertake advanced professional development in these areas and to ensure that all aspects of diversity issues are addressed in one's practice.

Whether for pleasure, pure curiosity, a higher degree or as required by your employer, an increasing number of counsellors and psychotherapists are motivated to carrying out research and may wish to draw on a variety of different research methods to do so. In their chapter on this topic (Chapter 11), Annette Fillery-Travis and David Lane help to guide the reader through the various stages of planning and conducting research. They have vast experience in this area and they convey a number of helpful ideas and skills for planning and conducting research. More importantly, they have produced a chapter which is both inspiring and helps to reduce any anxiety one may have about approaching the whole enterprise of research as a practising clinician. Having completed your research, there may be many possibilities and opportunities for writing it up for publication. In Chapter 12, David Winter and Del Lowenthal address the fact that some practitioners may lack the confidence and skills to translate their research or theoretical ideas into a publishable format. This chapter describes how to approach the challenge of writing for publication and provides hints for how to improve the chances of material being accepted by publishers and editors. In the final chapter, Kasia Szymanska addresses the important topics of stress and burnout, which has personal resonance for all practitioners. She highlights the fact that many of us are required to cope with increasing work pressures, sizeable clinical loads, teaching and supervisory responsibilities and seemingly limitless bureaucracy in our jobs, without adequate support. These in turn may have an impact on our overall effectiveness as practitioners as well as our personal relationships. The final outcome can be burnout. This chapter discusses stress and burnout relating to clinical practice, and how best to prevent this from occurring. Finally, Appendix A is a list of suggested useful reading and Appendix B contains contact details of relevant organisations.

Whilst the book is aimed primarily at qualified practitioners, it is likely that trainees who are at an advanced stage in their professional training will be interested in many, if not all, of the topics discussed. Hopefully, over time, postgraduate training courses will incorporate some of these themes and material into their basic training. After all, one's professional training needs to reflect as best possible the demands and requirements of the qualified autonomous practitioner. We recognise that a book of this kind cannot cover all of the themes that are relevant, nor can we anticipate with accuracy those which may emerge in the future. For this reason, we see this as an ongoing project and that future editions of this book will hopefully come to reflect the contemporary issues that challenge us at the time of publication.

We hope that you enjoy reading the book and derive pleasure, as well as personal and professional benefit from its contents.

1 HOW TO DEVELOP YOUR CAREER AND ORGANISE YOUR CONTINUING PROFESSIONAL DEVELOPMENT

Sarah Corrie, Nicola Hurton and David A. Lane

INTRODUCTION

Graduating from a counselling or psychotherapy training is a significant achievement. The nature of knowledge, skills and competencies may vary between the professions and professional bodies which confer formal registration but whatever the training body, graduation represents an official endorsement that an individual is appropriately qualified to offer therapeutic services to the public, and that these services have the potential to facilitate constructive change. However, as Schön (1987) observed, it is doubtful whether any professional training can create a curriculum that is capable of addressing the complex world of practice in any definitive or enduring sense.

A similar dilemma has been identified in relation to continuing professional development (CPD). As Guest (2000) notes, it was once possible to obtain an initial qualification and be reasonably confident about keeping well informed. Attending courses and conferences and reading journals was deemed to be sufficient to ensure that one's knowledge remained up to date (Lane, 1991). However, this is no longer the case. Today's rapidly evolving professional, social and economic climate and the increased emphasis on CPD as a requirement for on-going registration means that we need to think increasingly about embedding our professional development within a specific learning journey and career development plan.

In this chapter, we offer the reader some hints and guidance on how to approach career planning and CPD. We start by offering a definition of career development which provides a backdrop to the discussion that follows. We then consider career development at three separate but inter-related levels: the individual, the organisational and the societal levels. Finally, we identify some general themes which we see as essential to effective career planning.

WHAT DO WE MEAN BY 'CAREER' DEVELOPMENT? TOWARDS A HOLISTIC DEFINITION

There are currently many ways of providing a service as a counsellor or psychotherapist. We see this diversity as a strength of the therapy professions, leading to what Lane and Corrie (2006) describe as a rich tapestry of creative and informed models of practice that can benefit an increasingly wide range of clients.

However, in the context of career planning and CPD, such diversity poses a number of challenges. For example, there is now a multitude of career paths we might carve out for ourselves, stemming from the vast range of settings in which therapists offer their services. These include (but are by no means restricted to) the public sector, the voluntary sector, private sector services, private practice, academic and training institutions and commercial organisations. Other therapists will have portfolio or peripatetic careers rather than seeing themselves embedded within any particular organisational context. Therapists may also play out a variety of roles at work – for example, working as a generic or specialist practitioner, researcher, supervisor, trainer or manager – and will combine these with other life roles such as parenting, and positions in the family and community.

How then, can we define career development in a way that takes account of this diversity and that empowers us to make informed and rewarding choices in this era of change?

Bezanson (2003) has defined career development as 'the lifelong process of managing learning and work in order to live and work with purpose and create a quality life' (p.9). We find this a useful and appealing definition for several reasons. First, by viewing career development as a lifelong process, we can reflect upon how our career concerns may change over time (e.g. according to our 'life stage' or 'career stage'). Second, this definition invites us to reflect on our careers from a personal and subjective perspective (e.g. in relation to our interests, values and personal meanings/interpretations) and also in relation to the contexts in which we work and live (e.g. organisations and families). Third, this definition views us as actively managing and constructing our own careers and learning, and managing transitions between (and within) the two. This is very much in accordance with today's emphasis on sustaining employability and employment through lifelong learning and career-management skills, and with this chapter's commensurate focus on managing one's own career and CPD.

We further believe that Bezanson's definition encourages us to take a 'holistic' view of our career development, which may resonate with many therapists and counsellors. That is, it encourages us to reflect on our career development in a way that integrates work life and non-work life, and in ways that make these feel more 'purposeful, energised and connected' (Bezanson, 2003, p.10).

Taking account of Bezanson's notion of career development as a lifelong and holistic process, we have found it relevant and useful to explore career planning and CPD at three interacting levels:

1. **The individual level:** our interests, values, 'career anchors' and life/career stage.
2. **The organisational level:** the institutions which shape how we practice and confer on-going registration, the organisations in which we are embedded and the CPD requirements that might be specified by both.
3. **The societal level:** national and global influences such as trends in employability, social and cultural diversity and advances in knowledge and technology.

Each of these levels of influence is considered in turn.

THE INDIVIDUAL LEVEL: WHO AM I?

When considering career planning and CPD, an essential starting point is having a good idea of one's motivations, interests and career/life-stage needs, as well as one's strengths and limitations. There are several career theories that may serve as useful frameworks for reflecting on these areas.

Holland's theory of vocational/occupational choices is based on the assumption that we are most likely to succeed and be satisfied in work that is congruent with our interests. According to Holland, people, careers and work environments can be characterised by six 'types', or combinations of types. The assumption is that 'congruence of person and job environment leads to job satisfaction, stability of career path, and achievement. Conversely, in-congruence (i.e. person and job are mismatched) leads to dissatisfaction, instability of career path, and low performance' (Holland, 1996, p.397).

For those readers who are interested in reflecting on their personality type and how this may relate to preferred occupational activities and environments, we have summarised the six personality types below (adapted from Holland, 1996):

1. **Realistic:** sees self as practical and having manual and mechanical skills. Values material rewards for tangible accomplishments. Prefers activities and occupations involving manipulation of machines, tools and things.

2. **Investigative:** sees self as analytical, intelligent, sceptical and academically talented. Values development or acquisition of knowledge. Prefers activities and occupations involving exploration, and understanding and prediction or control of natural and social phenomena.

3. **Artistic:** sees self as innovative and intellectual. Values creative expression of ideas, emotions and sentiments. Prefers activities and occupations involving literary, musical or artistic activities.

4. **Social:** sees self as empathic, patient and having interpersonal skills. Values fostering the welfare of others and social service. Prefers activities and occupations involving helping, teaching, treating, counselling or serving others through interpersonal interaction.

5. **Enterprising:** sees self as having sales and persuasive ability. Values material accomplishment and social status. Prefers activities and occupations that involve persuading, manipulating or directing others.

6. **Conventional:** sees self as having technical skills in business or production. Values material or financial accomplishment and power in social, business or political arenas. Prefers activities and occupations that involve establishing or maintaining orderly routines, and the application of standards.

Although some interests and values may be obvious to us from the outset of our careers, others evolve or only become apparent to us after a period of time. Schein (1980) proposes that as a person's career and life unfold, there is a gradual clarification of self-image around needs and motives, and talents and values. He conceptualises this as a process of finding a 'career anchor', where the anchor is that set of needs, values and talents which the person is least willing to give up if forced to make a choice.

Schein (1990) has identified eight career anchors: technical/functional competence; general managerial competence; autonomy/independence; security/stability; entrepreneurial creativity; service/dedication to a cause; pure challenge and lifestyle integration. Being able to identify one's anchor is helpful in that it enables us to plan and choose wisely when choices have to be made. To guide you in this process, we have provided descriptions of each anchor below (adapted from Schein, 1990). You may feel that several or even all of these anchors are important, but which one would you prioritise if you *had* to choose?

1. **Technical/functional competence:** what you would not give up is the opportunity to apply, and continue to develop, skills and knowledge in your area of expertise. You derive your sense of identity from the exercise of your skills and are most happy when your work permits you to be challenged in your specialist area.

2. **General managerial competence**: what you would not give up is the opportunity to climb to a level high enough in an organisation to enable you to integrate others' efforts across functions and to be responsible for the output of a particular unit of the organisation.

3. **Autonomy/independence**: what you would not give up is the opportunity to define your own work in your own way. If you are in an organisation, you want to remain in positions that allow you flexibility regarding when and how to work. You may even seek to have a business of your own in order to achieve a sense of autonomy.

4. **Security/stability**: what you would not give up is employment security or tenure in a job or organisation. Your main concern is to achieve a sense of having succeeded so that you can relax. The anchor also shows up in concern for financial security (such as pensions).

5. **Entrepreneurial creativity**: what you would not give up is the opportunity to create an organisation on your own initiative, built on your own abilities and your willingness to take risks and to overcome obstacles.

6. **Service/dedication to a cause**: what you would not give up is the opportunity to pursue work that achieves something of value, such as making the world a better place, solving environmental problems or helping others.

7. **Pure challenge**: what you would not give up is the opportunity to work on solutions to seemingly unsolvable problems, to win over tough opponents or to overcome difficult obstacles.

8. **Lifestyle integration**: what you would not give up is a situation that permits you to balance your personal needs, your family needs and the requirements of your career. You need a career situation that provides enough flexibility to achieve such integration.

In thinking about lifelong career development, several writers (e.g. Erikson, 1959; Levinson *et al.*, 1978; Super, 1957) have also found it useful to think about various stages of development. For example, Super (1957) suggested that individuals pass through four stages of vocational development (exploration, establishment, maintenance and disengagement), involving different developmental tasks at each stage. Life-stage theories can help us to reflect on where we are in our career development, and suggest appropriate stage-related goals and activities. As Super (1980) has also noted, at any given age or life stage our career development needs to be examined in the context of the multiple roles we might occupy (e.g. worker, spouse, parent or homemaker).

Although these are just three of many possible frameworks drawn from the career theory literature they enable us to identify questions relevant to the individual level that can enhance effective career planning. In particular, questions arising from a consideration of these models might include the following:

- When have I felt most and least fulfilled at work? What does this tell me about my personality/interests, values and career anchors?
- How might I need to take account of these interests and career anchors in the future (e.g. through reading, courses, supervision, networks of colleagues, job/role/project changes and non-work roles and hobbies)?
- What is my current stage of career development? What are the primary goals, activities and learning targets for me, given my career and life stage?
- What opportunities does my career stage present for me to learn and to prepare for the future (e.g. the next stage)?
- What are the various life and career roles I occupy? Which ones have greatest psychological value? How might I blend these roles successfully?
- What types of activity and context would best support the development and expression of my interests and abilities in the present and future? How can I create congruent opportunities?

THE ORGANISATIONAL LEVEL: WHAT IS MY PROFESSIONAL CONTEXT?

Being aware of our abilities, interests and values is not in itself sufficient for effective career and professional development. Professional practice is embedded in a range of contexts which influence, or may even determine, how our careers unfold. As such, these contexts represent a network of potential opportunities and constraints that we must negotiate in order to arrive at a specific career development plan. So what are some of the opportunities and constraints at this level?

As noted earlier, therapists work in a diverse range of contexts. Even so, our collective behaviours are shaped, and largely determined, by the professional associations that we belong to, and have been trained by. In this sense, we would view our profession/occupation as our primary organisation/institution (also see Arthur, Hall and Lawrence, 1989). Similarly, Kanter (1989) has noted that professional careers 'are not automatically based in a single organisation' (p.511), and are mainly defined by skill, monopolisation of socially valued knowledge and reputation, with the latter being largely conferred by fellow professionals. These perspectives could lead us to consider career development as a series of projects (e.g. professional opportunities that involve growth in transferable knowledge, skills and competencies). Such projects may occur within, or across, organisational or occupational contexts. Furthermore, the professional community is an important organising factor in this development (e.g. we need to comply with certain CPD and conduct standards to maintain and enhance our reputation).

We could conceptualise a project-based career as a 'boundaryless career' (Arthur and Rousseau, 1996). A boundaryless career is defined as 'a sequence of job opportunities that go beyond the boundaries of a single employment setting' (DeFillippi and Arthur, 1996, p.116). Building on the idea of boundaryless careers, it has been suggested (Arthur *et al.*, 1995; DeFillippi and Arthur, 1994) that there are three interdependent types of competencies that individuals need to develop to navigate employment settings:

- **Knowing why**: knowing one's overall work motivation, beliefs and values, and the nature and extent of one's identification with a given employment context.
- **Knowing how**: knowing the skills and knowledge one brings to employment settings. The ability to use employment contexts to apply and enlarge the skills and knowledge one has to offer.
- **Knowing whom**: knowing career relevant networks of interpersonal relationships (e.g. clients, other professionals, previous employers, mentors, family and friends); maintaining and investing in these networks to provide career support, promote reputation and learning, and to generate business.

The above analysis – thinking about why, how and whom – can encourage us to think about features of ourselves (such as those discussed in the 'individual level' section) in relation to our context, and the things we can do to emphasise learning and mobility/employability. This context is primarily an occupational context, and so we have chosen to devote the remainder of this section to consideration of how our 'knowing' activities may serve as a basis for the attainment of important professional credentials.

Within our professional bodies, there is increasing emphasis on compulsory re-accreditation and compulsory CPD. For example, The British Association for Counselling and Psychotherapy has an annual review of accreditation in which evidence of CPD must be presented, alongside a development plan established with the support of a CPD advisor. The British Association for Behavioural and Cognitive Psychotherapies, which re-accredits its therapists every 5 years, similarly links re-accreditation to evidence of ongoing CPD.

The British Psychological Society (BPS) (2004) has also developed an explicit policy on CPD which makes this mandatory for professional psychologists who wish to retain their chartered status. The policy states that CPD must cover at least some aspect of each of the following:

1. developing, implementing and maintaining personal and professional standards and ethical practice;
2. applying psychological and related methods, concepts, models and knowledge derived from reproducible research findings;
3. researching and developing new and existing psychological methods, models, theories and instruments;
4. communicating psychological knowledge, principles, methods and policy requirements.

For a long time, the therapy field has emphasised the importance of a commitment to CPD in the field of personal, as well as professional, development. This reflects a broader philosophical commitment to intersubjective experience and the use of self-knowledge as part of the shared enterprise with the client. The BPS' CPD policy has now adopted a similar approach, requiring psychologists to demonstrate that they have identified personal development needs, planned appropriate development activities to meet these identified needs and reflected upon learning and its application to practice. However, the specific forms that such personal development might usefully and appropriately take are yet to be substantively explored (see Lane and Corrie, 2006, for a more detailed exploration of this issue).

In considering CPD more broadly, a number of conclusions can be drawn. The first is that we are witnessing a growing trend towards viewing CPD as an activity that is individually tailored, according to the stage of professional development and working context of an individual. The second is that as learners, we are all different, possibly as a function of our individual learning styles, vocational interests and career anchors as well as the multitude of work settings in which we might find ourselves. A third conclusion is that we are all lifelong learners. The guidelines of our professional bodies highlight that we can never fully 'arrive' at mastery but spend out careers working towards it. CPD becomes a means of maintaining growth in our thinking and practice, providing opportunities for transformational rather than accumulative learning. A fourth implication we shall mention briefly here is how professional development might also be supported through work-based learning as a means of improving and critically challenging practice.

As a rapidly developing discipline, work-based learning is not about the location of learning but rather about forms of learning specific to practice and how they may be developed and applied. Experience from organisations such as the National Centre for Work Based Learning

Partnerships (Middlesex University) and the Professional Development Foundation has led to the development of ways in which practitioners can share learning, and research about learning, from analysis of their practice. Tools that have added value to a consideration of how to tailor CPD to the needs of both the organisation and the individual include:

1. A 'learning review': including a personal knowledge and skills audit in order to establish what knowledge and skills the practitioner has acquired to be applied to future learning.
2. Programme planning: creating learning that aligns service focus, client and personal need, stakeholder commitment and access to related structural capital.
3. Work-based research: addressing the forms of analysis applicable to the issues that the practitioner faces in order to capture, use and enhance the capital of the organisation.

A work-based learning model of CPD and career development represents a commitment to address the needs of the organisation and the clients the organisation aims to serve. It moves closer to the idea of CPD as part of developing a knowledge culture framework of systems, values and behaviours (Lane and Rajan, 2005). It also ensures that the work setting can become a context for lifelong and transformational learning.

Recognising how our learning is embedded within specific contexts enables us to become more aware of and think creatively around the opportunities and dilemmas to which different working contexts give rise. One critical question might be the extent to which our individual interests and values are congruent with the organisations in which we find ourselves. For example, if our 'career anchor' is security/stability but the organisation in which we work emphasises entrepreneurial creativity, how can we resolve this incongruence? How much room do we have to negotiate and what is the point at which we seek an alternative context in which to offer our services?

Thus, when considering the impact of organisational factors, important questions become:

- How might I obtain information about job opportunities? How might I negotiate a mutually agreeable contract with the organisation, taking into account my development needs, career stage and life circumstances?
- How might I best use and expand my professional/organisational networks to realise my goals? Who are the most important people within and outside my organisational network (e.g. support systems, mentors, managers)?

- How do the different contexts in which I am embedded enable and constrain my choices around career development and CPD?
- What would a personal knowledge and skills audit reveal about what I bring to my work setting/s and how can I ensure I apply this knowledge to my future learning?
- What forms of CPD are most important for my current learning journey? How do these 'fit' with my own personality type and anchor groups?
- What do I want the outcome of my CPD to be? What do I hope to achieve for myself, my clients and my organisational setting/s? How will I take this new learning back into my work setting/s?

THE SOCIETAL LEVEL: WHAT IS MY GLOBAL CONTEXT?

Current thinking around career development and the guidelines laid down by our professional bodies and employing organisations are clearly also occurring in a specific context. We can negotiate this context more effectively if we appreciate some of the issues at a national and global level that are shaping organisational decisions about who we are and what we offer.

One obvious (and contentious) example of change in global thinking about therapeutic practice is the emphasis on 'empirically supported interventions' stemming from growing pressures to provide cost-effective services. This is readily apparent within the National Health Service in the UK, in which evidence, quality control and standards have been publicly endorsed (see for example, Department of Health, 1996, 1997, 2001). However, there can be little doubt that these values are shared in other countries, by other sectors (including industry, education and private practice) as well as shaping the expectations of those who use our services (Corrie, 2003).

Thus, in some service settings, certain types of therapy service may be favoured over others, with potentially significant implications for our identities, activities and roles. For example, we may need to consider how we respond when our service offer appears to be different from apparently neat prescriptions pertaining to the 'treatment of choice'. Should we prioritise such approaches in our career and professional development? When and why should we surrender our own values to 'what works best'? How do we justify our choices?

In an increasingly diverse society, therapists are also expected to be able to work in effective and empowering ways with clients whose abilities and racial, cultural and sexual identities differ radically from our own (see for example, Disability Discrimination Act, 1995). However, as noted by Corrie and Supple (2004), the ability to respond effectively to diversity requires skills in innovation which are rarely prioritised in basic therapy trainings. Moreover, such flexibility of approach does not necessarily fit comfortably with the growing trend to offer 'empirically-supported' interventions. We are, therefore, presented with the potential paradox of having to combine knowledge of 'best practice' with an inventive approach that takes account of the needs of individual clients.

In addition to these therapy-specific dilemmas, is the need to negotiate a professional climate that favours employability over employment. Major changes to the workplace in the UK in the 1990s (see Lane and Corrie, 2006) heralded the end of the job-for-life culture and a move towards inter-industry and transferable skills. As a result, career development is now less organised around progressing through an organisational hierarchy and more oriented towards individuals taking control of their own careers, including their own 'marketability'.

For many therapists, taking control of their employability, whether in the context of an organisational, peripatetic or portfolio career, may seem very familiar. However, when reviewed in the light of the rapid pace of technological change, we can see many potential challenges. An obvious example of this is the multitude of therapists now listed, or advertising, on the internet. The internet will likely become a major source of self-referring clients, and if we do not advertise in this competitive market, we run the danger of losing out. Moreover, these technological developments may also become a source of clients in their own right (e.g. those seeking help with 'internet addiction').

Reports in journal articles already hint at the ways in which therapists are engaging with technology (see for example, Kaltenthaler, Parry and Beverley's (2004) review of computerised cognitive behaviour therapy). In addition, there is now a *Journal of Technology in Counseling* (http://jtc.colstate.edu). A brief look through its table of contents reveals many ways in which therapists can, and may be required to, keep up with technological developments to advance their practice. Examples include counselling over the internet (by email), computer-assisted instruction in counsellor education, virtual reality therapy for treatment of phobias and computer-based supervision. These developments also highlight the prospect of new career opportunities, such as the potential to develop a 'global practice', offering therapy services, training or supervision to an international clientele through the gateway of technology.

We must, therefore, develop a means of ensuring that our knowledge remains current, even when information is proliferating at an exponential rate. We must also consider the kinds of innovations in knowledge and technology that we might be facing in the next decade and how we can maintain an approach to learning that will enable us to acquire new skills with optimum effectiveness. In a sense, then, we need to develop our own individual approach to 'knowledge management'. Questions that can guide an informed approach to career planning in this context include the following:

- In the context of my particular specialty, what national and global factors are likely to shape my clients' and referrers' expectations of what I can provide? What opportunities and constraints might this create for me, now and in the future?
- What is my own personal 'knowledge management' strategy? What methods will I use to update my knowledge and technology skills (e.g. courses, private study, reading, supervision, seminars, IT support and building networks with like-minded practitioners)?
- How will I establish the effectiveness of my efforts to keep my learning up to date?
- How do I manage the tension that comes from having to be inventive in order to meet the needs of individual clients and needing to be responsive to changing ideas about what the literature suggests 'works best'? How will I explain my choices to referrers and clients?
- What do I offer that is unique? How do I 'market' myself and my services?
- Based on current trends in my sphere of practice, what changes do I anticipate in the next ten years? How can I prepare for these (e.g. what knowledge and technology might I need? What types of personal learning and self-promotion will enable me to respond to this need)?

BUILDING ON MY CHOICES: HOW WILL I GET THERE?

What emerges from the themes discussed so far is the need for every individual to take charge of their own learning, professional development needs and career planning. This may seem neither strange nor unreasonable to many therapists. Indeed, it could be argued that with the emphasis our professions places on developing self-awareness and reflective practice alongside our technical expertise, we are well placed to respond to these challenges.

However, what is perhaps different is that we are no longer dealing with relatively straightforward questions about a commitment to best practice but rather how – in a climate in which we are exposed to a proliferation of social groups, knowledge and technology – we must make explicit how we are taking control of our careers. Now more than ever, skills must be revised and knowledge updated, with evidence of this becoming a prerequisite for on-going registration by our professional bodies.

So how can you integrate individual, organisational and more global influences into a coherent strategy for professional development and career planning?

If you engaged with the questions identified in the previous sections, you may well have an emerging sense of where your career might be headed. For example, your values and interests may lead you to suspect that an enterprising career will be the most personally rewarding career trajectory, offering high-prestige roles in ways that enable you to develop your natural leadership and strong interpersonal skills. Alternatively, your career anchor may highlight a desire for autonomy and independence. The sense of reward that comes from selecting projects that stimulate your interest and the freedom to establish your own working patterns will perhaps point you towards seeking out networks of like-minded colleagues, rather than organisational embeddedness. And of course, at least some of these influences will be filtered through a range of organisational and global influences as well as priorities stemming from career and life-stage issues.

Given that the choices facing us are likely to be complex and multifactorial, we see career planning and CPD essentially as an on-going process rather than a specific task. Managing this process will require self-awareness, a reflective approach to enquiry and an openness to changing priorities and needs that will enable new opportunities to be embraced and old ones to be discarded.

As a starting point, therefore, we would advise you to conduct a regular skills and knowledge audit, to help you identify the learning journey you have undertaken so far and its implications for your subsequent learning and career choices. We would see a consideration of influences at the individual, organisational and societal levels as essential to this type of review, as well as the opportunity to share your reflections with others (whether managers, supervisors, mentors or colleagues).

To guide your reflections in the first instance, however, we offer the following questions as a useful aid for supporting the development of your individual approach to career planning and CPD (see Box 1.1).

SOME FINAL THOUGHTS

In today's rapidly evolving world it can no longer be assumed that the knowledge gained in an initial training is sufficient to guarantee effective practice in the longer term. However, given the diversity of settings in which therapists now practice, there can be no single, correct approach to career planning or CPD. In this chapter we have, therefore, avoided any attempt to

BOX 1.1   REFLECTIVE CAREER PLANNING: SOME SUGGESTIONS TO GUIDE YOUR THINKING

- Looking at my career to date, which aspects of my work have I enjoyed most and least? What might this tell me about my career aspirations?
- Do I have a robust understanding of my values/priorities and interests at this time? Do I know what my strengths and limits are? How can I accommodate these in my career planning and CPD?
- What skills do I currently lack that are central to the development of my practice and career? How would my needs be most effectively met (e.g. through acquiring new knowledge, new technology, a different type of supervision, creating new networks of colleagues, attending a course/conference or reading)?
- How will I monitor the impact of my learning on an on-going basis to ensure that it meets my needs, as well as the needs of my clients and the requirements of my work settings?
- Can my needs be met through the organisational contexts in which I work, or will I have to look outside or even leave?
- How do the organisations and institutions in which I am embedded impact on me, my work and my choices around CPD? In what ways do they facilitate and constrain my choices? How might I capitalise on the opportunities and manage the constraints?
- What is my long-term vision of my career? To what extent might this be accomplished within the current organisations in which I am working or will a more radical change be required?
- What skills might I need to get there? What current opportunities exist and what new avenues might I need to explore to achieve my goals?

offer prescriptive advice, favouring facilitative questions which we believe might encourage greater reflection and shared discussion around what is arguably, a neglected issue in the therapy literature.

It is still the case that many choices around career planning and CPD come down to individual preference with relatively few substantive guidelines on how to approach this task. Although we applaud the opportunities that this creates for flexibility and creativity, we believe that therapists need substantive frameworks that can guide their thinking and planning to ensure that their choices are systematic, informed and empowering for themselves, their clients and their employers.

This chapter has identified several frameworks that can help you think about the direction in which your learning and career could be headed, and why. These frameworks are clearly neither exhaustive nor definitive. We hope, however, that they might open up avenues for exploration, discussion and creative planning that you will find a useful companion on your journey as a lifelong learner.

As Rose (2001) suggests, we each have the ability to create our own futures, even if this is not always in circumstances of our own choosing. We hope that, through drawing on the issues discussed in this chapter, you might be empowered to develop a personalised career plan that reflects a broader vision of how you want to offer your services to the clients you seek to serve.

REFERENCES

Arthur, M. B., Claman, P. H. and DeFillippi, R. J. (1995) Intelligent enterprise, intelligent careers. *Academy of Management Executive*, 9 (4), 7–20.

Arthur, M. B., Hall, D. T. and Lawrence, B. S. (1989) Generating new directions in career theory: the case for a transdisciplinary approach. In M. B. Arthur, D. T. Hall and B. S. Lawrence (eds) *Handbook of Career Theory*. Cambridge: Cambridge University Press.

Arthur, M. B. and Rousseau, D. M. (eds) (1996) *The Boundaryless Career: A New Employment Principle for a New Organizational Era*. New York: Oxford University Press.

Bezanson, L. (2003) Career development: policy, proof and purpose. *Careers Education and Guidance,* October, pp. 5–10.

British Psychological Society (2004) *Continuing Professional Development*. Leicester: British Psychological Society.

Corrie, S. (2003) Keynote Paper: information, innovation and the quest for legitimate knowledge. *Counselling Psychology Review*, 18 (3), 5–13.

Corrie, S. and Supple, S. (2004) Seeing is believing: adapting cognitive therapy for visual impairment. *Clinical Psychology*, 44, 34–37.

DeFillippi, R. J. and Arthur, M. B. (1994) The boundaryless career: a competency-based perspective. *Journal of Organizational Behavior*, 15, 307–324.

DeFillippi, R. J. and Arthur, M. B. (1996) Boundaryless contexts and careers: a competency-based perspective. In M. B. Arthur and D. M. Rousseau (eds), *The Boundaryless Career: A New Employment Principle for a New Organizational Era*. New York: Oxford University Press.

Department of Health (1996) *NHS Psychotherapy Services in England Review of Strategic Policy*. London: Department of Health.

Department of Health (1997) *The New NHS: Modern, Dependable*. London: Department of Health.

Department of Health (2001) *Treatment Choice in Psychological Therapies and Counselling: Evidence-Based Clinical Practice Guidelines.* London: Department of Health.

Department of Social Security. *Disability Discrimination Act* 1995 London: HMSO.

Erikson, E. H. (1959) Identity and the life-cycle. *Psychological Issues*, 1, 1–171.

Guest, G. (2000) Coaching and mentoring in learning organizations. *Conference Paper TEND United Arab Emirates*, April, 8–10.

Holland, J. L. (1996) Exploring careers with a typology: what we have learned and some new directions. *American Psychologist*, 51 (4), 397–406.

Kaltenthaler, E., Parry, G. and Beverley, C. (2004) Computerized cognitive behaviour therapy: a systematic review. *Behavioural and Cognitive Psychotherapy*, 32 (1), 31–55.

Kanter, R. M. (1989) Careers and the wealth of nations: a macro-perspective on the structure and implications of career forms. In M. B. Arthur, D. T. Hall and B. S. Lawrence (eds) *Handbook of Career Theory*. Cambridge: Cambridge University Press.

Lane, D. A. (1991) *Personal Development Planning: The Autonomous Professional Model.* London: Professional Development Foundation.

Lane, D. A. and Corrie, S. (2006) *The Modern Scientist-Practitioner. A Guide to Practice in Psychology.* London: Brunner-Routledge.

Lane, D. A. and Rajan, A. (2005) Business psychology: the key role of learning and human capital. In P. Grant (ed), *Business Psychology in Practice*, London: Whurr.

Levinson, D. J., Darrow, C. M., Klein, E. G., Levinson, M. H. and McKee, B. (1978) *The Seasons of a Man's Life.* New York: Knopf.

Rose, S. (2001) Moving on from old dichotomies: beyond nature-nurture towards a lifeline perspective. *British Journal of Psychiatry, Supplement* 40, 178, S3–S7.

Schein, E. H. (1980) *Organizational Psychology,* 3rd edition, Englewood Cliffs, NJ: Prentice-Hall.

Schein, E. H. (1990) *Career Anchors* (Discovering Your Real Values). San Francisco: Jossey-Bass Pfeiffer.

Schön, D. A. (1987) *Educating the Reflective Practitioner.* San Francisco: Jossey-Bass.

Super, D. E. (1957) *The Psychology of Careers.* New York: Harper & Row.

Super, D. E. (1980) A life-span, life-space approach to career development. *Journal of Vocational Behavior*, 16, 282–298.

2 HOW TO GIVE A LECTURE AND RUN TRAINING WORKSHOPS

David G. Purves and Neha Pandit

Some of us experience an irresistible urge to stand up, for an hour or more, in front of a group of strangers and talk about our interests. What can be more fun than that? It could be thought of as narcissism, pomposity or even arrogance that we think what we have to say might be of the remotest interest to anyone, and yet we continue to do it year after year and people continue to listen. In fact, giving lectures and running workshops is a rewarding way to work within the fields of counselling, counselling psychology and psychotherapy, which stretches you intellectually and offers the potential for endless learning opportunities. It allows you the full play of your creativity; there are no limits on the number of different ways that the transfer of knowledge can take place.

THE PROSPECT OF TEACHING IS FRIGHTENING

When we suggest to people that they might give a talk in a class, or heaven forbid at a conference, there are looks that range from fear and loathing to surprise and incredulity. When we suggest that they could run a workshop designed to teach people how to do something specific they are even more horrified. Responses vary, but common ones are; but I won't know what to say or do; people will criticise me; I will be embarrassed; I will make a fool of myself. These concerns become magnified such that attempting to overcome them seems like it would take a lifetime of effort, they usually side step our urging with a 'next year for sure' excuse. These doubters are the ones that are missing out.

Our goal is to encourage you to start to think of yourself as someone who is willing and able to teach in a variety of forums. Counselling and psychotherapy are professions where there are numerous opportunities for teaching and running workshops. There are very few impediments to dipping your toe into this forum and most of these are self-limiting and erroneous. Communication is intrinsically rewarding. So we want you to join us, it is not as daunting as it seems.

WHY CROSS THE FLOOR?

We do not learn how to teach when we ourselves are in school. Most new lecturers learn how to teach by immersing themselves in the subject material and using their first classroom as their testing ground for future practice, a process otherwise known as trial and error. Given the expected work and anxiety involved, why would anyone want to teach in the first place? Think back to all the years that you have spent studying. Who was your favourite teacher and why? Most probably it was not a teacher who simply restated facts, facts that you could have found out on your own, it was a teacher who enthusiastically presented information not in your book; someone who synthesised materials from many different resources, challenged you, excited you and made you want to know more. And, most importantly, it was probably a teacher who made you think. They helped you to see the world differently and so changed you forever. What an engaging prospect – through teaching, you have the opportunity to do the same for someone else. To give your listeners the power to be able to take what you give them, combine it with their own understanding and apply it to their own practice.

I HAVE NOTHING TO SAY, SO WHAT WOULD I DO?

'I have nothing to say' is a common thought for beginners to lecturing when they are asked to lecture or run a workshop. The reason for this feeling is simple and once you recognise this it is much easier to overcome. When you think about yourself teaching a subject you have not researched yet, you realise that you do not hold enough information in your memory to perform the task. Consequently, you feel unprepared and vulnerable. If you stay with that feeling, you will never teach. Attempt to contextualise your thoughts. Consider that until you have researched a topic you cannot feel secure in the knowledge necessary to do a good job. Once you delve into your topic, you will see that many possibilities open up.

Beginners fall victim to unrealistic ambition about what they should accomplish in the classroom. They often think they could and should share, not only everything they know about the subject, but also everything that has ever been written or said. The seasoned lecturer knows that students would retain very little of this information. One of the most effective ways to reduce your anxiety about what you will say is to think about the three most important ideas or themes that you would like your students to retain. Although this may limit the breadth of what you will cover, it will certainly increase the depth, and the probability that your students will walk away with strong memories of your lecture or workshop.

IF YOU WANT TO LEARN SOMETHING THEN TEACH IT

One of the greatest joys for someone who likes to learn is to teach. There is an old, and absolutely true, adage in education: if you want to learn something then teach it. No matter how well you think you know a topic, you will need to know more before you feel comfortable enough to stand in front of an audience. The acquisition of knowledge, as a by-product of the need to be well prepared, not only makes you feel that you really do know your subject, but also gives you some genuine level of expertise. No matter how much your audience know or think they know, you invariably know more than they do on a topic. Once you accept this notion you can relax and enjoy the experience of imparting knowledge in a systematic way. Furthermore, you get to keep the knowledge you have acquired, which gives you a much deeper understanding than you had previously. It also provides important confidence for the next time you are asked to teach.

TEACHING CAN PROVIDE AN INCOME

It is undoubtedly the case that if you are interested and willing to create opportunities, then you will be able to create additional income from lecturing. Whilst this sounds like a good thing generally, it is equally true that if you costed out the time you need to prepare for the period you spend in front of the class, then your hourly rate is likely to make you think that the whole enterprise is not worth pursuing. The financial argument, however, misses the point.

Teaching is a different kind of activity to working with clients. Although it is equally creative, it does require a different kind of engagement. It uses other aspects of your personality and skills. You can draw on therapeutic skills to become a good facilitator and indeed you should do so, but lecturing helps turn you into an educator and a communicator. These are additional facets which are complimentary to those of being a therapist. Each profession can feed the other but when you are teaching you are not a therapist and vice versa. The goals of each role are quite different. Additionally, it is always helpful to include variety in your working week as a buffer against 'burnout', and losing your passion for the work. In other words, alternative activities such as lecturing and running workshops can help replenish your therapy batteries.

KNOW YOUR AUDIENCE

If you have decided that you would like to move towards the lecturing circuit, it is important to position yourself at a level within which you will feel initially comfortable. There are numerous courses in counselling and psychotherapy, and many of these are constantly looking for people who can teach an aspect of their course. Often a simple telephone call will result in expressions of interest. But at what level should one begin? In universities, it is usually considered that you need to be at least two years (of education or experience) above the level you are teaching. This seems to be a reasonable and reliable rule of thumb. If you have finished a course of four years duration, you may think about teaching at year one or year two of that course. The minimum two years gap gives you a valuable sense of seniority and confidence.

When you approach a potential institution to teach for them, should you have something already prepared, or should you ask what they want to have taught? This question is only really difficult for the absolute novice. Most people ask you what you can teach, and in reality, as long as it does not involve foreign languages or mathematics (unless these are your forte) you can teach most subject areas because once you have researched it you can. However, it may be useful to have subject areas that you can say are your preferred subjects, at least to begin with. Again this helps build confidence and starts you on a level with which you are most familiar.

PREPARATION, STRUCTURE AND DELIVERY ARE THE THREE ESSENTIALS OF TEACHING

PREPARATION

We will deal with preparation first, as it naturally comes before structure or delivery. Preparation is doing the research that is necessary for you to acquire the knowledge you need to impart. In general, this involves knowing your material, knowing what you want to impart, developing an outline and structuring your session to achieve your learning outcomes.

This begs the question: how much material should I prepare? There is an inverse relationship between lecturing experience and quantity of prepared material; there are two things to consider. First, remember, most of the work involved in giving a lecture takes place well before you step into the classroom. If you prepare thoroughly, your chances of delivering a good enough lecture are excellent. Preparation and research are enjoyable, and interesting, which can both be a security blanket to the novice lecturer.

It is inevitable that you will prepare more than you need to present. Accept this fact, and consequently, do not bind your presentation to the material. All teaching material is disposable or amendable if it does not fit the learner's need. Never present material simply because you have it prepared. And never speed up your teaching beyond the speed of knowledge acquisition; simply because you have prepared the material in advance, just accept that you may not always be able to go through all of your material. Only you will know what has not been presented. However, if your lecture was entitled: 'The Romans BC100 to AD100' and you only got to AD 67 before you ran out of time, then the audience may feel cheated and it would be obvious that you failed to reach your self-allotted end point. However, if you called your talk: 'The Romans at the beginning of the millennium', then you have much more flexibility as to where you judge the end point to be.

It is easier to finish a lecture or workshop before you have completed all of the material, if you consider the following points:

1. Select topics that are more focused on process than content;
2. Make sure you cover the essential points first and then move into increasing elaboration;
3. Be prepared to have a question and answer session 10 minutes from the end to tie up loose ends;
4. Be sensitive to the needs of the audience to receive clarification of concepts.

However long the time you have to teach, until you are experienced, you will inevitably be unable to do everything you want to do. Therefore any structural planning you do in advance will always pay dividends.

WHO WILL I BE TEACHING?

This may seem like an obvious question, but recognise that your own experience is necessarily going to be vastly different from your student's experience. You must consider their learning capacity. If they are new to a subject they will have less contextual information upon which to hang new data. Teaching A-level students will be very different from undergraduates or graduates in the same discipline. Ask yourself how much will they already know about the subject? How interested will they be in the material? What experiences have they had thus far? Similarly, if you hope to impart difficult concepts, it is wise to consider the potential ability of the weakest students you might reasonably expect to have in your class. The speed at which your class can go is often determined by those who find it more difficult, rather than those who have a better understanding of the concepts being presented. Try to judge the likely general background of your audience, and pitch your lecture accordingly.

HOW LONG SHOULD THE SESSION BE?

While it may seem a blessing to have a shorter session, in reality a longer session will enable you to achieve a more satisfactory knowledge and skill transfer. Until you have tried, it will be confusing to calculate the relationship between teaching aims and time. As mentioned earlier, the novice lecturer always tries to do too much and leaves feeling frustrated because the last part of the lecture that tied everything together was hurried or missed completely. The experienced lecturer reduces their expectations of the amount of information they can get through in a given time. A part of this process is explicable because the experienced teacher spends more time explaining and giving illustrative examples, while the beginner feels most secure sticking to the points they have previously worked out. While the traditional model of the university lecturer standing at the front of a large auditorium talking for 50 minutes with students rapidly writing every overhead projected word is alive and well, it is a very poor model upon which to base your practice. There are many more creative ways to teach than to simply lecture and the most effective of these have at their heart the learning needs of the audience.

TO LECTURE OR DISCUSS: THAT IS
THE QUESTION?

The debate between a lecture format (which will be discussed later) and a discussion format is determined by the purpose of your presentation, and what your audience needs to know when they leave. This will inevitably have an impact on how and what you prepare. Where the primary goal is knowledge transfer of large amounts of information, then the lecture format would seem more appropriate. Your preparation will be guided by the knowledge that your students need to acquire. On the other hand, when the goals are more process oriented, then a discussion format would seem to be more effective. In which case, you may still need to prepare a mini-lecture, but you will also need to devise questions and/or exercises that would facilitate an understanding of the relevant process such as allowing an opportunity to practice what has been learnt.

WHAT DO I WANT THE STUDENTS TO TAKE AWAY
FROM THE SESSION?

In an introductory course you may be covering topics that you have either never covered before, or topics that you have not been exposed to in a long time. Read up on the area you are expected to teach and begin to anticipate questions. Review the literature to assess whether there have been any new developments, begin with a recent review paper and read recent articles specialising in the area to be covered. For more specific guidance, you can even examine the syllabus, materials, readings and assignments of other colleagues who have taught the course in the past. If working in an academic setting, review the department or course guidelines for the topic in question and set your broad course goals based on these. For example, the goals of an introduction to psychology course might include motivating students to do further study into topics areas that interest them, while giving them an adequate foundation to investigate a range of interests. Next, compile a list of subjects you feel are important to include. Try to anticipate how much time you would need to address each topic, then double that estimate, to allow for discussion and questions. Come up with an outline of approximately how much time is needed per section.

STRUCTURE

A wise teacher once said that the core of a good lecture is a clear and appropriate structure. The lecturer credo, he told me, is, 'Tell them what you are going to tell them, tell them, then tell them what you've told them'.

Having a sound structure will facilitate a stronger delivery and clearer message. Your efforts will be appreciated. After you have done all the preparations, you only have to present your work. But how do you do it? We have all sat through many lectures where the lecturer simply read the material from hand-held paper. This is the worst kind of educational experience for the learner, as well as being deeply boring. We acknowledge that it is tempting to figure out how fast you talk and write everything down. We also admit that as students we did this ourselves at some point. The logic of having every word prepared is obvious, you have nothing to remember and, as stress levels rise you can still deliver the words. So this may seem like a sensible strategy. The problems, however, outweigh the benefits. If you must write every word of your presentation out, do not for 1 minute believe that you can both read it and give an engaging talk. Unless you are highly seasoned as a public speaker or an actor, this simply is not possible. What actually happens is that you fail to learn the material as memorised text and you rely upon the black and white words. You will find that you cannot digress at all from the written text, otherwise when you go back to the text you will have lost your place or else messed up the order of presentation. This makes you feel confused and so drives up your stress levels, making the listeners feel nervous on your behalf, in essence a stressful experience for both you and your audience.

An alternative is to use tried and tested methods of structuring material so that it is effectively remembered and easily taught. Suppose you had written out a whole 50-minute lecture on your computer but decided instead to give an engaging talk using audiovisual equipment instead of simply reading from your paper copy. How would you transform one from the other? If we use this as an exercise, you will quickly see the method of creating structured talks. First, go through your talk and select the fundamental points that make your argument meaningful. Write each of these parts on a separate sheet. Then under each main point write no more than four subsidiary points that help to elaborate and explain the main point. Keep all of these points very brief indeed; remember that if they are screen projected, then people will take the time to read the slide which interferes with the listening process.

As you do this exercise you are actually going through the process of memorising each slide in a very structured way. For a 50-minute talk you should allow yourself adequate time to talk about each slide and so as a rule of thumb have no more than 15 slides, less if you intend to develop experiential exercises. All of the material you need to learn for each main point is contained within each subsidiary point. So for each slide you need to be able to talk a little about each of these points. Because they are so structured, with each point contributing to the overall argument, your brain easily remembers the story. And, with luck, you have transformed a dry and boring talk into one where you can look at the audience and engage with them, as you tell each part of the story. This technique relies upon the fact that the human memory is capable of remembering immense amounts of information, but only if that information is structured in appropriate ways that allow both for effective encoding and retrieval. The actual memory load for a highly structured talk is low because you only need to know what is associated with each subsidiary point. Each time you turn to a new point your brain automatically loads that information into your accessible memory store.

To aid making your story both memorable and enjoyable for the audience, prepare a detailed introduction: the more the audience knows at the beginning, the fewer problems will surface later on. Think of it this way, what's one of the first things you do when you go to the theatre, you open up your programme to get an overall peak into what the show is about. If you deviate from the introduction, be clear as to why. Make transitions from one topic to another clear by contextualising them. Remember, without background and context it is difficult for listeners to understand and retain information.

DELIVERY: ENGAGEMENT AND FLOW

Even if you use the technique outlined above, you will still need to practice the talk by yourself so you remember what you need to say and have a smooth flow between topics and subtopics. If you have to give an important talk, with material you have not used before, go through the talk between four and six times in its entirety. For material that is well known to you perhaps twice will be sufficient for you to feel confident in your delivery. As seasoned lecturers, we still practise. To keep an audience engaged for 50 minutes requires energy and enthusiasm. This means that you not only know the material, but are able to tell a story in a way that engages the audience. It is performance really. And good performance comes when you stop worrying about what you are going to say and instead focus on the way you are going to say it.

AUDIOVISUAL (AV) EQUIPMENT

These days you are likely to have access to audiovisual equipment. You can use this quite effectively to help you structure your talk and also to relieve you of much of the burden of memory. Using AV equipment for a presentation, or a whole-day workshop can make your presentation run efficiently.

There are many different presentation software programs which allow you to structure main points as slides, with sub-headings as subsidiary points that will provide the basis of your elaboration. There are also places in the software for you to make notes that appear on your screen, but are invisible to the audience. You are also able to print your lecture slides as pages of handouts for the audience to take away; something that is increasingly done and is usually greatly appreciated.

DELIVERY FORMAT

Now you know what you are going to do, but how are you going to do it? This can often be the hardest part of the process. But remember, at this point, you know what you need to know, which means you have everything you need to deliver. In relation to the delivery of the material itself, research shows that utilising varying methods of instruction is often the most effective strategy. Choosing different formats, which fit the material content, keeps your audience actively engaged. There are many different ways of doing this:

1. An expository lecture is what is commonly known as the traditional lecture format. It looks at one question/problem, with major and minor points. It facilitates the dissemination of factual information, but minimises the active participation of the audience. Some things to avoid when preparing this type of lecture are don't use too many tables/figures to illustrate points, keep quotations to a minimum and use fewer overheads rather than more.
2. The interactive lecture centres on getting participants to come up with thoughts in response to a question. An example might be 'how do you think these phenomena might look in another culture'. The stream of

examples will range in their specificity and orientation, nonetheless, it encourages people to think independently.

3. In problem solving, the teacher will pose a stimulating question that triggers the student's interest, for example 'what might happen if …'. This again encourages students to think independently while incorporating what they have learned about a topic.

4. The workshop is a setting where over a longer period of time learners are able to gain a deeper understanding of a topic and acquire new skills. This format is particularly popular in counselling and psychotherapy as ultimately therapists have to provide practical solutions for clients to implement and so commonly attend training events.

CREATING EXPERIENTIAL EXERCISES

Fiction writers have long known that to tell a reader something results in dry prose, but to show a reader something brings the experience alive. The same principle applies to teaching. All teaching benefits from using experiential exercises; this is particularly true if you are teaching an applied subject such as counselling or psychotherapy. People have different ways of learning and a considerable amount of research has demonstrated that for the best educational experience there needs to be a match between mode of delivery and mode of learning.

There are a few fundamental principles that are wise to follow if you are planning experiential exercises:

- Decide how much time you realistically need for the exercise;
- Be clear about what you want to achieve in the exercise;
- Give very clear instructions;
- Give plenty of time for a general de-brief at the end;
- Have written instructions if possible;
- Make the exercise relevant to the general topic you are following.

WHAT ARE YOUR NEEDS?

Think about yourself. How do you deal with being nervous? It is not uncommon for nervous speakers to speak too quickly, to not take pauses and to not make eye contact with the audience. If you know this to be true of yourself, you need to think of ways to slow your pace down and try to engage with your listeners. Some teachers find it useful to make notations on their lecture notes that remind them to take breaks in their speech maybe even pause for questions. Breathing or relaxation exercises can help calm your nerves.

AUDIENCE NEEDS

Audience attention is highest in the first 15–20 minutes, then it decreases, and increases only slightly in anticipation of the end. Therefore, it is best to give the most important information first. In addition, to maximise attention, change the teaching format by breaking your talk up into 15–20 minute chunks whereupon you change what you and your audience are doing. In other words, vary the format. This will provide a much more engaged audience. This remains valid whether you are teaching for one hour or seven hours.

You already know what your audience needs to learn, but how can you help facilitate the learning process? Learning theory dictates that positive reinforcement is a key component in learning. As teachers, we can encourage our students through simple statements such as 'that is a good point', or 'good answer'. A little encouragement can go along way in the learning process.

HOW DID YOU DO?

Feedback is always useful. Of course, positive feedback is always easier to hear than negative feedback, but negative feedback (otherwise known as constructive criticism) is often what helps us improve the most. Eliciting feedback, in the form of an evaluation, can also be immensely useful in future-course planning.

EVALUATION FORMS

The evaluation form should allow you to assess the extent to which the training achieved its objectives and to identify changes that could be made for future workshops. Some questions to bear in mind when designing the evaluation form are as follows:

1. Did the participants acquire the knowledge and skills you set out to provide?
2. Did the participants perceive you were adequately prepared?
3. Were the activities interesting and effective?
4. Was the format appropriate?
5. Do the participants need more training?

CONCLUSION

Teaching is inherently rewarding, if the process is managed by the lecturer for the benefit of the student. Whether you have a positive or negative experience will be reflected in the amount of effort you are prepared to put into adhering to the guidelines we have set out for you here. The skills of lecturing or running workshops need to be acquired through effort and practice. Model the learning experience for your students by trying to make every teaching experience better for you and better for them, through increased preparation and effort. In this way not only will your new skills contribute to your overall development as a professional, but also you will be providing a thoughtful and enjoyable service for your learners.

3 UNDERSTANDING PSYCHIATRIC AND MEDICAL ASSESSMENTS

Berni Curwen and Peter Ruddell

Counsellors, psychotherapists and counselling psychologists arrive at their professions from a wide range of backgrounds and receive widely differing knowledge consistent with their chosen therapeutic orientation and rigour of training. Only some will have had training in medicine and psychiatry (see Curwen and Ruddell, 1997; Ruddell, 1997). This chapter therefore outlines the major components of psychiatric and medical assessment, knowledge of which might benefit the above practitioners. It is important that practitioners do not attempt to practise beyond their training and competence. For example, the majority of counsellors and psychotherapists would not undertake a comprehensive mental state examination but knowledge of the process may widen their understanding (see Curwen, 1997; Lukas, 1993; Morrison, 1995). A psychiatric or medical assessment may be quite unnecessary for many referrals, but recognition of when one might be required is most important.

WHAT ARE PSYCHIATRIC AND MEDICAL ASSESSMENTS?

The psychiatric assessment is also known by other terms such as the clinical interview or the psychiatric interview. The medical assessment or physical examination in this context determines the extent to which a person's medical (non-psychiatric) condition impacts upon his or her psychological well-being.

The purpose of the psychiatric assessment is to:

- obtain the necessary information to make a diagnosis;
- understand the individual;
- understand the individual's circumstances;
- establish a therapeutic relationship;
- provide the individual with information about the condition with which they present, evidence-based treatment recommendations and prognosis.

The psychiatric assessment consists of the following main components:

- client history;
- medical assessment;
- mental state examination (MSE);
- risk assessment;
- formulation leading to diagnosis and treatment recommendation.

These are considered in the following sections.

CLIENT HISTORY

Taking a client history will be familiar to most practitioners and is essential to making a formulation leading to a psychiatric diagnosis with recommendation for treatment. This chapter is concerned with psychiatric and medical diagnosis and will not cover history taking in depth. Although histories may be best recorded systematically and in a logical, predetermined order, flexibility is important too, allowing questioning to be adjusted to problems that emerge as the interview proceeds (Leff and Isaacs, 1990). Information from a client may be supplemented with information from a person close to the client as well as reports and information from other agencies. Openness in record keeping is important and the information documented should be shared with the client. Information intended to be shared with a third party should have the agreement of the client: exceptional cases where this is not possible are best discussed with your supervisor.

Within the main history taking there are common components that are usually included. Histories with social aspects are personal, family, marital and sexual. Other history taking will include medical and surgical conditions, psychiatric background and menstrual history. The client's current life situation will be explored along with the circumstances which lead up to the client attending the interview. Information gathered about the client's current difficulties is considered alongside the client's description of his or her own personality to elicit recent changes.

Personal factual details held about the client such as name, date of birth and current address are also usually checked for accuracy within the client history-taking process.

MEDICAL ASSESSMENT

Medical factors and psychological functioning may significantly impact upon each other (Bynum, 1983; Engel, 1962; Tuke, 1872). For example, a study by Eastwood and Trevelyan (1972) found a positive association between physical and psychiatric illness, while Shepherd *et al.* (1966) found a high incidence of physical morbidity within clients with psychiatric illness and Querido (1959) found a high incidence of psychiatric disorders in patients with physical illness. Davies (1987) explored the interaction of commonly used medications on the incidence of psychiatric symptoms and it is important for the psychiatrist to eliminate whether any psychiatric symptoms may have been induced by a particular medication. Where a medical illness has been identified it is important to ascertain any associated psychiatric symptoms and treat these to prevent psychiatric disorder and suicide (Saunders and Valente, 1988). Clients who have severe physical illness are more vulnerable to experiencing a psychiatric disorder where there is a previous history of psychiatric disorder (Campbell, 1986).

A psychiatrist will take account of any known medical difficulties as part of the psychiatric assessment and will conduct a physical examination as part of the mental state examination to identify or exclude conditions where a suspicion has been raised during the assessment process.

MENTAL STATE EXAMINATION (MSE)

The MSE is a central component of the psychiatric assessment. In contrast to history taking, in which the client's symptoms up to the present time are recorded, the MSE focuses solely on the individual's current mental state, his or her symptoms and behaviour at the time of the interview. It is conducted in an orderly and systematic fashion and the components of examination are summarised in Table 3.1.

The purpose of an MSE is to detect abnormal features in a client's state of mind, and behaviour, at the time of the assessment. If abnormal features are found, this information contributes to the diagnostic process. Carrying out an MSE may at first seem a laborious task but the process is a practical skill that can be learnt by watching experienced interviewers and by practising under supervision (Leff and Isaacs, 1990; Wing *et al.*, 1974). Observations of interpersonal dynamics are also important when interviewing a partner or other family members. The family or partners will interact during the interview, and this may give important clues to both the contributing causes of the problem and the most appropriate help.

APPEARANCE AND BEHAVIOUR

GENERAL BEHAVIOUR

Keen observation of the client's appearance and behaviour is important. Behaviour means anything a client does, whether implicit or explicit.

Table 3.1 Components of mental state examination

Component	Assess
Appearance and behaviour	Facial expression Posture Movements Social behaviour
Speech	Rate Amount Continuity
Mood	Prevailing mood and associated symptoms Variations of mood Appropriateness of mood
Depersonalisation and derealisation	Preoccupations Obsessional or compulsive symptoms Delusions
Perception	Hallucinations Illusions
Cognitive function	Orientation Attention Concentration Memory
Insight	

Initial observations, such as healthy/unhealthy, clean/unkempt etc., may point to indications such as self-neglect or several other possibilities including alcoholism, drug addiction, depression, dementia or schizophrenia. Their bodily appearance such as body size may suggest the possibility of physical illness, anorexia nervosa, depressive disorder or chronic anxiety.

An individual adopting incongruous styles of dress, bright colours or oddly assorted clothes may indicate mania, psychosis or schizophrenia. The overall pattern and extent of symptoms are necessary to guide assessment rather than single observations. Any of the above examples of appearance and behaviour could have a non-pathological explanation.

When behaviour is recorded it is best given as a clear description of what the client actually does and not an application of labels as subjective terms which are stigmatising (Goffman, 1963) for example 'completely covers face with jumper' is preferable to 'bizarre'.

FACIAL EXPRESSION

Facial expressions may provide a telling insight into an individual's mood. An expressionless face suggesting flat affect in depression is common but so too is the constant adoption of a smile or frequent frowning. In anxious clients there may be raised eyebrows and dilated (enlarged) pupils. A wide range of emotions may be suggested through facial expression including elation, irritability and anger, together with the mask-like expression of clients taking drugs with parkinsonism side-effects.

POSTURE AND MOVEMENT

Posture and movement are important indicators of mood. The demeanour of a depressed client will usually be slow (both for movement and speech). They may lean forwards in their chair with hunched shoulders and head inclined towards the floor. The actions and speech of an anxious client are more likely to be quick and jumpy. Wringing the hands is common and general restlessness. Clients with an agitated depression, as with anxiety, may exhibit shakiness and restlessness, or constantly play with an item of jewellery or clothing. The actions or speech of a client with mania may be unmistakably restless or overactive.

SOCIAL BEHAVIOUR

Social behaviour is a general term concerning the way in which a person relates with others. It reflects a complex amalgam of inherent and learned ways of interacting with others mediated through the individual's personality and implicit to it is a body of social rules. It is because changes to an individual's social behaviour may reflect illness that this component is considered in the MSE. A client with schizophrenia may behave unusually. They may be overactive and socially disinhibited or withdrawn and preoccupied; others may be aggressive. Clients with antisocial personality disorders may also appear aggressive. The actual behaviour observed is accurately recorded. In both anxiety and depression a person's range of interactions with others may be temporarily limited.

SPEECH

The content of what a person says and the way it is said is recorded. Fast speech may suggest mania and slow speech could indicate depressive disorders. The amount of speech is increased in some clients, such as those who are anxious. Depressed clients or those with dementia may pause for long periods before replying to questions. Tone may be monotonous, speech may lack spontaneity, be hesitant or easily distracted. The flow may be suddenly interrupted. This could suggest the client is listening to a 'voice' but may also indicate poor concentration. Rapid shifts from one subject to another may suggest flight of ideas common in mania, schizophrenia or psychosis.

A prominent characteristic of schizophrenia is disordered thought: a lack of logical thread and general diffuseness may indicate this. Neologisms are private words often used to describe personal experiences and are a characteristic of some forms of schizophrenia.

MOOD

Mood is assessed using the factors already discussed under appearance and behaviour combined with the content of what the client says about how he or she feels. Where low mood is suspected, further sensitive enquiries are made. Changes in mood are important and it is informative to discover if the client's current presentation of self differs markedly from his or her normal outlook on life. Exploring for the presence of tearfulness, thoughts of pessimism and/or hopelessness about the future and guilt about the past are necessary. Presence of such thoughts may lead your enquiry towards open but sensitive questions about suicidal ideation (see risk assessment below). If anxiety is detected, questions about physical symptoms and the thoughts which accompany them are useful. A question such as 'What goes through your mind when you feel anxious?' will enable anxious thoughts to be detected and may lead to the client responding by talking about his or her thoughts and fears of fainting or of losing control or 'going mad'.

DEPERSONALISATION AND DEREALISATION

Depersonalisation is experienced as feeling unreal, detached, empty within and unable to feel emotion as if viewing oneself from the outside. Derealisation is experienced as viewing the world and people in it as lifeless, like cardboard cut-outs. These may be difficult to assess and clients may have difficulty describing their experiences. An example of a typical question asked here would be, 'Do you ever feel that things around you are unreal?' Discovering examples of the client's experiences are also useful in this context.

OBSESSIONAL ASPECTS

The terms 'obsession' and 'compulsion' are closely associated. A repetitive, intrusive and unwanted thought, feeling, image or impulse is known as an obsession. A compulsion is always an action (which may be a mental action such as counting). Clients with obsessional thoughts may be ashamed of them if they have particular themes such as violence or sex. A client may report that he or she is experiencing a thought over and over again that he does not understand and wishes would go away, but cannot stop himself thinking no matter what he does. The client is asked for examples of what thoughts keep coming into his mind, so that the theme may be established.

Compulsions can be observed but are more often performed unobtrusively. Clients will often be embarrassed or humiliated when speaking about their compulsions. They may say that they know what they are doing is 'crazy' or 'silly' but they must do it and cannot stop themselves. Rituals are also fully explored as they may have a significant impact on a client's quality of life. It may take a client hours to wash his or her hands because the client has to repeat the action many times in exactly the same way. Most compulsions cluster around one of three types of actions: counting, repetitive cleaning or washing and checking.

DELUSIONS

A delusion is a fixed, firmly held false belief out of keeping with the client's culture, unaltered by evidence to the contrary and for which the client has no insight. Some common types are persecutory delusion where an individual may believe others are attempting to inflict harm upon them (see Freud, 1911); delusions of control where a client may believe that someone or something is controlling what they do, say or think, or what they can do to others (Schneider, 1949); ideas of reference where a client believes that significant or unrelated events in the world have a secret meaning aimed at them. Delusions can sometimes be difficult for the practitioner to detect but a gentle, persistent, enquiry aids the process. Cultural differences must be carefully observed as beliefs may be culturally determined (Rack, 1982). A helpful guide is to discover if a client's belief might be shared by others from a similar background.

PERCEPTION

ILLUSIONS AND HALLUCINATIONS

Illusions are misperceived sensory events, such as a dressing gown hanging on a bedroom door being misperceived as an intruder or a departed loved one. A hallucination is similar, but has no external stimulus. Both may relate to any of the five senses – sight, smell, taste, touch and hearing – but hallucinations are most common in the auditory and visual senses. It is helpful to pose questions within a normal framework of experience by preparatory statements such as, 'Some people have unusual experiences when their nerves are upset...'. The client may then be more prepared to elaborate and say he has seen the antichrist (a visual hallucination) or hears his absent father's voice criticising him (an auditory hallucination) or smells putrid flesh (an olfactory hallucination). A tactile hallucination, where the client believes they are being touched or have insects crawling under their skin, is more unusual, as is a gustatory hallucination where a client may believe that they can taste poison. Some auditory hallucinations occur in normal experience when falling asleep (hypnagogic) or waking (hypnopompic).

COGNITIVE ASSESSMENT

This consists of orientation, concentration and attention, memory and insight as outlined below. Awareness of these aspects of the client's cognitive functioning will have become apparent throughout the process of the assessment and further specific questions may not be necessary at this stage.

ORIENTATION

Orientation in this context refers to time, place and person. Time orientation is assessed by asking questions about the current day, month or year. To further assess orientation of place the client is asked about where he or she thinks they are, how they got there and so on. Orientation of person is assessed by asking questions about the client's spouse or children and what their relationship is to him or her. Healthy people do not always know the exact date or the day of the week!

CONCENTRATION AND ATTENTION

Where unsure about the client's current concentration and attention, formal tests may add to previously gathered information. It is usual to ask the client to subtract 7 from 100 and then to take 7 from the remainder repeatedly (Rose, 1994, p. 35). However, errors may be due to lack of skill in arithmetic. If poor performance is due to this then you may ask the client to recite the months of the year in reverse order.

MEMORY

Three aspects of memory are assessed: immediate or working memory, short-term memory and long-term memory. When there are doubts regarding an individual's ability to remember, standardised psychological tests may supplement the general assessment. These provide quantitative assessment of the progression of potential memory disorder (Wechsler, 1945).

A client's immediate memory may be assessed by asking him or her to repeat sequences of digits that have been spoken slowly enough for him to reasonably register them. A normal response from a person of average intelligence is the ability to repeat back seven digits correctly. Short-term memory is assessed by asking about news items from the last day or two, or asking about recent events in the client's life. Long-term memory is assessed by asking the client questions such as what town she lived in as a 12 year old and names of earlier political leaders. When assessing elderly people, standardised ratings of memory for recent personal events, past personal events and general events help to distinguish between people with cerebral pathology and those without (Post, 1965).

INSIGHT

Insight refers to the client's degree of correct understanding of his or her condition and its cause coupled with a willingness to consider treatment. At this stage of the MSE the assessor will have a good idea of how far the client is aware of the state of his health. Direct questions can be asked to ascertain whether or not his perception of his problem is reasonably accurate. For example, a person with a problematic relationship might unrealistically attribute all problems to his partner, whereas another person in a similar situation might recognise, and wish to deal with, her own input to the problem. The answers to these questions are important because they determine in part whether the client is suitable for therapy.

RISK ASSESSMENT

The risk assessment as part of the medical and psychiatric assessment is mainly focused on the degree of risk a client may be to themselves and others taking into account their current and changing mental condition. Risk to self may best be viewed as a range from most extreme, when the client is actively suicidal and may end their life, to least extreme where the client has no suicidal ideation, is well supported and is largely in control of their life despite psychological difficulties. Even where risk of suicide is low, the client may be a serious threat to themselves, such as when a person with hypermania engages in numerous acts of unprotected sexual activity, possibly being exposed to sexually transmitted infections. It is beyond the scope of the current chapter to discuss these factors in detail but the reader might wish to become knowledgeable about assessing for suicide and being aware of the factors that might best identify those at risk (see for example Palmer, 2007; Ruddell and Curwen, 2002, 2007). A range of resources are available for helping in this process, such as questionnaires that aid in the detection of suicidality. For example: the Reason for Living Scale (Linehan, 1985) for measuring adaptive characteristics in suicide, the Scale for Suicidal Ideation (Beck et al., 1971), the Hopelessness scale (Beck, 1993; Beck et al., 1974b) to help in assessing risk of suicide, the Prediction of Suicide Scale (Beck et al., 1974a), the Los Angeles Suicide Prevention Scale (Los Angeles Center for Suicide Prevention, 1973) and the Beck Depression Inventory (Beck, 1978; Beck et al., 1996).

Risk to others is equally important and the factors helping to identify predictors are well established. For example, Maden (2003) in reviewing a major Study of psychiatric risk assessment by Monahan et al. (2001) called *Rethinking Risk Assessment. The MacArthur Study of Mental Disorder and Violence* notes that 'there were few surprises here, and future surveys will recycle the main variables of personality, previous violence, substance misuse and cultural influences…the unanswered questions are about intervention'.

Where the psychiatric assessment identifies that a person is a risk to self or others, the assessment of risk will be a continuing process and in many cases it will be necessary to involve a multi-disciplinary team of professionals the composition of which will depend on the nature and severity of the risk identified.

THE MAJOR CATEGORIES OF PSYCHIATRIC DISORDER

This section is intended to help practitioners become aware of the major categories of psychiatric disorder. It is not intended to enable the reader, unless appropriately trained and qualified, to make a diagnosis. A disease classification system is common to all branches of medicine. In psychiatry diagnostic labels are more often defined by clusters of symptoms or clinical features. Two widely accepted classification systems are used in psychiatry to aid the diagnosis of psychiatric disorders. They are the *International Classification of Diseases* (ICD 10), published by the World Health Organisation (2004), and the American Psychiatric Association's *Diagnostic and Statistical Manual of Mental Disorders,* fourth edition, text revision – DSM IV TR (2000). The classifications are broadly similar with codes and terms which are fully compatible. Accurate diagnosis is important to the client and practitioner as it best enables an appropriate and collaborative treatment plan to be made. An appropriate diagnosis can provide the client and other professionals with a framework for understanding and treating their difficulties and developing client-led treatment programmes (Appleby and Forshaw, 1990; Institute of Psychiatry, 1973).

Much information is required before an accurate diagnosis can be made and this is drawn from the MSE and the client history discussed above. A diagnosis matches signs and symptoms of sufficient intensity and duration, derived from this information against known descriptions of disorders. A psychiatric formulation is primarily used to summarise descriptive information which may be used to integrate it into a hypothesis about the causes, precipitants, and maintaining influences of an individual's problems.

Tables 3.2–3.8 outline the major categories of psychiatric disorder. Information is included in this form to aid brevity and for ease of reference. Most of the major categories of disorder (such as anxiety disorders, or mood disorders) have a designation, 'not otherwise specified' abbreviated to NOS which is used when symptoms suggest a mental disorder falling within the larger category but where the cluster of symptoms does not meet the criteria

Table 3.2 Anxiety disorders

Acute stress disorder	Anxiety lasting 2 days – 4 weeks, within 4 weeks of a traumatic event with at least three dissociative symptoms.
Agoraphobia without history of panic disorder	Agoraphobia with fear of developing panic symptoms – no history of panic disorder.
Anxiety disorder due to a general medical condition	Panic attacks, obsessions or compulsions associated with a specified medical condition.
Generalised anxiety disorder	Persistent, excessive, hard to control worry and anxiety. May be associated tension, fatigue, insomnia and impaired concentration. No focus on panic attacks.
Obsessive-compulsive disorder	Obsessions and/or compulsions recognised as excessive or inappropriate by client.
Panic disorder with agoraphobia	Recurrent panic attacks with agoraphobia.
Panic disorder without agoraphobia	Recurrent panic attacks with persistent worry of feared implications of attack (losing control, heart attack, 'going mad').
Post-traumatic stress disorder	Re-experiencing of traumatic event. Avoidance of reminders of trauma with numbing of general responsiveness and increased arousal. Symptoms last more than 1 month.
Specific phobia	Avoidance of feared object or situation with associated anxiety.
Social phobia	Anxiety and avoidance associated with unknown people or expectation of negative judgements – may include panic attacks.
Substance-induced anxiety disorder	Anxiety symptoms as physiological consequence of drug use or withdrawal.
Anxiety disorder NOS	Anxiety or phobic avoidance where the criteria do not reach those above.

Table 3.3 Mood disorders

Depressive disorders

Dysthymic disorders	Predominantly depressed mood (not continuous) for 2 or more years and not meeting criteria for other disorders.
Major depressive disorder: single episode or recurrent	One or more depressive episodes (2 weeks of depressed mood and loss of interest). No manic, hypomanic or mixed episodes. Change from usual functioning.

Bipolar disorders

Bipolar I disorder	One or more manic or mixed episodes often with depressed mood and/or hypomania.
Bipolar II disorder	One or more major depressive episodes with one or more hypomanic episodes. No manic or mixed episodes.
Cyclothymic disorder	Hypomanic symptoms for 2 years and numerous episodes of depressive symptoms – insufficient to reach major mood disorder. Not due to other mental or physical conditions or substance use.

Continued

Table 3.3 cont'd

Mood disorders

Mood disorder due to a general medical condition	Mood disturbance directly physiologically linked to a general medical condition.
Substance-induced mood disorder	Disturbance in mood directly physiologically linked to drug use, toxin exposure or withdrawal.
Mood disorder NOS	Mood symptoms but not reaching criteria for specific mood disorders.

Table 3.4 Personality disorders

Cluster A

Paranoid	Distrust and suspiciousness.
Schizoid	Social detachment, restricted emotional expression.
Schizotypal	Discomfort of close relationships, eccentric in behaviours, perceptions and thinking.

Cluster B

Antisocial	Disregard and violation of other's rights. May be aggressive or destructive, breaking laws and rules.
Borderline	Impulsive; instability in interpersonal relationships, self-image and emotions.
Histrionic	Attention seeking through exaggerated emotions and excitability.
Narcissistic	Grandiose sense of self-importance; lacks empathy; needs admiration.

Cluster C

Avoidant	Social inhibition, feelings of inadequacy, hypersensitivity.
Dependent	Seeks care through submissive clingy behaviour.
Obsessive-compulsive	Orderliness, perfectionism and control are dominant.
Personality disorder NOS	Traits common to other personality disorders but not meeting the specific criteria of any one.

Table 3.5 Eating disorders

Anorexia nervosa	Refusal to maintain minimum body weight, refusal of food, distorted perception of shape/size of body; fear of weight gain; amenorrhoea; deny seriousness of low body weight.
Bulimia nervosa	Control of body weight by binge eating, self-induced vomiting, laxatives, diuretics, fasting, excessive exercise.
Eating disorder NOS	Some of the symptoms of either anorexia or bulimia nervosa but does not meet the criteria of any specific disorder within that category.

Table 3.6 Somatoformorm disorders

Body dysmorphic disorder	Preoccupation with real or imagined defect in appearance of body.
Conversion disorder	Symptoms (not intentionally produced but where psychological factors are evident) affecting voluntary motor or sensory functions suggesting a neurological or other general medical condition.
Hypochondriasis	Misinterpretation of body symptoms leading to preoccupation with fears of serious disease for 6 months plus; persists despite contrary medical evidence.
Pain disorder	Physical pain not intentionally produced where psychological factors seem to affect its onset, severity, exacerbation or maintenance.
Somatisation disorder	Starts before age 30. Multiple physical symptoms medically unexplained.
Undifferentiated somatoform disorder	Physical complaints not fully explained by a medical condition or use of drug(s).
Somatoform disorder NOS	This designation abbreviated NOS can be used when the mental disorder appears to fall within the larger category but does not meet the criteria of any specific disorder within that category.

Table 3.7 Dissociative disorders

Dissociative amnesia	Inability to recall important personal information, usually of a traumatic/stressful nature leading to distress in social and occupational areas of functioning.
Depersonalisation disorder	Feeling of detachment from self and diminished sense of control. Surroundings experienced as unreal.
Dissociative fugue	Sudden onset with unexpected travel away from home surroundings, where recall of past and memory of identity is impaired.
Dissociative identity disorder	The presence of two or more identities which take control of a person's behaviour. There is impaired recall between identities.
Dissociative identity disorder NOS	Some of the symptoms of above disorders but does not meet the criteria of any specific disorder within category.

of any specific disorder within that category. The tables below generally refer to adults – the criteria for children usually reflect their different developmental stage in life. Another general feature is that a diagnosis is usually made only when the symptoms cause clinically significant distress or impairment in social, occupational or other important areas of functioning.

The complaints or *symptoms* a client presents with are all considered by the qualified clinician and matched against all the possible disorders from which they might result. This list of possible illnesses is the differential diagnosis. The clinician must then begin a methodical process to discover

Table 3.8 Schizophrenia and other psychotic disorders

Schizophrenia	Delusions or hallucinations, disorganised speech, disorganised or catatonic behaviour, negative symptoms such as flat affect, social/occupational dysfunction. Symptoms present at least 6 months.
Schizophreniform disorder	Symptoms equivalent to schizophrenia but for 1–6 months. Social/occupational functioning may not be impaired.
Schizoaffective disorder	Same as schizophrenia plus major depressive, manic or mixed episode; hallucinations/delusions for 2 weeks without mood symptoms.
Delusional disorder	Non-bizarre delusions for at least 1 month but symptom criteria from schizophrenia not met.
Brief psychotic disorder	Psychotic symptoms persist for less than 1 month and resolve completely.
Shared psychotic disorder	Disorder influenced by another who already has delusions.
Psychotic disorder due to a general medical condition	Psychotic symptoms physiologically linked to a (specified) general medical condition.

the correct diagnosis. This process is known as 'ruling out'. Ruling out refers to the medical diagnostic process of eliminating possible illnesses or causes one at a time by considering clinical information from history, examination or testing that is not consistent with the diagnosis being ruled out. This process may require gathering further information. When all other diagnoses in the *differential diagnosis* have been ruled out, the correct diagnosis is presumed to remain. The specified diagnostic criteria for each mental disorder contained in the diagnostic manuals mentioned above are used as guidelines for making diagnoses, because it has been demonstrated that the use of such criteria enhances agreement among practitioners.

There are two groups of disorders the practitioner may encounter, which are not included in the tables. First are sleep disorders in which there are two main groups: the dyssomnias and the parasomnias. The dyssomnias are disorders where difficulties are experienced in going to sleep, staying asleep or excessive sleepiness (where they are a disorder of wakefulness). The parasomnias relate to difficulties (e.g. nightmares, sleepwalking) during a particular episode of sleep. Second are the *factitious disorders*: signs and symptoms of physical, psychological or both physical and psychological difficulties are intentionally produced to enable the client to assume the role of a sick person.

A further group of disorders that may be encountered are the mental disorders due to a general medical condition. These disorders are diagnosed when there is clinical evidence from the history, physical examination or laboratory tests that are caused by a specific medical condition. These disorders are grouped into two main categories: catatonic disorder and personality change. In the first, the presence of catatonia is evident and is indicated by signs including motor immobility (such as stupor), excessive activity (excitement), rigidity or posturing (such as waxy flexibility where a limb will retain the position into which it is placed by another). Personality change due to a general medical condition may be diagnosed where a persistent disturbance of personality takes place away from the person's previous and usual pattern of personality.

REFERENCES

American Psychiatric Association (2000) *Diagnostic and Statistical Manual of Mental Disorders* (4th edn, text revision). Washington, DC: American Psychiatric Association.

Appleby, L. and Forshaw, D. (1990) *Post Graduate Psychiatry Clinical Foundations*. Oxford: Heinemann Medical Books.

Beck, A. T. (1978) *Depression Inventory*. Philadelphia: Centre for Cognitive Therapy.

Beck, A. T. (1993) *Beck Hopelessness Scale*. San Antonio, Texas: Psychological Corporation.

Beck, A. T., Kovacs, M. and C (1971) Assessment of suicidal ideation: the scale for suicidal ideation. *Journal of Consultancy and Clinical Psychology*, 47, 343–352.

Beck, A. T., Schuyler, D. and Herman, I. (1974a) Development of suicidal intent scales. In A. T. Beck, H. L. P. Resnick and D. J. Lettie (eds) *The Prediction of Suicide*. Maryland: Charles Press.

Beck, A. T., Steer, R. A. and Brown, G. K. (1996) *Depression Inventory II*. San Antonio, Texas: Psychological Corporation.

Beck, A. T., Weissman, A., Lester, D. and Trexter, L. (1974b) The measurement of pessimism: the hopelessness scale. *Journal of Consulting and Clinical Psychology*, 42, 861–865.

Bynum, W. F. (1983) Psychiatry in its historical context. In M. Shepherd and O. L. Zangwill (eds) *Handbook of Psychiatry*, Vol. 1. Cambridge: Cambridge University Press.

Campbell, T. L. (1986) *Families' Impact on Health: a World Review and Annotated Bibliography*. NIMH Series DN6. Washington, DC: US Government Policy Office.

Curwen, B. (1997) Medical and psychiatric assessment. In S. Palmer and G. McMahon (eds) *Client Assessment*. London: Sage.

Curwen, B. and Ruddell, P. (1997) What type of Help. In S. Palmer and G. McMahon (eds) *Client Assessment*. London: Sage.

Davies, D. M. (1987) *Textbook of Adverse Drug Reactions* (3rd edn). Oxford: Oxford University Press.

Eastwood, R. and Trevelyan, M. H. (1972) Relationship between physical and psychiatric disorder. *Psychological Medicine*, 2, 363–372.

Engel, G. (1962) *Psychological Development in Health and Disease.* Philadelphia: Saunders.

Freud, S. (1911) Psychoanalytical notes upon an autobiographical account of cases of paranoia (Schreber). In *The Complete Psychological Works* (standard edn), Vol. 12. 1–82. London: Hogarth Press, 1958.

Goffman, E. (1963) *Stigma: Notes on the Management of Spoiled Identity.* Harmondsworth: Penguin.

Institute of Psychiatry (1973) *Notes on Eliciting and Recording Clinical Information.* Oxford: Oxford University Press.

Leff, J. P. and Isaacs, A. D. (1990) *Psychiatric Examination in Clinical Practice.* Oxford: Blackwell.

Linehan, M. M. (1985) Reason for living scale. In P. A. Keller and L. G. Ritts (eds) *Innovations in Clinical Practice: A Source Book*, Vol. 4. Sarasota, Florida: Professional Resource Exchange.

Los Angeles Center for Suicide Prevention (1973) *Los Angeles Suicide Prevention Scale.* Los Angeles: LACSP.

Lukas, S. (1993) *Where to Start and What to Ask: An Assessment Handbook.* London: W. W. Norton.

Maden, A. (2003) Rethinking Risk Assessment. The MacArthur Study of Mental Disorder and Violence: *Review in Psychiatric Bulletin*, Vol. 27. 237–238. The Royal College of Psychiatrists.

Monahan, J., Steadman, H. J., Silver, E., Appelbaum, P. S., Clark Robbins, P., Mulvey, E. P., Roth, L. H., Grisso, T. and Banks, S. (2001) *Rethinking Risk Assessment: The MacArthur Study of Mental Disorder and Violence.* New York: Oxford University Press.

Morrison, J. (1995) *The First Interview.* New York: Guilford Press.

Palmer, S. (ed) (2007) *Suicide: Strategies and Interventions for Reduction and Prevention.* London: Routledge.

Post, F. (1965) *The Clinical Psychiatry of Late Life.* New York: Pergamon Press.

Querido, A. (1959) Forecast and follow-up: an investigation into the clinical, social and mental factors determining the results of hospital treatment. *British Journal of Preventive and Social Medicine*, 13, 344–9.

Rack, P. (1982) *Race, Culture and Mental Disorder.* London: Routledge pp. 121–2.

Rose, N. D. B. (ed) (1994) *Essential Psychiatry* (2nd edn). Oxford: Blackwell Scientific.

Ruddell, P. (1997) General Assessment Issues. In S. Palmer and G. McMahon (eds), *Client Assessment.* London: Sage.

Ruddell, P. and Curwen, B. (2002) Understanding suicidal ideation and assessing for risk. *British Journal of Guidance and Counselling*, 30(4), 263–272.

Ruddell, P. and Curwen, B. (2007) Understanding suicidal ideation and assessing for risk. In S. Palmer (ed) *Suicide: Strategies and Interventions for Reduction and Prevention.* London: Routledge.

Saunders, J. M. and Valente, S. M. (1988) Cancer and suicide. *Oncology Nursing Forum*, 15(5), 575–580.

Schneider, K. (1949) The concept of delusion. Reprinted and translated in S. R. Hirsch and M. Shepherd (eds) *Themes and Variations in European Psychiatry*. Bristol: John Wright, 1974.

Shepherd, M., Cooper, B., Brown, A. C. and Kalton, G. W. (1966) *Psychiatric Illness in General Practice*. London: Oxford University Press.

Tuke, D.H. (1872) *Illustrations of the Influence of the Mind upon the Body in Health and Disease*. London: J. and A. Churchill.

Wechsler, D. (1945) A standardised memory scale for clinical use. *Journal of Psychology*, 19, 87–95.

Wing, J. K., Cooper, J. E. and Sartorious, N. (1974) *Measurement and Classification of Psychiatric Symptoms*. Cambridge: Cambridge University Press.

World Health Organisation (2004) *International Statistical Classification of Diseases and Health Related Problems* ICD-10 (10th revision; 2nd edn). Geneva: WHO.

4 HOW TO PREPARE A REPORT ON A CLIENT

Robert Bor

Therapists may be called upon to formally assess and submit a report of their findings to a client, an employer, lawyer or other agency, such as a court. Such requests place a significant burden of responsibility on the therapist as many sensitive and complex issues are potentially at stake. These include issues of safety and risk to the individual or to others; the possibility of the person losing his or her job, career and future work prospects; as well as the individual's personal esteem and the likely impact on family or dependents. This chapter describes the place of psychological assessment and reporting in therapy, the essential requirements for these, and also presents an illustrative report to convey a sense of what might be considered appropriate for this undertaking.

Psychological assessments are undertaken for three main reasons. First, because a client requests it and assessment seems relevant to the concerns that the client presents in therapy. Second, when requested by a third party such as another therapist or a lawyer acting for the client in relation to a specific matter (e.g. custody dispute, immigration matter, litigation following psychological trauma etc.). Third, when the therapist's expert opinion is solicited by the courts.

This chapter is mostly concerned with the third scenario which, by definition, is exceptional and therefore never conducted as a matter of routine within the course of psychological therapy. Psychologists and less frequently therapists are most likely to be called upon to undertake psychological assessments. Those which involve mental state and psychopathology assessments, as is a fundamental requirement in the third category, will almost certainly be carried out by specialist clinical or counselling psychologists; however, any therapist may be required to produce a report containing their opinion of the client's problem and what they have covered in their therapy sessions with the client. It is imperative that the psychologist or therapist's report is of the highest calibre. It must be in a format and of a quality that can be submitted as evidence in a court of law. The reasons are threefold: first, the client will normally have access to his or her report and may question some of the findings; second, given the possible deleterious effects on the individual's circumstances, his or her legal counsel may mount a challenge to the findings and the report is likely to be closely scrutinised by other experts; and third, the therapist may be required to defend his or her report in a court of law.

Not only, therefore, must the assessment be comprehensive and robust, but it must also be conducted by a professional whose experience and specialism is conducting mental health assessments. Many different aspects of the assessment and report may come under scrutiny by lawyers and other psychologists. One that invariably diminishes the veracity of the report is the qualifications and expertise of the therapist who undertook the assessment. The following is a short excerpt from a verbatim transcript between the barrister and psychologist in court from one such case that highlights the potential problem:

Barrister: Can you please tell the court, Dr. Harvey, what your professional qualifications are?

Psychologist: I am a Chartered Occupational Psychologist with a doctorate from X university.

Barrister: Can you also please tell the court something about your experience of conducting mental state examinations and assessments of clients?

Psychologist: I have completed more than fifteen reports; I was trained to carry out psychological assessments in my university course. On a day-to-day basis, I consult to Airline G where I am responsible for selecting new pilots and conducting appraisal interviews. I also contribute to the assessments where staff are being considered for a promotion.

Barrister: So you are not specifically qualified to carry out *clinical* assessments using *clinical* instruments?

Psychologist: Well, I do have experience in these and ...

Barrister: (interjecting) Then why are you not licensed as a *clinical* psychologist?

Psychologist: Ummm...

In this case, the challenge to the conclusions of the report started by undermining the qualifications of the psychologist which, in turn, diminished the strength of the evidence presented. This excerpt illustrates that it is not sufficient to claim expertise in using a particular psychometric test when reporting on an individual. The therapist must also demonstrate that he or she has the training, qualifications and experience to interpret such tests and present a balanced account of the individual's performance in the context both of their background and their mental state at assessment.

The quality of psychological reports has never been the subject of a systematic study and therefore it is difficult to gain insight into the extent of their use or usefulness. However, there is anecdotal evidence to suggest that some are fundamentally faulty and may unfairly jeopardise an individual's case. The shortcomings are varied and include incomprehensibility, lacking in validity, being based on faulty assumptions or interpretations, inappropriate use or choice tests or overreliance on testing, lacking in rigour and plainly biased. This is regrettable as, if used correctly, and taking into account certain limitations, psychological insights and methods have made an important contribution to understanding complex psychological problems and in assisting in legal cases. Psychology and therapy may not be *precise* sciences, but this does not diminish their potential for value and usefulness.

Therapists themselves face significant challenges in their assessment of clients. The person requesting assessment may place unrealistic or unattainable demands on the assessment process and outcome. Apart from clear and incontrovertible cases (e.g. an individual who sustains a severe and irreversible head injury following a fall whilst enjoying recreational rock climbing), the therapist more usually has to make recommendations in his or her report based on probability, degree and risk. The degree of complexity increases even further where the individual client's pre-morbid state has to be inferred. The ability to predict a person's behaviour in given situations nearly always poses a significant challenge.

Therapists may be required to comment on whether an individual might be suffering from a specific disorder. These are most likely to include those from the list below:

- psychosis;
- affective disorders, including bipolar disorder;
- personality disorders (especially where there has been evidence of overt acts of violence, a pattern of interpersonal problems or any other acting out behaviour);
- substance dependence (alcohol, sedatives, hypnotics, anti-depressants, recreational and illicit drugs, and inhalers);
- neurosis;
- self-destructive acts;
- disturbance or loss of consciousness;
- transient loss of control of nervous system functioning without satisfactory explanation of the cause;
- epilepsy or convulsive disorders;
- progressive disease of the nervous system.

Some therapists might argue that it is not within their area of expertise to 'diagnose' clients or work within the framework of *Diagnostic and Statistical Manual of Mental Disorders* (DSM) (American Psychiatric Association, 2000) categorisations. They would nonetheless be expected to have a working knowledge of basic psychopathology and be familiar with the medical model of assessment and diagnosis. Assessment of clients is by interview and appropriate tests where indicated. Collateral information may be requested from the client's family, employer, line manager, occupational health department or personal family physician or general practitioner, where permission has been given to do so by the client.

Psychological assessment is conducted in order to determine whether the individual currently suffers from a psychological problem. The therapist must, therefore, describe and report the *presence* of psychopathology or clinical syndromes. A further requirement is to offer an opinion as to the extent or severity of the problem and the likely impact that it will have on the individual's life. Prediction in this context is almost always challenging and in this section of the report, the therapist should seek to draw on findings from published research to substantiate his or her opinion. It does not diminish the usefulness and quality of the report to state that it is not possible to speculate as to the likely consequences of having the problem if, indeed, this is the case. It is most important to be truthful and fair and to give a balanced account of probabilities. For this reason, it may be both appropriate and necessary to point out several possible outcomes without stating with certainty which one is most likely to occur.

The definition of 'caseness' and specific criteria for diagnosis is usually made in relation to the American Psychiatric Association's classification system for mental illness (American Psychiatric Association, 2000). This nosologic system defines clinical syndromes and lists the unique symptoms that must be present in order to diagnose an individual as suffering from a particular condition.

PURPOSE OF REPORTS

Therapists are trained to communicate with and to other professionals about and with their clients in various ways. An essential part of the communication is report writing. Reports facilitate the sharing of information, mapping and formulation of clinical problems and describing possible psychotherapeutic interventions. Therapists should aim to produce accurate, clear, credible, useful and persuasive reports (Benn and Brady, 1998). It is an unfortunate fact that many reports are criticised for not being sufficiently useful. They may be deficient in certain or many respects. This may be due to the fact that some of those who undertake such assessments have learned more from experience than formal training. The more frequently cited deficiencies of reports include vagueness, excessive speculation, failure to include data from which inferences are drawn, excessive use of jargon and unbalanced (i.e. overly negative or positive) opinions being expressed.

The UK Data Protection Act (1998) and Access to Health Records Act (1990) enable people to have access to their health records and therapists' reports are no exception. Any information written about the individual, including rough notes or the results of psychological tests, is included within the scope of this legislation. The only exception to access is where there is a risk of serious harm to the individual or to others. The individual may also challenge the accuracy of information held about him or her, although the therapist can stand by his or her opinions or recorded facts as long as a note is made of the disputed sections. It, therefore, almost goes without saying that any client who is assessed can request access to the report and therefore should always be written with this outcome in mind. This is distinct from who *owns* the assessment. The report is the property of the person or agency that requested it. Psychological reports should always be used in their entirety and never in edited sections.

The purpose of a report of a clinical assessment of a client is guided by the need to answer four main questions:

1. What psychological problems, if any, does the client currently experience?
2. Could these psychological problems adversely affect or impair the client's behaviour?
3. Are the problems likely to be transient or more permanent?
4. Are these treatable problems and, if so, is psychotherapeutic intervention or treatment likely to be effective?

Reports are typically structured in a format that allows the reader to follow the process and outcome of the assessment and the judgements made. This enables other specialist psychologists and therapists, as well as anyone who is not a therapist (e.g. lawyer, doctor) to make sense of:

(a) the problem that has been assessed and the context in which it occurs;
(b) how it has been assessed;
(c) what has been found through the assessment;
(d) the therapist's opinion as to the likely implications of the problems; and
(e) the therapist's conclusions and recommendations.

The first section of the report contains biographical details about the client and also includes important contextual information. Included in this section are the client's name, date of birth, the place and date of assessment, the date of the report, reason for referral and the name of the referrer. Some therapists also summarise their qualifications and experience in this section. If intended for court, this first section will also include a short CV or resume of the therapist writing the report. The second section outlines the different sources that the therapist has drawn on to undertake the assessment. This might include psychological tests, previous tests carried out on the client, their health records and related information, such as information gleaned from other sources (e.g. interview with the client's partner). The third section typically describes the background to the problem and the client's account of this. A summary of what the client tells the therapist should be included in this section. The results of the clinical and mental state assessment of the client are described in the fourth section. The person writing the report should keep in mind that technical information should be presented in a format that is easy to understand. It is normal practice to include references to the tests used. The fifth section is optional and may summarise the findings from any additional relevant information that has been gathered (e.g. interview of a line manager). The therapist's formulation and opinion comprises the sixth section. The therapist includes an 'educated guess' as to the causes of the problem in this section. The limitations of the assessment should be included here. Only claims that can be substantiated should be included in the report. Finally, the author makes his or her recommendations in the seventh section. This may include recommendations for further assessment and psychological treatment. Some authors attach a brief summary of the report at the end and also include a legal declaration that the report reflects the therapist's best professional judgement and has not been unduly influenced by the person who has requested or paid for the report.

All statements in the report about the individual should be credible and persuasive. The conclusions reached should be consistent with the data presented. Opinions that are based on the professional's personal thoughts or subjective reactions to the client have no place in a therapist's report. Care should be taken to present a succinct, readable and balanced report comprising several sub-headings that is free from jargon, typographical errors, wordiness or unsubstantiated findings. It is also important to keep in mind the person for whom the report is written. Specialist knowledge of the reader should not be assumed. Terms that may be more familiar to therapists (e.g. *transference* or *neurotic*) but less well understood by others should be avoided.

It is most important for the report writer to bear in mind his duties not only to those commissioning the report, but also to the client and third parties to whom the report will have relevance. If, for example, the report is written in the light of legal proceedings, the writer must feel confident that the report is accurate, based on well-established scientific reasoning and that it will stand up to cross examination. Above all, the writer must be satisfied that the report is true and believed to be true. To compromise on this point could lead to the report writer having to explain himself in a criminal court. Therapists and other experts who are able to establish themselves as unbiased and balanced whilst able to address all relevant issues based on scientific reasoning will make a good impression on the reader and the fear of being contradicted can therefore recede. A good reputation should surely follow.

CONCLUSION

Those who have specialist training (such as in the course of their continuing professional development) should preferably write psychological assessment reports of clients that address mental health concerns, although any therapist may be required to produce one for the courts. The findings of the assessment should always be presented in a balanced and useful way. The report should follow a clear structure and be comprehensible to a non-specialist audience. Whilst the report is the property of the person requesting it, the author should keep in mind that the client and others might view it and have comments to make about its accuracy. For this reason, the report should always be of a medico-legal standard (see Appendix 4.1).

APPENDIX 4.1: SAMPLE REPORT

The following is a sample report that is entirely fictitious and included for illustrative purposes only. Some sections are briefer than is normally the case due to space considerations.

SAMPLE REPORT

TOUCHDOWN AIRLINES
PSYCHOLOGIST'S REPORT

Name:	First Officer John Smith
Date of birth:	31 May 1969
On the instructions of:	Dr. Stephen Harris, Authorised Medical Examiner
Location:	Touchdown Airlines Head Office, One Mile Island, United Kingdom
Date of assessment:	15 January 2006
Date of report:	20 September 2006
Reason for referral:	F. O. Smith was referred for assessment of his psychological state and to determine whether he is mentally fit to return to full flying duties having been off work for more than 21 days due to marriage difficulties.
Psychologist and author:	Dr Peter Johnson

BASIS OF THE REPORT

This report is based on my:

(a) clinical interview of F. O. Smith;
(b) interpretation of a psychometric test completed by F. O. Smith;
(c) understanding and interpretation of background information supplied to me by Dr. Stephen Harris, Aeromedical Examiner at Touchdown Airlines; and
(d) understanding and interpretation of information supplied to me during a meeting with Captain Jane Elford, Chief Pilot, Boeing Fleet at Touchdown Airlines.

BACKGROUND HISTORY AS
F. O. SMITH PRESENTED IT TO ME

(A) PERSONAL AND PILOTING
BACKGROUND:

F. O. Smith is a 36-year-old man who grew up in Canada. After completing his schooling, he was accepted into Bank Airlines pilot *ab initio* pilot scheme, where he obtained his commercial pilots' licence and for whom he flew for ten years. He later joined Practical Airlines where he also flew commercially, mainly operating Boeing types. He has been employed at Touchdown Airlines for the past eight years and he currently operates Airbus types.

(B) FAMILY HISTORY AND PERSONAL
BACKGROUND:

F. O. Smith's parents and two younger brothers all live in Canada. He married his wife, Juliet, ten years ago. They have two daughters, aged eight and six years and an eighteen month old son. He told me that he has a good relationship with his children.

(C) THE PRESENT PROBLEM:

He told me that his wife has recently questioned him about his relationships with female crew and she has expressed concerns that he has been having an extra marital relationship with one particular flight attendant. Things came to a head two months ago when his wife threatened to leave him to go back to her parents in Scotland. F. O. Smith told me that he has been experiencing problems in his marriage for several months. He said: 'I have had personal issues with my wife; we have not been seeing eye-to-eye since the beginning of this year'.

F. O. Smith explained to me that his wife comes from a very close and emotionally 'claustrophobic' family background. He told me that his in-laws telephone his wife three to four times a day and give her advice as to how she should manage her life both in terms of major decisions as well as in seemingly insignificant details such as where she should shop for the cheapest milk. He explained that he has sometimes felt displaced by his in-laws and has argued with his wife about her overly close attachment to her parents.

I asked him to explain more about the nature of the marriage problems. He told me that it was difficult to pinpoint the precise cause of the problems, but they amounted to a breakdown of trust. He explained that there had been several situations in which trust had presented as a problem; for example, his wife's concerns about his relationship with a colleague at work. F. O. Smith also pointed out to me that he felt that his wife confiding in her parents about issues that he felt were personal to them as a couple made him feel wary of discussing some things openly with her as he could not trust her not to convey the issue to his in-laws.

When the problem came to a head two months ago, his wife threatened to return to Scotland; she told him that she needed the physical space to reflect on the future of their relationship. Recognising the emotional repercussions to himself of this decision, F. O. Smith took himself off line and presented himself to one of the specialist doctors in the airline's Aeromedical service and he also arranged for counselling through the airline's Employee Assistance Programme.

He told me that while he is able to normally maintain separation between his working life and his domestic/personal life, he said: 'It is important to take the responsibility onto myself and to remove myself from a situation if I think that there is any danger'. He told me that in his work context, he is able to take charge in challenging and difficult situations and apply the lessons taught in Crew Resource Management training programmes. He recognises though that he cannot manage problems in the same way in his personal relationships. He explained that work is an antidote to his personal difficulties as it is somewhere where he can feel good about himself and where his mind is taken off his domestic problems.

I asked F. O. Smith to explain how he felt at the time that his wife threatened to leave. He told me that he was shocked that his wife should want to leave him and was very distressed that she should want to return to Scotland, taking the three children with him. He also felt resentful and lacking in personal control when 'the rumour network in Touchdown [Airlines]' became involved in his personal situation. He said that the rumours about him made him feel very angry, as he did not feel that he had control of aspects of his personal life.

I understand from F. O. Smith that his own parents in Canada are aware of his marriage problems and they have encouraged him to 'sort things out' within the relationship.

I asked him what he was hoping to achieve through counselling and psychological support. He said: 'I am prepared to face my demons. I need to know what is causing this [the problems in the marriage relationship]'. He explained that he felt that he was more motivated to overcoming the problems at this time than he perceives his wife to be. Nonetheless, he expressed an interest in couples' therapy.

In order to determine whether he has a realistic sense of the possible outcomes, I asked F. O. Smith what he thinks may happen to him if his wife decides to leave him. He replied in a calm tone: 'If she leaves me, I accept this; she is entitled to move on. It would be traumatic at first, but I would heal in time'.

F. O. Smith told me that he was surprised that his personal situation had 'got out of control' and he felt both confused and resentful that his taking the positive step of voluntarily and proactively coming off line had resulted in the need for a specialist report. Whilst he understood that his exceeding the 21-day threshold for sick leave necessitated a report in the light of the automatic suspension of licence pending medical clearance, he emphasised that this was a very stressful time for him. He told me that with the threat of the loss of his marriage relationship and his licence, the situation was beginning to feel like a witch-hunt. He acknowledged that some of his recent behaviour might be an excessive reaction to these threats, which in turn, might have increased people's concerns about him.

I discussed with him several hypothetical outcomes to the assessment and recommendations. These ranged, on the one hand, from loss of licence to a recommendation that he be deemed fit to return to work, as well as other outcomes. He said that he understood and accepted these possible outcomes.

ASSESSMENT OF F. O. SMITH

F. O. Smith is a 36-year-old male pilot employed by Touchdown Airlines. He arrived on time for the assessment. He was neatly, though casually, dressed. He appeared clean, well kempt and physically healthy.

In interview, he was pleasant, friendly and fully co-operative. He answered all questions I put to him in an open and honest way. He maintained good eye contact. He gave clear answers to both open and closed questions. His affect was at all times appropriate. A good rapport was established and, overall, he seemed to be at ease in the situation. He displayed good insight into his difficulties although evidence of his insight required some prompting from my side at times.

He was fluent in English, this being his first language although he was brought up in a French-Canadian community and he is bilingual.

There was no suggestion of any major deficit when he was asked to recall things from both his short- and long-term memory. Verbally, he was fluent and his pace of speech measured suggesting no major cognitive problems.

There was no evidence of delusions or hallucinations, and he was fully oriented in time and place. There were no psychotic features or suicidal ideation.

In order to emphasise some points, he gesticulated in a confident manner. There was no evidence of any involuntary behaviour, inappropriate gestures or responses, or thought disorder.

Overall, his manner was pleasant. It was clear from his background, educational achievements, demeanour and communication skills that he is probably of at least average intelligence.

He told me that his mood is usually 'jovial' and 'happy-go-lucky' though he has felt more depressed since he has been unable to resolve his marriage problems. He also has a tendency to become 'moody' after a night flight.

F. O. Smith told me that his appetite and weight are both 'fine' and 'stable'.

For recreation, he enjoys fishing, golf, aerobics and aerobatics. He owns his own light aircraft.

He told me that he drinks alcohol, although in moderation and most only socially. He denies using any recreational drugs.

I explored with him how he manages stress and conflict both in the work place as well as in his personal life. He seemed to give a balanced account of some of his personal shortcomings. I noted his inability to respond flexibly to certain problems. His need to be in control is consonant with this. At times, he can be impulsive and demanding, and he may lack insight into some of his own behaviour. Where his needs are not met, he responds in certain situations by becoming more demanding and dominant. He then looses the ability to be diplomatic and empathetic to others. Some of this pattern can be quite child-like. He may pull on others for a response and is unremitting in this until he gets a reaction; after which, he then backs off. One consequence is to alienate himself from those around him, as he appears to lack insight into the effect his behaviour has on others and especially into how his relationship with his wife has deteriorated.

When he feels frustrated, this may be marked by a rapid change in his temper. It appears that he does not always adequately manage his personal stress. Where this is the case, he has a tendency to become defensive and argumentative. He may place self-interest above all else when he feels threatened in a situation. When challenged or threatened, he either acts aggressively or tactically in order to achieve his goals.

I confined my **psychometric assessment** to his personality. I asked F.O. Smith to complete the Personality Assessment Inventory (Morey, 1991), which he did. I personally undertook the scoring and interpretation of his test. He was fully co-operative and the results of each of this measure were usable. A brief description of the instrument together with the results in his case is presented below.

Personality Assessment Inventory – The PAI is a rigorously constructed psychometric instrument designed to provide clinicians with a reliable and valid measure of personality and psychopathology. The PAI contains 344 items and respondents are required to answer whether each item is 'totally false', 'slightly true', 'mainly true', or 'very true'. The items of the test are scored onto twenty-two non-overlapping scales, some of which help to determine whether the respondent is consistent, careful and honest in relation to the test items.

VALIDITY OF TEST RESULTS

The PAI provides a number of validity indices that are designed to provide an assessment of factors that could distort the results of testing. For this protocol, the number of uncompleted items is within acceptable limits. Also evaluated is the extent to which the respondent attended appropriately and responded consistently to the content of test items. F. O. Smith's scores suggest that he did attend appropriately to item content and responded in a consistent fashion to similar items. The degree to which response styles may have affected or distorted the report of symptomatology on the inventory is also assessed. The scores for these indicators fall in the normal range, suggesting that he answered in a reasonably forthright manner and did not attempt to present an unrealistic or inaccurate impression that was either more negative or more positive than the clinical picture would warrant.

CLINICAL FEATURES

The PAI clinical profile is entirely within normal limits. There are no indications of significant psychopathology in the areas that are tapped by the individual clinical scales. According to F. O. Smith's self-report, he describes no significant problems in the following areas: unusual thoughts or peculiar experiences; antisocial behaviour; problems with empathy; undue suspiciousness or hostility; extreme moodiness and impulsivity; unhappiness and depression; unusually elevated mood or heightened activity; marked anxiety; problematic behaviours used to manage anxiety; difficulties with health or physical functioning. Also, he reports NO significant problems with alcohol or drug abuse or dependence. F. O. Smith, however, acknowledges that he sometimes looses his temper and is prone to lose control when he is emotionally stressed.

SELF-CONCEPT

F. O. Smith's self-concept appears to involve a generally stable and positive self-evaluation. He is normally a confident and optimistic person who approaches life with a clear sense of purpose and distinct convictions. These characteristics are valuable in that they allow him to be resilient and adaptive in the face of most stressors. He describes being reasonably self-satisfied, with a well-articulated sense of who he is and what his goals are.

INTERPERSONAL

F. O. Smith's interpersonal style seems best characterised as friendly and extraverted. He will usually present a cheerful and positive picture in the presence of others. He is able to communicate his interest in others in an open and straightforward manner. He usually prefers activities that bring him into contact with others, rather than solitary pursuits, and he is probably quick to offer help to those in need of it. He sees himself as a person with many friends and as one who is comfortable in most social situations.

BACKGROUND OF F.O. SMITH AS PRESENTED TO ME BY HIS FLEET CAPTAIN

I learned from the Chief Pilot Boeing Fleet that F. O. Smith's flying skills are excellent. All of his line checks have been to a high standard. There have been no reports of risk-taking or actions that would pose a danger. There have been no reported interpersonal problems in the work place.

OPINION

1. F. O. Smith is not currently suffering from any psychological condition that would prevent him from resuming flying duties.

There is specifically **no evidence that he suffers from any definable mood or personality disorder.**

2. His marriage relationship has deteriorated over the past few months and this has given rise to **significant personal stress.** It was a positive decision and also a measure and sign of his prudence that he elected to take himself off line whilst undergoing counselling for his marriage problem.

3. The present crisis in his life was precipitated by his wife's threat to leave him. His reaction to this demonstrated that he is prone to behave impulsively at times with the aim of trying to stabilise or control events. This may also signal an urge to control his own mood, as he fears personal loss and being exposed to unpleasant feelings (e.g. low mood or depression). This tendency to act defensively and to try to control events is not a definable psychological problem *per se*, but a sign that he has **traits of personality problems.** The most likely of these are a tendency towards paranoia and narcissism, particularly when he is under stress. In my opinion, his personal problems have exacerbated several personality traits, which in turn, have compounded his difficulties with other people. This pattern escalated significantly in the past week. However, there was clear evidence to me that under professional guidance and by confronting him with how he mismanaged his problem, this pattern all but dissipated.

4. When he is under stress, his logic and reasoning tends to become one-sided. He has a tendency to become self-referential, child-like in his behaviour and display a lack of empathy for others. His attributions to events and situations can be impaired or biased by his determination to view problems only from his perspective. His solutions to certain problems exacerbate his personal and interpersonal difficulties. He also has a tendency to act out his feelings (e.g. anger, feeling out of control; lacking in trust) when he feels stressed, rather than finding solutions to the problems he faces. His reactions to events may, at times, be inappropriate or disproportionate. He has a tendency to compound his difficulties by misjudging problems and solutions. An example of this was his reaction to his misjudging the clerical problem that arose over his exceeding the 21-day limit for being sick after which he would be grounded. There are times when he experiences intense anger and this can break through when he is under pressure.

It must be stressed that there is no evidence that any of these traits, tendencies or behaviours occur in the workplace.

On the contrary, it appears that these traits are confined to his domestic situation and personal relationships. In my opinion, he is currently suffering from an **adjustment reaction** (as distinct from an adjustment disorder) to an adverse life event. The fact is that this event has not passed and a solution to his marriage problem is not imminently at hand. This must imply that he continues to be prone the self-defeating cycles of behaviour relating to stress, as outlined above.

5. In my opinion, given his pre-morbid personality and psychological state, his track record as a pilot, as well as the opinion of a senior colleague whose opinions I was able to solicit and from my own clinical assessment of F.O. Smith, **most of his psychological difficulties are transient** and not that dissimilar to those seen in some other pilots. **They reflect personal shortcomings rather than gross or enduring psychopathology.** I would expect his problematic behaviour to dissipate once the source of his stress has been resolved. There is evidence, however, that some of his personality traits and behavioural patterns cause ongoing difficulties.

RECOMMENDATIONS

In the light of the above findings, my recommendations are as follows:

1. To give F. O. Smith the opportunity to bring resolution to his marriage problems through his own efforts as well as with the help of a marriage therapist. It would be prudent to take him off line whilst he undertakes this.
2. To encourage him to undergo psychological counselling for a minimum of ten sessions with a trained, sympathetic specialist therapist who can help him to gain insight, both into his behaviour when under stress as well as into his personality traits, and to help him to acquire more adaptive skills for dealing with anger. There is no evidence that long term psychological treatment would produce more favourable results in his case (Bor *et al.*, 2004).
3. To enable him to maintain currency of his pilots' licence through simulator sessions; and to maintain professional involvement in the airline.
4. To review and reassess his situation in not less than three months with a view to determining the extent to which he has resolved his marital difficulties and demonstrated that he can apply alternate

responses to challenging situations. This could be in the form of a report from his therapist and/or further psychological assessment.

DECLARATION OF THE AUTHOR

1. I understand that my duty in writing this report is to provide an accurate professional account of my work with this individual. I understand that this duty overrides any obligation to the person from whom I have received instructions or by whom I am paid.
2. I confirm that I have complied with that duty in writing this report.
3. I believe that the facts I have stated in this report are true and that the opinions I have expressed are correct.

Dr Peter Johnson PhD
Consultant Clinical Psychologist

REFERENCES

American Psychiatric Association (2000). *Diagnostic and Statistical Manual of Mental Disorders* (4th edn, text revision). Washington, DC: American Psychiatric Association.

Benn, A. and Brady, C. (1994). Forensic report writing. In M. McCurran and J. Hodge (eds) *The Assessment of Criminal Behaviours of Clients in Secure Settings* (Chapter 6, pp.127–145). London: Jessica Kingsley Publishers.

Bor, R., Gill, S., Miller, R. and Parrott, C. (2004) *Doing Therapy Briefly*. Basingstoke: Palgrave Macmillan.

Data Protection Act (1998). London: HMSO.

Morey, L. (1991). *Personal Assessment Inventory Professional Manual*. Odessa, FL: Psychological Assessment Resources.

National Health Service Management Executive (1991). *Health Service Guidelines: Access to Health Records Act (1990)* HSG (91) 6. London: Department of Health.

5 HOW TO COMMUNICATE EFFECTIVELY WITH COLLEAGUES

Alan Frankland and Yvonne Walsh

Basic training probably gives most practitioners some awareness of the need to develop professional competence in formal communications, and by the end of your training you probably felt that, through direct teaching or apprenticeship whilst on placement, you had developed a sufficient grasp of the most visible professional communication issues such as constructing reports, making presentations and writing for publication. We would hope that your induction into the skills required for these areas of work also offered you insight into why it is as important to be as competent in this part of your work as in the theory and practice of therapy itself.

The reasons for developing proficiency in clear professional communications in these areas include:

- The avoidance of ambiguity or uncertainty in reports or case notes caused by loosely framed sentences or the confusion of observation, evidence and opinion, (which is particularly important because such documents are a matter of public record and they can easily become a part of legal or quasi-legal proceedings).
- The avoidance of misunderstandings between agencies (or colleagues) which can lead to clients not receiving the services they need, or to peer professionals feeling short changed or mistrustful of one another, making it harder to work effectively, creating additional work stress or ultimately putting clients at risk.
- Maximising the opportunities for colleagues and teams to learn from each other at every level of work, from administrative procedures to practice, professional issues and theory.

You were probably also made aware during your training (particularly in relation to case notes and communications about clients) of a range of developing issues concerned with confidentiality and data access and data-protection issues.

Other texts cover these issues in more detail than we have space for here (see for example various chapters in Bor and Watts, 2006) and the major formal communications are covered in some depth in other parts of this book. This chapter is about the somewhat less public communications that nevertheless make up a very significant part of our professional lives, and the same issues still hold. Without clear communications in the office, in emails or letters between colleagues the same kinds of problems, as those identified above for a badly written report or a poorly delivered presentation, can occur. It is not just the showpiece documents or evidence to a tribunal that require attention and care because they might lead to confusion and difficulties for clients or between colleagues or become the subject of disciplinary procedures or litigation.

We have divided this chapter into two rather uneven parts – written communications and spoken communications. Some of the 'principles' we focus on in the section on written communications apply across the board as we shall indicate; we are not implying that spoken communications are less important or interesting. Whilst we have occasionally been aware of psychological research which relates to the material presented here, for the most part support for what we have to offer comes from our combined 40+ years of professional life in psychology and psychotherapy in a wide variety of contexts.

WRITTEN COMMUNICATIONS BETWEEN COLLEAGUES

THE FIVE 'C'S

Let us begin with something which is apparently very straightforward:

Memo 5.1

To: Lucy Starr
From: Malcolm Jennings
Re: Workload/CPD and Testing Policy Review
Thursday 19th Jan. 2006

Dear Lucy,

I think it would be good to meet to clarify these issues and make some decisions together.

Specifically I think we need to make a clear decision on the following:

1. Whether you will be taking on the extra client sessions?
2. What needs to be dropped or re-allocated if you do?

3. Your (potential) IGA training – costs and time etc.
4. Progress on the Testing Policy Review.

I know you have admin time next Tuesday morning; I'm free first thing (8.45 to 10.00) and before lunch (12.00 to 1.00) could you arrange your morning to make a meeting at either of these times? If not, what does your Thursday p.m. look like next week? I want to get this more sorted by the Friday so that I can get on with the departmental estimates etc. from Monday.

Please ensure that we have a date/time fixed before you finish tomorrow and preferably by close of play today. Maxine has my diary if I'm not around.

Nothing heavy in this, no great change of direction envisaged etc., just think we need to get it more sorted before I do the budget. I'm not expecting lots of docs and preparation before we meet, although some notes on where things are up to on the Testing Review could help us both.

Noticed you still limping a bit when I saw you yesterday – hope the ankle not troubling you too much and mending properly.

See you soon

Malcolm

Dr. Malcolm Jennings
Consultant Psychologist and Psychotherapist
Head of Adult Services, KISMHT

Memo 5.2

To: Malcolm Jennings, Head of Adult Services
From: Lucy Starr, Counselling Psychologist
Re: Workload/CPD and Testing Policy Review
Thursday 19th Jan. 2006

Dear Malcolm,

Thanks for the email.

The ankle's mending well, physio is happy and I've not a lot of pain, just a bit weak so I'm Hopalong Lucy when I get tired!

I'll do a bit of re-arranging and see you 4.30 to 5.30 Thursday if that's OK. I've got a day's leave earlier in the week (remember? I did check it with you), and leaving meeting 'til lateish on Thurs will give me time to get my act together and put a progress update on paper re the Review before we meet.

Cheers

Luce
Lucy Jennings
Chartered Counselling Psychologist
Adult Services, KISMHT

Memo 5.3

Hi Jess,

Need a chat before I can do the budget, hop along to my office (ha, ha) when u've got a mo. No big deal.

Cheers

Zak

Memo 5.4

Hi Zak,

Will be diffcult 2 c u b4 Thurs next – reely bizzy and hav bked a day AL.

Thursday 5ish be OK?

Jess

PS whats it about?

The delightful Joanna Lumley in a television advertisement for car insurance asserts, 'You don't have to be posh to be Privileged' and it is not our intention to suggest that you have to be 'posh' to be a good communicator – but you do need to be clear, concise, coherent and to cover the ground, and you need to make contact with the person (or people) you are aiming to communicate with: if you don't, the whole thing fails. It is not the 'txt-type' shorthand that is the problem with the Zak and Jess (Memos 3 and 4) exchange above (although we would not advocate writing that way in professional communications which once in a while may become part of some kind of formal procedure where that style would simply seem casual and unprofessional). The problem is that these messages have failed to cover the ground that is needed for both parties to know what is required and how it might be achieved.

Both pairs of communications given above contain a message from a teamleader to a member of the team, and the team member's reply, but the same principles apply in all the communications that make an office, a team, a professional relationship run smoothly and effectively. These qualities can be summed up as the five 'C's in communication.

C1 – CLEAR

If a communication is to be of value, it needs to be expressed in a way that is readily meaningful to those who receive it. It needs to actually say what the author intends. One of the ways of ensuring this is the old clerical saying about a good sermon, 'Say what you are going to say, say it, then say what you've said'. In a brief memo this threefold repetition is probably unnecessary (and would clash with C2 below), but belt and braces is not a bad idea. In Malcolm's memo (Memo 1), this is achieved by a carefully thought out 'Re' line that actually tells the reader something, plus a straightforward indication of what the writer wants – a meeting of an identifiable length within a particular timescale. It would have been easiest to just head the mail 'Various', but that would have told the reader nothing and wasted an opportunity for usefully focusing the message from the outset.

C2 – CONCISE

As emails and other messaging systems proliferate, and because most professionals experience a sense of pressure in their work, it is more effective (and arguably more polite/compassionate) if professional communications are relatively brief and certainly concise. Zak scores highly on brevity, but there is such a thing as being too concise. As Jess' reply shows: too brief a message does only part of the job. On the one hand abbreviations may be misread – does 'hav bkd' indicate half baked or have booked? And on the other hand, Zak's brevity has left Jess completely in the dark about what the requested meeting is for. A quick scan of the fuller communication attributed to Malcolm might indicate that there is some room for tightening up (e.g. there may be more information in the third paragraph than Lucy needs to make a good decision) but in general the message is quite tightly edited without becoming so compact it becomes positively difficult to read and rather chilly.

C3 — COHERENT

The communication between Zak and Jess has something of the feel of a stream of consciousness: the idea pops into the writer's head and is jotted down and sent off without much thought and certainly without checking that it will make sense to someone other than the writer. You may have had experience of these kinds of communications, 'I just wanted to explore the issues around …'. Unless the writer has a particular facility for language and thinks in an unusually straightforward and linear manner such 'communications' often fail (even if the ideas they contain are really good) because they lack coherence and structure. Malcolm's message on the other hand flows well between ideas – this is what I want to happen, this is why, here is a suggestion about how it might be achieved, this is the margin of tolerance. It offers the reader a coherent experience which itself invites a positive response.

C4 — COVERAGE

As Jess' plaintive PS indicates, it is important to check not just for coherence, but that the necessary content is covered. Malcolm's message does this well; Lucy can be in no doubt what is required and is enabled to make a meaningful response which contains a reasoned reaction to the request (Memo 2). Whereas poor Jess has no idea what it is all about and may have inferred from Zak's casual tone that this is nothing very important and that half an hour at going home time will cover it.

C5 — CONTACT

This is where Zak's original note might score most strongly, it's very informal making a non-hierarchical affiliative overture to Jess which might make it more likely that she will not feel threatened and will want to respond. However, informality does not always work and may seem juvenile (or nerdy). If you have to tell someone you are being informal and light-hearted (ha, ha), there must be the suggestion that you know that your humour might well miss the mark. Shades of 'The Office' here then. Malcolm on the other hand makes contact through a simple enquiry about Lucy's well-being (which she is then able to respond to warmly and lightly in her reply) and that human touch may well have had the effect of enabling her to put herself out ('I'll do a bit of re-arranging') to enable the original communication to be effective.

Although we have used the example of a very simple office communication it is important to emphasise that we see these principles as applying to most of the interpersonal communications that professionals and colleagues might generate and receive, up to and including letters and referrals. The five 'C's represent an assertive and informative communication style and it is arguable that attention to these issues would also be desirable in professional conversations (although they are more difficult to manage in that medium where review and editing are not an option).

There are some additional points that we want to make, which may be slightly less universal in application but are still important where they do apply. Imagine if you will, a continuum between principles (derived from research, experience or rational analysis) and prejudices (reflecting one's own likes and dislikes) we would have to acknowledge that whereas we think a case could be made that the five 'C's and what we have called the EBCs – evidence, boundaries and confidentiality – are close to the principles end of the continuum, the others (Communication Preferences, having more of an aesthetic element) are probably situated towards the 'prejudices' end of the line. Let us therefore move on to considering the EBCs and their place in professional communications.

EVIDENCE, BOUNDARIES AND CONFIDENTIALITY

EBC1 – PROVIDING THE EVIDENCE

There will be many inter-colleague communications which have (as at least part of) their purpose a motivational or persuasive function: a team memo advocating a change in current procedures, a request for new staffing, rejection of a shift in departmental policy and so on. Where such communications use official forms or templates these will often include a request for the argument to be made in evidential terms, but we would argue that even where this is not the case or when the communication is still relatively informal it is nonetheless effective professional practice to adduce and marshal the evidence which supports your point of view. To do so is not only persuasive, it is also respectful and in many ways democratic or collegial.

Indicating the evidence on which my rejection of your proposal is based gives you grounds to re-assess your position: it shows that I am interested in getting you on board, not just in silencing you with rhetoric or authority, and it is one of the general indicators of a professional who is engaged in their work. As in essays in academic life the evidential base for an argument may come from very hard quantitative and outcome studies, from qualitative research, from other published sources (in which case it is not strictly evidence but 'expert opinion' but we will let that pass here) or from other empirical sources including one's own professional and personal experience. These may have differential value (depending on the issue being discussed and the style and predilections of each correspondent), but the inclusion of some sort of evidence is surely a good practice for professionals who can no longer proclaim their right to act in particular ways and to exercise certain privileges unless they can give a rounded account of the reasons behind their actions. Simple assertion of a point of view without a review of the evidence which supports it is surely just arrogance.

There will of course be occasions when the assertions made are too trivial to require evidence 'we usually meet at 3.30 for an hour' does not require reference to the departmental diary to validate it, but it seems wise in a world in which we cannot be certain of agreement about what we take for granted (viz where 400 plus models of therapy (Kovel, 1981) vie for acceptance) not to assume too much common ground with diverse readers. An unsupported statement like 'It is perfectly clear that the relationship lies at the heart of therapy...' may seem incontrovertible to some writers (including us actually), but it needs to be evidenced when writing for people outside our usual circle of known colleagues and co-professionals or for a more general audience. It is not difficult to get used to citing a key study in support of such data (in this case we'd choose Hubble, Duncan and Miller, 1999) and we would strongly advocate doing so.

As in this brief section, there will be occasions when there is no clear evidence available, where ones own views are founded simply on a generalised sense of what is right or helpful. In such cases we fall back on the persuasive argument and the well-made case – not strictly evidence at all. We would certainly advocate leaving the language of advertising (and of angry coercion) out of professional communications altogether. Tempting though it may be to start your rejection of the department's proposal to change the current assessment tool with 'Only an ill-intentioned nerd or an ignorant fool would propose sweeping away our current practice for an ill-conceived mess of quasi-scientific dogma...'. It is probably more effective not to do so, but to try to proceed rationally and with the evidence to hand to demonstrate the weakness of the proposals. Of course writing (but not sending) the intemperate and insulting outburst may help you get to the place where you can marshal evidence and arguments to make a powerful and persuasive case, but be careful not to hit the send button!

EBC2 – BOUNDARIES AND CONFIDENTIALITY WITHIN COMMUNICATIONS

In all client-focused communications we have to be aware that there are ethical and legal constraints on what we can and cannot share. We are constrained by the Data Protection Act, 1998, to treat all personal information whether computer based, written or spoken as 'belonging' to the person concerned. We need to keep in mind that 'Counsellors owe clients clear duties to keep confidences and maintain the privacy of dealings, but clients can release the obligation and courts can order confidence broken', (Scoggins, Litton and Palmer, 1998).

If a client's information is passed on without his or her permission or against his or her will, the client can then make a formal complaint and you will be open to disciplinary action from professional bodies and/or your employer. If the client has suffered loss or injury because of this, he or she may also have a case for legal redress.

Scoggins *et al.* (ibid) remind us that clients will be open in helping relationships in the expectation that what is offered will not be revealed without their consent. However, we need to be aware that there are certain circumstances in which a counsellor or other professional working with a client/patient can be obliged by law to disclose what transpires in a confidential situation.

There are six principle occasions on which disclosure of confidential material will be justified or required. Scoggins *et al.* (ibid) have described these as:

- with the patient/client's consent;
- by order of a court trying a civil dispute;
- by order of a court in criminal proceedings;
- by order of a tribunal that holds the power to compel the giving of evidence;
- under statutory powers compelling disclosure in the course of investigations by official agencies;
- where the public interest justifies the volunteering of information even though the client refuses consent and there is no court order or statutory compulsion to disclose the particular information.

Note that except in a very few cases there is no duty of disclosure unless and until someone who has power to make such an order does so.

Maintaining boundaries and ensuring you comply with the law and good practice around confidentiality is your responsibility. It is your responsibility to ensure that this permission is given; it can be no defence to say 'my manager told me to': check and then check again. Also, be aware that laws change and that policies change in line with developments in the law. Good practice dictates that we keep abreast of professional codes and that we comply with them in all areas of professional life, but especially with regard to our client's confidentiality.

We also need to be aware of inadvertent or careless communications. Any confidential information needs to be kept safely. The NHS practice of requiring confidential information to be stored under double lock (locked in a filing cabinet in a locked room) is not 'overkill'. Think about how many people have access to the buildings you work in; cleaning staff, contractors, office staff (not to mention clients and their families) and not all of these will have knowledge of or perhaps respect for confidentiality.

When we have documents containing confidential information in use, it is important to remember that they still need protection and not leave pages open where they may be visible to a passer by, or leave files or documents where they might (perhaps innocently) be picked up by others. Many organisations dealing with confidential material will have procedures to protect those documents when out of the office (guidelines about keeping them in a locked case out of sight in your car for example). Even if the material in the file is of no great moment, you have to consider only for a few seconds how you would like it if notes about your relationships or health were to be dropped near where you work, to come to a higher regard for what might otherwise seem irksome or unnecessary restrictions.

Being careful about confidentiality is important in spoken communications too. Often people will stand and discuss issues in corridors or over the coffee machine. Where individual cases or examples are involved this is inappropriate and disrespectful and it could lead to information being overhead or misunderstood and to you developing a reputation for being a gossip. Choose your settings for these kinds of discussions carefully and take into consideration what you are trying to achieve and how your behaviour will be perceived. Remember that your client's stories belong to them and need to be held respectfully even when you cannot be overheard.

COMMUNICATION PREFERENCES

PREFERENCE 1 – FORMAL LANGUAGE, GRAMMAR AND PUNCTUATION

The style of writing in this chapter must show plainly enough that we are not particularly formal and we are not advocating a stuffy or very 'correct' style of writing all the time. Nevertheless, it must be the case that the more formal the function of a piece of writing, the more formal its style should become, gradually moving from the colloquial (first person, use of abbreviations – which can't/won't always be wrong etc.) to the fully formal third person, without abbreviations or casual structures – like asking the reader direct questions – and without using 'relaxed' syntax and grammar.

We do take the view that there are some speech forms that do not readily transfer into even the most informal professional written communications (innit), and that even though grammar and syntax may be simplified and relaxed there is no case for just ignoring grammatical forms. As Lynne Truss (Truss, 2003) pointed out, grammar and punctuation are, for the most part, aids to clarity and communication. It is usually worth preserving them for this end and for the impression that a well-crafted message gives. On the whole professionals do not turn up for work in their gardening (or hiking) gear – to do so might be perfectly acceptable to many clients and colleagues but would lose them credibility with others. If it is worth spending a little time thinking about our personal appearance and creating the right impression, it is also worth considering whether our written communications are also 'properly dressed' (turned out in a way that is fit for purpose). The linguistic martinet who makes no allowances for colleagues with genuine difficulties with language (dyslexia, or being in the early stages of transition from another language community, for example) is at best an unattractive figure, but in the age of word processors there is not much excuse for most spelling errors or grossly inappropriate grammatical forms, and they do grate.

PREFERENCE 2 – WORD CHOICE

It is important to 'keep it simple' and to try to find the right word for the job. There is nothing wrong with jargon where it is part of a shared vocabulary or where it is the only term which fully holds the desired meaning, but the unnecessary use of jargon or choosing longer and more obscure words in place of straightforward ones tends to obfuscation (or should we say 'might well make your meaning less clear'?). All jargon (and the use of initials and TLAs – three-letter abbreviations) runs the risk of excluding some readers and potential participants in a conversation and it is important to be aware of this. In some cases that will be what you want to do, or be justified by the technical requirements of what you are trying to communicate in others it will show a disregard for some receivers and limit the value of your communication. The risk of using jargon or complex vocabulary that is not genuinely familiar to you is that when you get it wrong it makes your readers or listeners uncomfortable and could lead to you seeming to be a fool or a charlatan!

Whilst the old journalistic rule of not repeating key words in any one paragraph can lead to very torturous structures and some pretty gnomic sentences, written communications do generally read better without undue reiteration. This is not only an aesthetic issue. It seems likely that a communication in which sentences and paragraphs are well crafted will give the appearance of being thoughtfully presented. Thus not only will it read more fluently but it may also be more persuasive.

PREFERENCE 3 – MANNERS

We are really beginning to sound like the estimable Ms Truss (Truss, 2005). This is simply a plea for consideration in writing – especially emails.

- Ensure that you only send emails to colleagues who need to know, i.e. avoid creating additional spam: we all get enough already.
- Whilst it may not be necessary to start every email as if it were a letter, surely it helps to use your correspondent's name somewhere in the email and the form of a letter gives your response a simple and comprehensible shape. Very brief unnamed responses can seem taciturn or sometimes rude.
- Whilst it may sometimes be important to express (even strong) feelings in written communications, do be aware that when something is written down it may sound harsher (or ruder) than if it was spoken. Sticking to the guidelines of expressing yourself through 'I statements' and avoiding finger pointing probably makes a lot of sense here (viz 'I am very angry that it was decided to undertake this re-organisation without consulting me' cannot reasonably be seen to be inflammatory or libellous but 'This is just a crap decision that you have taken without sufficient consultation and you should be ashamed of yourself' is neither respectful nor helpful (because you might be shooting the messenger) and it could be libellous and so dangerous as well as lacking consideration).

LETTERS ABOUT CLIENTS AND REFERRALS

Whilst all the above principles apply here we think there are also some additional items that it is worth bringing to your attention in relation to this particular aspect of professional communications.

1. Before writing about clients to any third party do try to ensure that they have a right to or a need for the information that you are giving them, this is particularly important if writing in response to a request. Remember that the medium is also a message and just writing back

to acknowledge that Jim Jonson is a client of your service tells the reader something they may not be entitled to know. Double check the confidentiality issues through supervision and/or with your client.

2. Letters about clients should always be on the more formal end of the communications continuum and follow an accepted template for such correspondence.

3. Unless your organisation uses some other unique identifier, these letters should use the date of birth and the address of the client as a header to enable accurate identification (there may be more than one Augustus Brown in the house or known to the referrer).

4. When reporting information gained from the client this should be in terms such as 'Mr Jones describes', or 'Mrs Jones reports'. Use surnames and titles – it may be acceptable to call your clients by their given name, but the use of their family name in correspondence is courteous and demonstrates respect. If you really do not like using titles, it is acceptable to call the client by their full name 'Robert Jones describes' or 'Francine Jones reports', but it then takes some care and skill to write sentences that do not seem unbalanced or awkward.

5. When reporting information about the client be clear what the source of that information is and do not generalise too much beyond it. ('I have observed Jim Jonson working in both therapy groups and in the drop-in setting. Although he appears to lack some social skills he is usually friendly and quite well-received by peers' makes much more sense than 'Mr Jonson is affiliative but socially unskilled'.) If you are using standardised tests or procedures to establish data about a client state that is the case and give the information in a form that is digestible by the reader. Avoid giving raw scores unless you are sure that the reader is as familiar as you are with the test used.

6. Letters should, in the main, contain factual information and any opinion should be stated as such.

7. Remember that your reader is probably also busy, so a rough guide is to write letters that are only one side of A4 in length, practice précising information so that it retains it's meaning, but is concise.

8. Always ensure that there is a clear statement of your name and title below your signature and that it is clear how to contact you if any clarification or follow-up is required.

AGENDA, MINUTES AND MEETING NOTES

Writing formal minutes is a particular skill and if it becomes a formal part of your work role, it would be sensible for you to seek specific training, and to be clear what the minuting conventions of your organisation are and work within them. Less formal minute taking and the creation of notes of a meeting, however, is a common part of the work of many professionals, so some quick additional notes and guidelines must be offered here.

The process of minuting or taking notes of meetings ideally starts well before the meeting takes place, in that some kind of agenda or proposed content of the meeting has already been fixed. For minuted meetings the agenda will usually take the form identified in Example A. Some meetings adopt the convention that items are numbered and taken in the order printed, as decided beforehand by those convening the meeting. This means that participants have some sense of what will happen, and when, before they attend the meeting. Other groups will adopt the convention that the chair determines the order of the agenda with participants early in the meeting (usually after taking apologies and confirming the minutes of the previous meeting). Where meetings are not formally minuted there may well be less formality in structuring the meeting around apologies, minutes etc., but if a record is to be kept of a series of meetings, it needs to be checked and agreed, and people need to know what the event is about, so something very like an this agenda is also likely to emerge.

During the meeting the minute taker (or the person who has agreed to make less formal notes) should attempt to make a record of the main arguments and discussions which will usually appear in minutes as 'discussion of', with points that were particularly salient 'noted' and anything which is actually agreed marked as agreed. Often an action point will arise as part of an item agreed and it is helpful to note the agreed action and who is to carry it out. Example B is an extract from the minutes of the KISMHT meeting from Example A. You will note that the account of proceedings is pretty concise; more content does not necessarily mean more clarity in this context: the language chosen and the level of detail need only be fit for purpose: in this case keeping some record of the fact and content of the meeting, to be able to track decisions and jog people's memory about agreed actions. With the exception of disciplinary hearings or similar events (when professional record keepers should be employed), it is not necessary to attempt a record of every speaker or a verbatim account of every contribution. Where there is a real requirement for a complete record it makes more sense to use a tape recorder in the meeting and transcribe from that (again a specialist function).

EXAMPLE A

KISMHT

Friday February 17th 2006 09.30 to 11.00 in the Meeting Room, Providence House.
(Phyllis Salter to Chair, all team members expected to attend, apologies for absence to Rick Pepper by Wednesday 15th where possible please)
Welcome
Apologies for Absence
Minutes of the previous meeting
Matters arising from the Minutes

Standing Items	Patient numbers this month
	Onward referrals
	Availability and Leave
Item for Discussion 1	Change in criteria for patients requiring emergency response
Item for Discussion 2	Redevelopment of Trust mission statement
Item for Information 1	Changes in Central Management staffing
Item for Information 2	New Car Parking policy

Any other business
Date and time of next meeting
The meeting will close by 11.00 am.

EXAMPLE B

KISMHT

P2
        as members of the new Management team were not well known to ERT staff.
17.02.06#9
PS tabled a paper from Estates about the new parking regulations that would come into force in the Autumn
Discussion Of whether these were in line with Government and Trust policies on green issues
Noted 1 That Trade Union reps had not been consulted whilst the plans were being drawn up.
Noted 2 That provisions for disable users and essential users (such as ERT members on duty or on call) seemed inadequate or unclear.
Agreed That PS would write urgently to Estates for clarification of these issues and raise the matter at the next Sector Managers meeting.

17.02.06 #10
There was no other business.
17.02.06 #11
The next meeting will be on March 17th – usual place and time. PS will chair, Daley Sinclair to do Agenda and Minutes.
The meeting closed at 10.55 a.m.

SPOKEN COMMUNICATIONS

Spoken communications are more directly personal than written communications. They expose more of you, the person, and information flows between you and the person that you address in other ways than just via the words you say. The process of communication is interactive and multi-dimensional and therefore much less easy to control. Whilst written communications can be reviewed and edited before being sent, verbal communications are generally much more spontaneous and may even take the speaker by surprise at times.

Given the importance of the non-verbal dimensions in all communications (not just in therapy), it is surely sensible to remember that how the message is conveyed will affect how it is heard. If you wish to be considered as a level-headed, knowledgeable colleague whose views and opinions count, it will be important to maintain a calm, informative and fairly precise manner of speaking, avoiding heavy use of colloquialisms and, even when discussing professional matters with a close colleague, avoiding being over-friendly or 'matey'.

How you say something, the tone and pace which you use, your presentation as well as the language content all combine with the message you are wishing to convey set the 'scene' of this message (Argyle, 1988). Thus in professional verbal communication confidence in presentation, clarity and conciseness are essential and these are the result of careful preparation. We can perhaps illustrate some of these issues through the case studies in Examples C and D and draw on them for guidelines for action.

EXAMPLE C

PREPARATION MAKES A DIFFERENCE

Anne and Amy are two psychotherapists involved in a multi-site research trial. They are on the same distribution list for memos and emails. They attend many

Continued

EXAMPLE C cont'd

of the same meetings. Anne repeatedly comments 'I wasn't aware' or 'I didn't know' and shows up for meetings without the relevant background information. Whereas Amy has the necessary material to hand, and it is obvious when she speaks, from the notes that she refers to and her grasp of what is transpiring, that she has done her 'homework' and has prepared in detail – she hasn't just read the 'Executive Summary' on the train as she made her way to the meeting. When Amy speaks, her colleagues pay attention – she has proven herself worth listening to.

The guidelines we might derive from Example C are:

- Know who your audience is and their communication needs and preferences.
- Know what your message is; do the preparation – both on gathering knowledge and on how you wish the message to be perceived. Do your homework by reviewing appropriate material in advance, making notes on the sequence and details you want to get over and completing tasks agreed in previous interactions.
- Know why you want to convey your message, what you are hoping to achieve by giving this message and clarify this with those you are talking to, so they will know what you are trying to achieve and can work with you to make this happen. They need to understand the objective, background and context that your message rests within and their role in response to the communication so that the aims of communicating with them can be achieved.
- Know what response you hope for from giving this 'message'.

EXAMPLE D PART 1

GETTING YOUR MESSAGE ACROSS: ANN

Amy and Ann were both at the same seminar; they were there representing their teams and were expected to feed back what they had learnt on their return. Ann found the presentation interesting, but didn't take notes. She knew she would remember the salient points and that minutes would be forthcoming in time. On the day of her presentation to her team she left the handouts she had been given on her kitchen table and so was only able to promise that she would 'get the handouts to the team tomorrow'. She spoke for 5 minutes 'off the cuff'.

EXAMPLE D PART 2

GETTING YOUR MESSAGE ACROSS: AMY

Amy took full-detailed notes – including some reflections on her own reaction to the subject matter. Before her presentation to her team she reviewed the preparatory reading she had done before the seminar, jotting down some additional points which she added to her notes for her presentation. She prepared a PowerPoint presentation and included in this her conclusions and recommendations for the team to take forward. She also prepared her own handouts for the team so they would have something to take away and reflect on. Amy filled the full half hour she had requested be set aside by the team; her colleagues were interested in what she had to say and her manager felt that the cost of sending her to the seminar was money well spent; the case she made for taking her recommendations forward was both cogent and practical.

The guidelines we might derive from Example D are:

- Once again the importance of preparation: although spoken communications are more fluid and less controllable than written work, they can be supported by effective preparation and notes.
- It is often useful to follow up a spoken communication with a written record of what was discussed and what was agreed. This will enable participants to review what was said and pace their intake of new material in a way that suits them. It may also aid acceptance of what you are saying because participants have been given a kind of gift – which may make them feel better disposed to you and your message.
- With many kinds of spoken communication events (not just 'talks' and feedback sessions) it will be useful to follow up with a written record of what was discussed and agreed to enable you to both clarify that you have gotten your message across accurately and that you have understood the recipients response in addition to your shared understanding of what should happen next.

These principles apply to both group communications and one-to-one communications. If done well, all the consultations, meetings, phone conversations and video conferences that you participate in should accomplish a greater amount than you can accomplish without them. Your challenge is to do these things well.

CONCLUSION

It has undoubtedly proved easier for us to write about written communications than about spoken or conversational communications. Although we hope that what we have offered on spoken communications will be helpful, it is comforting for us to recall that we are writing for an audience of professionals who are already expert in interpersonal communications: so perhaps we only really have to remind you that what is true about communications with your clients in personal therapy or group work (in relation to non-verbal behaviours, attention span, assertion skills, open or multiple questions etc.) is also true when you are communicating with professional colleagues.

REFERENCES

Argyle, M. (1988) *Bodily Communication*. Routledge: London.

Bor, R. and Watts, M. (eds) (2006) *The Trainee Handbook*. Sage: London.

Data Protection Act (1998) HMSO: London.

Hubble, M. A., Duncan, B. L. and Miller, S. D. (1999) *The Heart and Soul of Change. What Works in Therapy*. Washington, DC: The American Psychological Association.

Kovel, A. (1981) *Complete Guide to Therapy*. Pelican Books: London.

Scoggins, L., Litton, M. and Palmer, S. (1998) Confidentiality and the law. *Counselling Psychology Review* 13(1), 6–12.

Truss, L. (2003) *Eats, Shoots & Leaves: The Zero Tolerance Approach to Punctuation*. London: Profile Books Ltd.

Truss, L. (2005) *Talk to the Hand: The Utter Bloody Rudeness of Everyday Life (or Six Good Reasons to Stay Home and Bolt the Door)*. London: Profile Books Ltd.

6   FRAMEWORK OF SUPERVISION FOR PRACTITIONERS AND TRAINEES

Riva Miller

INTRODUCTION

Professional competence and appropriate accountability are key considerations of practising therapy in the modern era. The professional
registration of counsellors and psychotherapists with recognised bodies
such as BACP, UKCP, BPS in the UK meets this requirement. There is
therefore increasing demand on qualified practitioners to supervise and
mentor trainee therapists, those recently qualified, as well as colleagues
with experience and competence. Supervision, in its widest sense, is an
integral part of the on-going practice development for qualified therapists.
The requirement for therapeutic practice to be supervised and accountable
may well lead to a more rigid requirement for supervisors to be trained to
do this task.

Therapy with clients is influenced by complex personal, professional and
contextual factors. Client situations and difficulties can trigger feelings
and reactions from therapists that, in turn, impact on how therapy
proceeds. The management of this reciprocal reverberation of relationships
is a key element of therapy. Additional challenges for the therapist may
arise from working alongside other professionals, who hold different
perspectives. Supervision is an ideal context for the therapist (supervisee)
and supervisor to address these issues creatively, effectively, safely and
efficiently.

Outside the realm of therapy, different forms of workplace supervision
exist, usually based on a hierarchical model of a more experienced
practitioner working with a trainee or more junior member of staff.
Supervision in counselling and psychotherapy is an intrinsic part of training
and a key way of linking theory to practice, and bringing together

personal and professional journeys for trainees and qualified practitioners. A unique feature of this supervision is that it strives to be collaborative between supervisor and supervisee, which is a key element of the process whereby clinical practice is supported and enhanced. Nevertheless, at the back of all supervisors and supervisees minds is the knowledge that this relationship can be hierarchical due to accountability to a line manager, head of department or in private practice, to relevant others. Whilst such hierarchical considerations may get in the way of true collaboration they provide safety for the client and ultimately the supervisee.

Certain questions come to mind when thinking about supervision.

- What is supervision?
- What part does supervision play in day-to-day clinical practice both in private sector and within institutions?
- Is there a difference between supervision, consultation, appraisal and personal and professional development, and can one supervisor cover all these roles?
- How different is the supervision of qualified practitioners from that of trainees?
- What parameters should be considered when setting up and providing supervision?
- What specific skills are required of a supervisor, and are these different to those used when working with clients?
- Do the supervisor and supervisee have to share the same theoretical approach to therapy?
- What are the key elements of supervision that help to keep it lively, effective and useful?
- How can supervision help when the supervisee feels 'stuck' (Elizur, 1990)?
- What can one do when there is an impasse between supervisor and supervisee, or in situations that point to concern about clinical competence of the supervisee or the supervisor to carry out their tasks?
- Can one be a supervisor if you are not currently engaged in clinical practice?
- What training and on-going supervision is needed for the supervisor?

These questions are explored in different sections of this chapter from a number of perspectives so that both the supervisee and supervisor can prepare for the work that lies ahead. In addition, a framework of supervisory practice is suggested with guiding principles and a structure or 'map' for the supervision session that can be readily adapted to a range of different theoretical models of supervision. Thought-provoking and well-considered supervision of therapeutic practice is a necessity, not a luxury, for all practitioners at every level in order to maintain and enhance practice skills.

WHY IS SUPERVISION NECESSARY?

Many factors make supervision a necessary and desirable feature of therapeutic practice.

- Supervision of clinical practice is part of the requirements for original and continued registration with the main recognised bodies in the UK (BACP, UKCP, BPS) for all levels of practitioner.
- The requirement for accountability (who is in charge) and responsibility (professional standards) in institutional settings (the NHS, social and educational services) and in private practice are regulated and monitored through supervision.
- Supervision has a role, especially with trainees, in ensuring an acceptable level of clinical expertise, alongside academic achievements that are more formally judged.
- Effective and confident practice can be confirmed, enhanced and developed through the process of supervision.
- Supervision provides a 'safety net' for client and supervisee. Therapy is a complex activity that draws on the knowledge and experience of the therapist. Many clients seek therapy at a time where they are vulnerable. Unless cared for professionally, empathetically and competently their feelings could be exploited or the severity of their problem exacerbated. Likewise, supervisees may face difficult and sensitive issues in daily practice that require thoughtful reflection, subsequent attention as well as support.
- Supervision provides an opportunity to consider different approaches to take when the supervisee feels 'stuck' in therapy with a client.
- Reflective supervision provides an appropriate context in which a measure of neutrality and objectivity can be regained.
- Key concerns in contemporary therapeutic practice, such as gender, race, culture and sexuality, are important issues to explore, not only in the supervisory relationship, but also in the supervisee's work with clients (McHale and Carr, 1998; Papadopoulos, 2001).
- Supervision should provide a forum for integrating personal experience and professional learning in an appropriate way that respects boundaries.

These points, amongst others that the reader may identify, make supervision of clinical therapy and counselling necessary. The next section expands on these points to define more precisely what supervision entails.

WHAT IS SUPERVISION?

Effective supervision can be achieved only when there is a clear definition about what it is, and this is shared between the supervisor and supervisee. Supervision can be defined as an opportunity to oversee, monitor and critically appraise a supervisee's practice. For the supervisee, supervision provides a structured opportunity to bring together and integrate personal experience, professional learning and practise and offers a measure of both challenge and support. There is often an element of learning from an experienced professional with the supervisor being a mentor.

Supervision provides a context in which issues for the supervisee can be examined from the broadest and the narrowest perspective, giving a second opinion to a problem, with 'two heads being better than one'. The supervisor gives the supervisee a chance to re-tell the client's story, elicit aspects that might have been missed during the therapy session and reflect on those that have an emotional impact on the supervisee (Hayward and Brown, 2003; Papadopoulos, 2001).

There is a difference between supervision, therapy, personal development, continuing professional development, appraisal and consultation. Clarity about the differences and the overlaps keeps the specific supervision focused.

HOW IS SUPERVISION DIFFERENT FROM THERAPY?

Supervision differs from therapy in that the supervisee is not a client in the sense of a client and therapist relationship. Issues may arise either in the supervisee's work with the client, or indeed in the relationship with the supervisor, or another colleague, which can trigger personal reactions in the supervisee due to past or present personal experiences. Some of these reactions are relevant for discussion in supervision, others may be more deep seated or personal and would be responded to or managed differently in the context of personal therapy. Supervision, nevertheless, is an appropriate forum for particular personal issues to be *identified* that might impact on the quality or work with clients. The supervisor, under these circumstances, might ask the supervisee to share his/her thoughts on the matter. This inquiry, in itself, might be sufficient to highlight meaningful connections and deepen understanding for the supervisee about the impact of their personal reactions on therapy with the client. At the other end of the scale, the supervisor might recognise a need for the supervisee to seek more appropriate help and encourage this to happen. It is the supervisor's responsibility to identify this boundary line between the two different roles and make decisions about how to proceed with the supervisee. An example of how a supervisor handled this boundary between supervision and therapy is given to help clarify this fine line.

Anna was a newly qualified psychologist working in an organisation dealing with disturbed adolescents. Two issues of a personal nature emerged as she talked about her difficulties in dealing with adolescent aggression. The supervisor asked if she had ever had to deal with aggression in her own life's experience. Anna replied promptly, looking up at the supervisor. She said that the relationship with her father was uneasy, dating from her late adolescence. He was very dictatorial with her, with one incidence of near physical abuse. Given her physical appearance the supervisor thought Anna might have eating problems and felt, after reflection, that it was worth risking raising this with her directly at this time about whether she ate regularly and adequately. The supervisor knew that such information was relevant in supervision only if it affected her work with clients. Anna admitted that as an adolescent, and again more recently, she was vulnerable to bulimia. The relationship with her father and the eating problem, were both issues with the potential to impact adversely on her ability to handle clinical work optimally and professionally. The supervisor considered the bulimia a relevant personal issue that might affect her work and thus stressed the importance of seeking expert help outside supervision. The supervisor, however, decided to explore further with Anna how she thought her family relationships might have an impact on how she was dealing with the adolescent aggression. During the interval between supervision sessions, Anna had managed to more confidently tell her father what she wanted from him in a forthcoming family visit. At the next session Anna realised that, through dealing better with her own family issues, she could be able to work more effectively with the adolescent challenges.

In this case, Anna was perceptive and able to identify the impact of her own family of origin issues on how she handled situations of conflict with adolescents. The supervisor was able to draw a line between management of Anna's clinical competence and those aspects pertaining to personal therapy and did not enter into a discussion about the bulimia other than urging that she seek immediate help.

PERSONAL DEVELOPMENT

This is a requirement for trainees on most therapy courses. It can be regarded as supervision specifically related to how personal issues and experiences impact on clinical work, as shown in the example of Anna and her father. It is almost a cliché but still apt to re-state that we all bring much of ourselves into our work, and in the context of therapy, it is important to understand how this might be put to positive use or best be kept out of the relationship with clients. A supervisor might carry out this task of personal development that is different from overseeing clinical work. Trainees usually have a separate supervisor in their placement for their clinical work with clients. In some circumstances one supervisor may have to fulfil both roles, and what is important is that there is clarity about the differences in aims and purposes.

CONTINUING PROFESSIONAL DEVELOPMENT (CPD)

CPD is different from personal development as it entails maintaining clinical skills and ensuring that knowledge related to therapy or counselling is current and relevant. Updating is done by attending courses and having appropriate supervision for clinical work. CPD is now a requirement to keep up registration with the recognised regulatory bodies.

APPRAISAL

The appraisal of aims, achievements and difficulties is an element of supervision that is built into many organisational structures. Within organisations appraisal is the way professional practice standards are monitored, and in some circumstances it may not always include all the collaborative elements of supervision. It is defined hierarchically and usually carried out by a line manager.

CONSULTATION

Consultation is different from supervision in that there is no defined task to oversee or have responsibility for clinical practice. It is a process in which a therapist, or other professional, seeks an opinion about a clinical or working dilemma from another therapist who has some authority of expertise regarding the nature of the subject. Such consultations do not have the formal structure of supervision and are free from the hierarchical constraints of clinical supervision. Nevertheless, within the consultation certain boundaries and parameters also need to be defined to obtain clarity and enhance the outcome of the meeting, often of two experts (see, for example, Bor and Miller, 1990; Kingston and Smith, 1983).

SOME CONTENTS OF SUPERVISION

The above definitions are a first step in providing 'good' supervision. However, it encompasses many other factors taken from different perspectives.

Some are listed here to stimulate thought and help the reader to bring yet others to mind.

CONTEXT

The context in which supervision takes place has a bearing on ethical and practical considerations in each different situation for supervisor and supervisee. Encompassing the context is an important first requirement when setting up and doing comprehensive supervision at the micro (relationship between supervisee and supervisee), macro (the workplace of both) and mezzo (the place supervision holds in therapy) levels. The context affects the views of supervisor and supervisee and unless considered with clarity can lead to assumptions being made that may influence the subsequent quality of supervision. Careful consideration of where the supervisee works, who else impinges on their activities, and where the supervisee is placed in any given hierarchy allows thought to be given to the restraints and opportunities placed on their clinical practice. Working as a multidisciplinary team member, in a team of the same discipline or in isolation in private practice has different parameters and perspectives. Liaison with other professionals across disciplines can influence therapeutic work and may be a source of stress to supervisees that is often not fully appreciated. The need to look beyond clinical cases and to help the supervisee to understand more about their work in the context entails discussion about:

- caseload management;
- review of written records and letters;
- relationships and liaison with other professionals;
- professional development and career aspirations; and
- how the context influences therapy, and how the supervisee can intervene in that setting most effectively.

FORMAT

Choosing the best format for supervision for each supervisee can enhance the overall benefits. The possibilities are wide but include one to one, small group, couples or a combination of these. One to one offers more focus on the individual supervisee, whilst group supervision increases the opportunities for different perspectives and support for supervisees who hear about how others manage similar concerns (Hildebrand, 1998; Proctor, 2000). Peer group meetings without a designated supervisor are more about mutual support and sharing ideas without the same emphasis on accountability that is necessary in most supervision.

TECHNIQUES

The techniques used in supervision depend on the experience and theoretical orientation of the supervisor. The most frequently and readily available techniques to review and reflect on practice are the use of tape recordings, self-reporting by the supervisee and written records. The use of role-play can readily enhance reflection and unblock situations when either supervisor or supervisee feels 'stuck'. Live supervision, with the supervisor in the room (Smith and Kingston, 1980) or behind a one-way screen, adds another helpful dimension, but is not always a possibility from a practical point of view. With live supervision the supervisor can more readily focus on the process in therapy and in giving feedback interventions with clients are more immediate.

LENGTH OF THE SUPERVISION PERIOD

Clarifying the length of time over which supervision or personal development is envisaged to take place is sometimes left vague and ill defined. Time frames need to be agreed from the outset as it adds to the clarity of the process. It might be that a year is initially set and the contract is then reviewed. In other circumstances, there might be a definite time period defined by either supervisor or supervisee, or in some instances the time might be restricted by other constraints, such as a fixed-term work contract. Some experienced supervisees might choose to use supervision from time to time and this too is feasible with both a flexible and disciplined approach by the supervisor. Trainees seeking personal development usually have a clearly stipulated number of hours of required hours.

DEVELOPMENT

Good supervision will seek to bring out and develop the supervisee's competencies and skills, and expand potential at appropriate stages of training and experience (Hawkins and Shohet, 2000). The supervisor should always be alert to clues that open up opportunities for discussion about the supervisee's clinical work that can enhance skills and knowledge and help the supervisee to feel emancipated enough for some risk taking. Helping the supervisee to reflect upon process in therapy by distinguishing between different kinds of data and information and to use this to build up a workable hypothesis is one aspect of supervision. The diffident or disorganised supervisee might not easily make explicit their skills and deficits. It is for the supervisor to inculcate a need for structure and to open up the discussion by exploring the strengths and any weaknesses in approach and introducing at times a lighter touch to the discussion – with playfulness and humour.

FEEDBACK

Identifying when, and reviewing how, the reactions of the supervisee to the client can be replicated in the supervision help supervisor and supervisee reflect and to use these responses positively to enhance therapeutic expertise. The style and manner of how the supervisee is given feedback and confirmation of competence by the supervisor may evoke reactions, for example, to problems related to authority. Such situations need to be dealt with sensitively and in a way that frees the supervisee from feeling constrained. Constraints to solutions in difficult cases are often found in how the supervisee has picked up and used clues given by clients. Simply inviting the supervisee to remember and re-tell his or her story with the client may unlock difficulties. Sometimes these constraints come about because of fears of risk taking that emanates from the supervisee's personal life story, and in other instances the supervisee may be trying too hard not to make 'mistakes'. The context of supervision is a place to experiment, often through role-play, with various approaches and thus increase confidence.

TRAINING FOR THE SUPERVISOR

Training the supervisor for supervision can provide a time for reflection, acquisition of skills and regulation of standards. However, much good supervision emanates from experience acquired over time and from the supervisor's own role model of supervision, and being clear about the responsibilities of the role.

RESPONSIBILITIES OF SUPERVISOR AND SUPERVISEE

The relationship between the supervisor and supervisee brings responsibilities for both. A key shared responsibility is to monitor clinical standards and the supervisee's competency in handling challenging issues whilst maintaining ethical practice.

The supervisor's main responsibilities are to:

- Discuss the supervisee and supervisor's expectations.
- Create the supervisory context by defining the parameters about what is appropriate to bring to supervision.
- Establish, with the supervisee, a relationship of trust that enables creative thinking and sharing of difficulties and differences.

- Encourage the supervisee to develop his or her unique professional style and approach.
- Define and outline practical details such as location, times, length and frequency of sessions, and payment as applicable.
- Clarify any unique or particular issues of accountability, and responsibility and any conflicts of interest if, for example, the supervisor is the manager as well.
- Take responsibility for discussing how issues of confidentiality will be handled, such as links with line managers and other professionals.
- Identify and respond to situations if it emerges that a supervisee is unfit to practise or when challenging dilemmas arise, for example the overconfident supervisee, one who shows incompetence, or one who says 'Yes, but...'.
- Give a different and creative perspective to difficult situations, where this is called for.

The supervisee has responsibilities that include to:

- Discuss, from the outset, any particular requirements or issues that might affect the supervisory relationship (obligation to have supervision for registration or training, completing supervision reports, cultural or gender restrictions).
- Reach an understanding with the supervisor about the main aims and objectives of supervision at his/her stage of practice and experience, and being clear about any particular needs (e.g. development of specific skills or theoretical ideas).
- Consider how to deal with any serious concerns, such as finding the supervisor 'incompetent' or unhelpful, which is less easily managed if without a separate line manager.
- Be prepared for sessions (having cases organised, thought given to dilemmas).
- Respect the supervisor's time (attending on time, being prepared).

Clarity about responsibilities helps when it comes to choosing a supervisor and selecting a supervisee.

CHOOSING A SUPERVISOR/SELECTING A SUPERVISEE

Before starting out in supervision, both supervisor and supervisee have some key issues to consider and possibly discuss prior to agreeing a contract for supervision which include:

- The qualities and broad approach that are required as the bottom line of supervision (monitoring, accountability, confidence for safe, confidential discussion of strengths and difficulties).
- Understanding the requirements of registering bodies, and whether the supervisee needs to be registered with the same registration body as the supervisor.
- Whether the supervisor's registration with a professional body is required and acceptable.
- Whether the supervisor should come from within the same institution or outside.
- Consideration of the relevance for the supervisor and supervisee to share the same or come from different theoretical orientations, and how differences might be resolved.
- Provision of opportunity for the attainment of skills being sought by the supervisee (family therapy, CBT, psychoanalytic, systemic) and matching these with and competence of those of the supervisor.
- Whether there are any particular gender or cultural issues that may be relevant to the supervisory relationship.

In choosing a supervisor the supervisee may simply base the initial decision on reputation or recommendation. A supervisee working privately may be free to choose a supervisor, whereas there may be limited choice for the supervisee in an organisation, and this should be brought into the open. Answers to each of the points itemised cannot be prescribed as each situation is different and they have to be considered by both the supervisee and supervisor.

TRAINEES, QUALIFIED THERAPISTS AND COLLEAGUES

There is some difference between supervision with trainees and with qualified practitioners. Supervision with trainees is a relationship to develop skills, provide support, monitor practice link theory with practice and sometimes help in decisions about suitability for the task. The supervisor is usually an experienced practitioner whose main role is to help the trainee to link academic learning with practice. As such, the supervisor carries some authority of knowledge. Any emotional reactions to clients can be used to help deepen self-knowledge and thus stabilise and enhance therapeutic skills. Emotional support during the learning process is an element of the trainee-supervisor relationship. Even though the supervisor is the 'expert', respect for what skills and resources trainees bring to their clinical practice is a hallmark of good supervision. The trainee therapist must surely have a rich array of personal, social and professional experience that can be reflected upon to develop more confident practice.

With qualified therapists supervision is more about providing an opportunity for enhancing skills and reviewing practice within a safe environment. If the supervisor is a professional colleague, there are particular boundary issues to consider such as how to keep the relationship professional when each might meet in other contexts, even outside of work. The supervisor must be explicit about handling confidentiality issues and liaison outside supervision. The bottom line will always be clinical safety with clients.

FRAMEWORK FOR SUPERVISION

Many of the guiding principles and steps in supervision sessions are familiar to supervisors and embedded in practice. Having a practice framework for supervision can facilitate achieving its aims. This framework includes overall guiding practice principles and a structure or 'map' for each supervision session which can be applied and adapted to suit the supervisor from a range of different theoretical approaches.

GUIDING SUPERVISORY PRINCIPLES

These are the key tenets that inform supervisory practice. Those for supervision are not dissimilar to those for therapy (Bor *et al.*, 2004). Having a set of aims in mind helps supervisors to achieve a positive working relationship with the supervisee, who in turn will be clearer and more secure about the overall goals and process of supervision. The following principles help to set the tone for 'good' supervision:

- To develop a positive working relationship that enhances trust, is non-judgemental and enables learning to take place.
- To clarify with the supervisee the supervision aims and parameters (what is and what is not appropriate, and any professional accountability issues).
- To make no assumptions about what supervisees might want from supervision and to seek to explore this with them, and review their goals from time to time.
- To recognise, draw out and respect the supervisee's capabilities and competencies.
- To set small, realistic, measurable and achievable goals for each session.
- To listen carefully to what is said and note what is left out by picking up clues from the supervisee's feedback. This helps to assess progress in

supervision with a view to raising points at appropriate times about, for example, the impact on the supervisee of a client's responses, such as anger outbursts.

• To share responsibility with the supervisee for the process and content of supervision.

• To recognise and respect the boundaries between supervision and therapy.

These principles are held in mind by the supervisor whilst carrying out supervision.

STRUCTURED SESSIONS

Having a *'map' or structure for the session* can act as a checklist to ensure that the most important aspects are covered. Supervision is but one task in the demanding practice for many therapists, and often means a shift in thinking and practise. This 'map' includes four distinct stages within supervision:

1. pre-session considerations;
2. the initial session;
3. on-going sessions; and
4. the final supervisory session.

Each stage embodies some key objectives that will be considered separately for clarity although the steps within them are similar. The supervisor, prior to starting, will have in mind how to best create the most congenial context for supervision and will also aim to address with the supervisee how his/her objectives might be achieved by the time supervision ends. Thus, in starting this process the ending is envisaged.

STAGE ONE: PRE-SESSION CONSIDERATIONS

Preparation before meeting the supervisee is important, the main consideration being how best to establish focused work with the supervisee and the steps include:

1. Reflection on who (supervisor, supervisee or a manager) and how (phone, email, letter) the initial contact was made as this sets the context and the pathway to explore expectations. Thus one of the first questions from the supervisor might be to clarify how the supervisee heard of the supervisor and, if the supervisee was sent, and the reason for the

present request or requirement for supervision. If the choice is based on reputation, expectations may be raised, if not discussed, which may lead to disappointment for the supervisee if they are not met.

2. Clarification as to whether supervision is part of the requirements of accountability and responsibility, and if it is a private arrangement, what issues of accountability might be relevant, with detailed discussion being left until the first face-to-face meeting.

3. Discussion of the supervisor's availability and whether the supervisee can fit in with those times as this simple aspect can realistically allow or deter supervision to go ahead.

4. A brief description of the supervisor's clinical setting (whether private work, several different settings or within an institution) and an explanation by the supervisee of their setting and requirements.

5. An initial clarification of some of the main parameters of supervision from the supervisor's perspective, including the theoretical approach to supervision (whether this is rigidly in one model or able to be flexible) and whether the supervisee and supervisor are able to agree that this is an issue in the first place.

6. Early discussion about fees is important if it is a private arrangement. Some supervisors might be willing to negotiate special conditions for trainees who are required to have a number of supervised hours.

7. If relevant, the supervisee's course or college tutor and any formal links that are required, including any paper work, should be discussed.

8. It is advisable for the supervisor to suggest an initial meeting before making any final commitment to ensure that the aims and wishes of both have been agreed and understood.

9. Finally, set the date, time and location of the first meeting.

Following this initial conversation the supervisor can reflect upon the information and any issues raised that can save time and help to make the first meeting more focused. The key issues include:

- How the supervisee came to contact or approach the supervisor.
- The sex, gender and age of the supervisee and whether these raise any dilemmas in the match between the supervisor and supervisee.
- The theoretical approach of both supervisee and supervisor.
- The nature of issues or problems likely to be encountered by the supervisee in his or her practice.
- Whether the supervisee is a trainee or a qualified therapist as this alerts the supervisor to pertinent aspects for each.

The following example is provided to illustrate how things might unfold if these preliminary details are not carefully considered.

David, a trainee counsellor, approached the supervisor who had taught a brief therapy model on a counselling course that he had attended. During the course David often questioned the value of the brief approach of the supervisor as he was more committed to psychoanalytic therapy. When David approached her asking for supervision, she was surprised at his interest as her impression was that he was sceptical and critical of the approach. However, she agreed to meet with him without first carefully attending to some of the preliminary questions described above. There was, in the first place, insufficient clarification that the initial meeting would be used to discuss and agree parameters and expectations for supervision. David cancelled the first appointment at the last moment. He later re-scheduled another first session but never returned for further sessions. On reflection it was clear that the supervisor did not pay sufficient attention to the reasons that David chose to come, nor were the parameters of supervision sufficiently explored. A collaborative relationship had not been established. Nor did the supervisor explore some of her intuitive misgivings about his approach to her in the first place. She was left with a feeling that he came to test her out and was looking for something that had not been made explicit.

This was an example of 'cutting corners' by not asking a series of initial questions and making assumptions that supervision could begin in the initial meeting, rather than using it to explore expectations, wishes and beliefs about the outcome of this arrangement. This case demonstrates how important the preliminary stage of supervision is for the on-going success of the process and highlights the supervisor's responsibilities for ensuring this happens.

STAGE TWO: THE INITIAL SESSION

The first meeting is crucial for laying the foundations for 'good' supervision. Each supervisor, from whatever theoretical background, has some notion of the structure of the session. There are a number of steps that it would be useful to follow.

INTRODUCTIONS AND SETTING THE PARAMETERS

The supervisor takes a lead in opening the session by clarifying names and how they will address each other. Having a brief discussion of expectations on both sides helps to establish whether or not the supervisee and supervisor have sufficient agreed aims to enter the supervision. Questions may include, for example:

- What are you looking to gain from supervision with me at this stage of your career?
- Have you given thought as to how these hopes could best be met?

Setting parameters in more detail is an important aspect of the first meeting and includes:

- What to bring to supervision;
- What issues are outside the brief of supervision and how these will be dealt with (personal difficulties);
- How often the supervisor and supervisee will meet;
- The time period over which supervision will take place, which varies according to the needs of the supervisee (context, registration, managerial, wishes).

Issues of accountability and responsibility must be clarified, especially if the supervisor is also the line manager and conflicts of interest could emerge. For example, a supervisee may wish to take a particular approach with clients and see them frequently over a period of time. This might conflict with the overall needs of the service for which the supervisor, as manager, is responsible. In other circumstances the supervisor may be responsible for clinical practice but may not be the line manager, and different issues must be clarified, for example,

> I am responsible for your clinical work but am not your line manager. Can you think of any issues from your point of view that might come up that you might want to be communicated to your line manager? How would you see that happening?

In asking this question the supervisor opens up the issue of context and at least has raised the topic in the supervisee's mind.

It is appropriate, at this initial contact, to consider how any differences in theoretical approach, if any, will be managed, for example the supervisor might state:

> Our theoretical approaches are in some ways different, however, I think that we can build on your CBT work and maybe introduce some different ways of approaching similar issues. Do you think this will present any difficulties for you? I suggest that we continuously review how well your needs are being met.

The supervisor should make explicit that notes will be taken to serve as a record of what is covered, expectations and objectives of supervision.

If future issues of conflict arise, the supervisee would probably have access to these notes; thus, everything should be written with thought and any controversial issues should be backed up with concrete examples. The supervisee should be encouraged to also keep notes.

ENGAGEMENT AND BEGINNING THE SESSION

This is the key element in developing a congenial working relationship and takes precedence in this initial meeting. Exploring the expectations of the supervisee is important for both supervisor and supervisee so that there is clarity about what the supervisee is hoping for from supervision. For example,

Supervisor: Let's return to what you are most hoping for from supervision. What are your main hopes?
Supervisee: I want to feel more confident in how I deal with clients. I need to be able to feel free to tell you my difficulties without feeling inadequate and exposed. I'm worried that what I do will sound bad to you and you will judge me on that!

A simple statement can help to start this process such as:

I would want to work with you to reach these goals, so we will need to plan together how to proceed.

Highlighting from the start that the emphasis will be on presenting work that the supervisee considers has gone well, alongside those that present problems, sets a tone of respect. The supervisor might begin by exploring the supervisee's view of their main strengths and areas of confidence. For example in relation to cases the supervisor might clarify early:

I would want to discuss your cases that you feel you manage well as we can learn as much from that as from those that present challenges.

What the supervisor expects from the supervisee is also an important step in engagement and establishes collaboration. Any possible blocks to effective collaboration should be highlighted as soon as possible. Bringing into the open any current concerns from the point of view of supervisee and supervisor is a key to good supervision. Two examples illustrate how this might be done. In the first, a supervisee said in the first session that she wanted a supervisor from the same culture (or gender). The supervisor used this request as an opportunity for reflection and exploration with the supervisee as to what benefits might arise rather than to how the differences appear to be a barrier to the supervisory process. The supervisee responded that she had not thought about it in that way. In the second example the supervisor herself was unsure about whether she felt competent enough to supervise a particular supervisee who was seeking for particular expertise with drugs and alcohol and she said:

> I feel able to offer you supervision over most of what you have described, but I have little personal expertise with the alcohol problems that interest you. We might see if you can find someone else to help with this in particular, but it should not impede our overall discussion about your work. What do you think of this proposal?

The supervisees after both these discussions were willing to try the supervision on offer.

GIVING AND ELICITING INFORMATION

This is a two-way process between supervisee and supervisor. At this initial meeting the supervisor may suggest in more precise detail how the sessions might be used and also elicits the supervisee's wishes. Issues regarding confidentiality need to be discussed from the outset, being one of the 'ground rules' of supervision. There should be clarity about feedback to others such as line managers, if this is appropriate. Without assurance about this matter the supervisee will never feel able to be really open in sessions. The supervisor must take responsibility for clarifying issues that might emerge that could, in some situations, present concern, such as supervisee incompetence and in the worst scenario malpractice. If this is done in a general way for all supervisees, it covers the topic in a straightforward, less threatening manner. The supervisor has to be prepared, should issues arise in supervision that are of concern either for client safety, or that of the supervisee. The supervisor might have to break confidentiality and consult appropriate others and should also clarify, at an early stage, that any feedback to anyone on his part would be done with the supervisee's consent and an agreed procedure between them. Most supervisees want to be assured of confidentiality. In a more concrete way information is given about how supervision will be managed through cases, caseload discussion and the working context.

ASSESSING WHETHER TO GO FORWARD

Making an assessment of whether or not to proceed with the supervisory contract is a step that both supervisor and supervisee might do silently before it is made explicit. However, the supervisor can lead the way by asking the supervisee if anything that has been discussed so far has changed their views of any possible obstacles or difficulties that might be encountered and should be further clarified before proceeding with the arrangement. Allowing time to invite any questions and comments from the supervisee also contributes to the assessment.

DECISION-MAKING

This is a phase that comes just before ending, and after the assessment is made by both supervisee and supervisor, for example the supervisor might say:

> From my point of view we seem to have covered most of the important issues. Even though there are some difficulties in finding a suitable time I think we can decide that today before ending. What are your thoughts about this?

ENDING

Closing the first meeting with clarity and optimism is the responsibility of the supervisor. The supervisee can be invited to summarise his or her views of the meeting. Summarising the main points helps each to hear the others' views. For example, the supervisor might say:

> You have been very open about your apprehensions concerning supervision, but also expressed some excitement at the thought of using our time to test issues and for you to get some support. I would like to offer you a date so we can embark on this journey of exploration.

EVALUATION

Allowing time at the end of the session for evaluation helps the supervisor to gain some further insight into the value of the meeting to the supervisee and also allows the supervisee to have the last word. An example of how this might be done is shown in the following discussion between supervisor and supervisee:

Supervisor: Give me one thought that you might take away from this meeting?
Supervisee: I feel a bit overwhelmed with all the things we have discussed and I am sure will reflect on them, especially the confidentiality. However, I also feel excited that is a place where I can be challenged without being worried about feeling incapable.

STAGE THREE: ON-GOING SUPERVISORY SESSIONS

The format for on-going supervision is very similar to that of the first meeting. Thus only specific differences are highlighted.

ENGAGEMENT AND BEGINNING THE SESSION

Introduction and re-engagement is led by the supervisor who can start the session with a general opening question, for example,

> Any thoughts from our last meeting that you want to raise before we get started?
> Any special thoughts for today?
> What kind of month have you had?

The supervisor can then invite the supervisee to set the agenda with him for that session, for example by suggesting:

> Let's start by making an agenda of issues you would like to cover today. What are the main things from your point of view? There are also a few things I would like to discuss.

GIVING AND ELICITING INFORMATION

Eliciting the supervisee's beliefs, values, principles and intentions is the key issue in a collaborative, respectful supervisory process. Some examples of opening questions are:

> What are the key values you hold that inform your practice?
> What are your main beliefs that help you when you meet problems with clients?
> What are your dreams for your future in this work?

ASSESSMENT

Assessment of the process and content of supervision comes towards the end of the session and is based on what is heard and seen, plus any additional information brought by the supervisee. It is a discipline that helps both supervisee and supervisor to evaluate the progress of supervision. Questions asked openly in the session or to themselves help in making this assessment:

> What am I feeling right now in relation to this case/the process of supervision?
> What issues have not been brought into the open that might be hindering progress?
> What could the supervisor and supervisee do to help the supervisee move forward?
> What needs to happen to enable this to occur?

ENDING

Allowing time for the supervisee to raise any additional issues not structured into the agenda is important at this juncture as it respects that the supervisee might have concerns or issues that may have been overlooked or even some that might come to mind during the discussion. The supervisor takes responsibility to allow this to happen by saying for example:

> Before we bring things to a close today is there anything you want to say or ask that we haven't discussed?

STAGE FOUR: THE FINAL SUPERVISORY SESSION

The last meeting should be a culmination of all that has gone before unless ending is unexpected. It is important to prepare for the ending in some detail in the last few meetings. Ending supervision is a time for review of expectations, what has been achieved and anything that might have been missed. A discussion might need to take place about the future contact between supervisor and supervisee, including the possibility of giving references in the future. Ideally, the last meeting is held in mind from the start, and during any review of progress. If the ending is unexpected, through circumstances that could not be foreseen, careful thought has to be given by the supervisor as to how this will be managed, which will vary according to the circumstances.

The stages and steps as outlined help to hold in mind the guiding principles of supervisory practice and the key aspects in each session that enhance good stimulating discussion between supervisor and supervisee.

CONCLUSIONS

All good clinical practice happens in a theoretical framework and likewise supervision has to be a thoughtful, logical and planned activity. At the heart of rewarding and challenging supervision is the relationship engendered by the supervisor with room to support the supervisee in times of need, as well as challenge and inform. Supervision clearly focuses on the skills, knowledge and experience that the supervisee uses to carry out clinical work. Providing a framework for this to happen can facilitate the process and lead to more effective supervision. Ultimately supervision is there to help the supervisee achieve safe, effective, efficient practice and in itself must be accountable. The supervisor should also have a forum to monitor practice of clinical and supervisory work.

REFERENCES

Bor, R., Gill, S., Miller, R. and Parrott, C. (2004) *Doing Therapy Briefly*. Basingstoke: Palgrave McMillan.

Bor, R. and Miller, R. (1990)*The Internal Consultant*. London: DC Publishing.

Elizur, J. (1990) "'Stuckness" in live supervision: expanding the therapist's style'. *Journal of Family Therapy*, 12, 267–280.

Hawkins, P. and Shohet, P. (2000) *Supervision in the Helping Professions* (2nd edn). Milton Keynes. Open University Press.

Hayward, M. and Bowen, B. (2003) Re-remembering – a supervision exercise. *Context, AFT Publishing*, 70, 23–25.

Hildebrand, J. (1998) *Bridging the Gap. A Training Module in Personal and Professional Development*. London: Karnac Books.

Kingston, P. and Smith, D. (1983) Preparation for live consultation and live supervision when working without a one-way screen. *Journal of Family Therapy*, 5, 219–233.

McHale, E. and Carr, A. (1998) The effect of supervisor and trainee therapist gender on supervision discourse. *Journal of Family Therapy*, 20(4), 395–411.

Papadopoulos, R. (2001) 'Refugee families: issues of systemic supervision'. *Journal of Family Therapy*, 2(4), 405–422.

Proctor, B. (2000) *Group Supervision*. London: Sage Publications.

Smith, D. and Kingston, P. (1980) Live supervision without a one-way screen. *Journal of Family Therapy*, 2, 379–387.

7 HOW TO MANAGE A COUNSELLING SERVICE

Colin Lago

> Each one of us has to develop our own (management) style and our own approach, using such skills and personal qualities as we have inherited ... management is an art rather than a science. The artistry lies in the combination of skills, perceptions, intuitions and combined experience which are brought to bear on problems which are continually different and almost invariably unique.
>
> Sir John Harvey Jones (1989)

This chapter has deliberately taken an apparently circuitous route towards addressing the task of 'How to manage a counselling service'. Somewhat paralleling the therapist's role of facilitating the clients' explorations of their own questions rather than directly responding to those questions with 'an answer', this chapter initially offers various general perspectives on the theme of management and encourages the readers, through the recommended exercises, to explore their own thoughts and position in relation to the management task.

This chapter is written in the recognition of:

1. The huge (and sometimes contradictory) body of literature that exists on 'managing'.
2. The wide range of personnel and personality types involved in management. (Obviously, managers are not all drawn from the same genetic mould.)
3. The wide range, yet relative short history, (in most cases) of counselling and psychotherapy agencies which serve completely different sections of the community (e.g. patients, students, employees, minority groups, citizens) in different contexts (e.g. education, employment, voluntary sector, city councils, national health service, etc.) and each having differing sets of aims, objectives, theoretical principles and operational procedures.
4. The value of a personal and experiential approach by each person towards his/her own fulfilment of development and potential within this management arena.
5. That there is no one right way of being a manager!

INTRODUCTION

Some years ago, a colleague and I wrote a book on the management of counselling and psychotherapy services (Lago and Kitchin, 1998), and despite our relative backgrounds, him as a management lecturer and myself as a manager of a counselling service, we found the task very challenging indeed. Our preoccupations were concerned with the tasks of making the 'right' choice of contents, the limits of book length we were working to and extracting the most relevant ideas from the sheer volume of existing texts on management and our own experience.

Having taken a building metaphor for the (above mentioned) book (e.g. the first two chapters are entitled 'Laying the Foundations' and 'Building a Sound Structure') it is interesting to note that it was only towards the completion of this text that we realised that the very dynamics and roles demanded of managers had been completely overlooked. In addressing the managerial tasks we had successfully avoided the implications! Consequently, a further chapter was then added, entitled 'Managing Managing'.

The focus in this chapter leads from considerations of how to be a manager before considering the particular elements and themes inherent in managing a counselling service. Exercises have also been included after various sections that are designed to assist your personal explorations on this topic.

Scant attention in the professional literature has been paid to the management of counselling services. This probably reflects the relatively recent historical development of counselling and psychotherapy as a distinct profession delivered in organisational and agency settings.

The management of counselling and psychotherapy services should be of concern to all practitioners, not just those appointed as managers. As Carroll and Walton (1997) have so succinctly expressed it:

> Understanding that there is more to counselling than what happens in the counselling room enables counsellors to have an eye and perspectives on the contexts in which the counselling takes place.

However, the reality for many therapists is that they often wish not to have anything to do with management and its tasks and processes. As was suggested in Lago and Kitchin (1998):

> ... at its most extreme, this attitude expresses itself in the over simplistic division between therapy as the pure, ethical, uncontaminated expression of honourable intention and management as a tainted and tainting experience full of compromise, domination and Machiavellian intent! (p.viii)

Added to the above complexities, Salaman (1995) suggests that most managers are promoted to management because they are good at something else-something other than management (p.4). Indeed, he goes on to assert that the earlier skills required for the previous tasks (in our case, being a therapist) are actually an obstacle to the development of management skills. Moreover he emphasises that previous skills may be 'in some cases and in some senses opposed to management skills'.

In summation, the task, then, of managing a counselling service is potentially an extremely challenging one for the following reasons:

- There is available an enormous volume of general management literature from which to gain advice and instruction. Much of this, however, tends to focus on the circumstances of the business world and, as Bendix (1956) noted half a century ago, has often reflected the historical period in which it has been written.
- Unfortunately, there is scant material available on management related to therapeutic organisations.
- In addition, many therapists actively choose not to become involved in management and if they do, their previous skills may not be fully satisfactory in the management role.

Despite the above somewhat seeming bleak perspective, management can also offer personal rewards and satisfaction as well as a deep sense of maximising potential, well beyond one's own capacity as an individual therapist to ensuring, as a manager, access to sound, sensitive, professional, therapeutic services for a wide range of distressed and troubled clients.

AN INTRODUCTION TO THE EXERCISES IN THIS CHAPTER

As mentioned above, please note that several personal exercises are included in this chapter. It is suggested, if you choose to respond to them, that it would be useful to contain your written thoughts and notes in one location, e.g. a personal diary or dedicated notebook or discreet file on your computer. This facility (of storing your recordings in one place) thus offers you the longer-term possibility for systematic reflection over substantial time periods on the theme of management. In addition, there then also exists the possibility of reworking and refining these elements in pursuit of your ongoing awareness, training and development.

EXERCISE 1

INTRODUCTION

This exercise process has been stimulated by the ideas contained in a new text about the uses of writing in therapy (Bolton *et al.*, 2004). The suggested task offers a method for quickly accessing and noting a range of your ideas and responses to a particular theme. Often, quite surprising elements may appear through this process in contrast with, for example, a longer essay of the same title. This exercise hopefully quickly helps you get an insight into some of the important elements that comprise your view of management.

1. For 5 minutes just write down a 'stream of consciousness' on the topic of 'management'. (Just try to keep the pen flowing over the paper; writing whatever comes into your mind on this theme. Do not concern yourself with grammar, punctuation, spelling and structure, even sense – just let the words pour onto the page.)
2. An alternative to this would be to write a similar 'stream of conscious-ness' on 'the manager who most inspired me and why'. (You may wish to complete both exercises.)
3. Have a short break from this task and lay aside the writing for the moment.
4. Afterwards, look at the writing again and spend some time reflecting on what you have written. (You may choose to do this either on your own, quietly, or in dialogue with a trusted friend, colleague, mentor or supervisor.)
5. Note what you have written about management (content) and how it has been described (attitudes/ behaviours). What learning can you take from this?

The notes that you have written as a consequence of the above exercise may give you a strong indication of some of the elements related to management that are of real significance and meaning to you.

HOW NOT TO MANAGE A COUNSELLING SERVICE

EXERCISE 2

INTRODUCTION

Though it may now appear somewhat confounding to the reader to lead with this section on how NOT to manage a counselling service, the exercise outlined below does provide material and a context from which you might subsequently elicit your own personal ideas and opinions on the management task. Considering what is not the case can sometimes guide us strongly in conceiving what we wish to be the case!

1. Again, without trying to bring deep or considered thinking to this task at this stage, brainstorm a list of points on the theme of 'how not to manage a counselling service'.
2. Take 10 minutes to complete this task and see how many points you can come up with. (This could also prove a valuable exercise for a team of therapists to participate in. It would be important, in this latter case particularly, to encourage the brainstorming behaviour rather than lapsing into discussion of each item as it is proposed.) The task is to see how many points on this theme you can generate.
3. Now take the time to reflect on each of the points you have listed and consider more deeply the implications.
4. In the light of the above list, consider the behaviours that you would now wish to avoid if you were a manager and then.
5. Attempt to create a new list of points, with brief ideas and details where necessary, of how you would now wish to behave as a manager.

One colleague who did these exercises reported the following:

> I did these exercises and found them very helpful indeed. In fact, I was fascinated that I too arrived at the same point ... as you do, because I recalled a manager who did not inspire me and it was this experience that led me to manage in a way that was opposite to that previous negative experience (Jordan, 2004).

SOME LEADING QUESTIONS ON MANAGING

> Management, like politics, consists to a large degree in the management of differences. Groups in organisations have different roles, different goal, and different skills, so have individuals. The blending of these differences into one coherent whole is the overall task of management (Handy, 1976, p.212).

The following (and many other) troubling questions have arisen out of my own experiences as a service manager over many years. Inevitably, many of the points below are linked to particular incidents, episodes and indeed crises with which the service teams and I were trying to face at that time.

It is appreciated that such a long list of questions might have the effect of completely stopping a prospective manager in pursuing his/her applications for management posts! However, that is clearly not the intention here. Rather, by including such a list, it is hoped that readers contemplating taking on a management role will be stimulated to consider carefully the many and varied aspects of behaviour that are required of and by managers.

- What do you think management is?
- How might you manage the tension, as a manager, between 'doing' (overseeing the administration in its entirety) and 'being' (with other staff members, with other tasks such as counselling, clinical supervision etc.)?
- How might this tension be managed where there are competing demands of authority, client concerns, group dynamics, personality and theoretical differences in the team, employment procedures and service policies?
- What might be the influence of your therapeutic theoretical model upon your style of management?
- What key principles (e.g. productivity, fairness, humaneness, financial probity, participation, planning, etc.) would you wish to base your work as a manager on?
- What effect, do you think, your personality and personal philosophy might have on your management style?
- The psychopathology of the leader can often be played out in the dynamics of the staff team. What effects might this have upon the management process? What is/are your 'shadow' aspect? What is it you are not able to see or appreciate easily (within your personality) which might well also impact upon your counselling team?
- How might you manage the tension between, at the one end, tending to the individual needs and requirements of staff members through to ensuring that the appropriate productivity is occurring within the agency through to, at the other end, tending to the interface between the agency and the outside world?
- This tension might also be re-stated thus: How would you wish to be (and wish to be perceived as) as a manager and how might these concerns be balanced and informed by how you would wish the service to be viewed and used by the community and clients?
- Are you competent at handling change and how might you also be a facilitator of change?
- How might you manage the competing demands of long-term planning and the inevitable everyday pressures and crises?

EXERCISE 3

INTRODUCTION

Space, unfortunately, does not offer us here the possibility of explaining more fully the stories behind each of the above statements. However, as they allude to some significant moments or factors within the collective experience of many counselling organisations, it is hoped that certain of these statements will speak to you directly, thus furnishing you with material for consideration.

1. Choose one or two of the above questions above that 'leapt out at you' whilst you were reading them.
2. Taking one at a time, ask yourself the following questions:

    - Why this question?
    - What memories, ideas or situations does it stir in you?
    - How does this question stimulate you? What feelings does it raise?
    - How might you, faced with such circumstances, respond to this dilemma?

3. As with the other exercises in this chapter, you may choose to consider these questions in discussion with a trusted colleague or a group of colleagues as well as writing about them.

Each of the above statements relate to challenging issues for managers, issues that can prove to be both in the foreground of what one is doing as a manager as well as constituting elements of the continuous background in which one is working. The nature of foreground/background issues (as they affect the manager) is of course an ever-changing scenario. However, this exercise offers the possibility of identifying some specific elements of critical managerial activity that are worthy of consideration, anticipation and possibly strategic development.

SOME RESEARCH OUTCOMES ON MANAGEMENT

> Where people have had prior management training coupled with astute organisa-
> tional awareness they find the process of setting up and managing a counselling
> service less difficult and so less stressful than others (Jordan, 2003, ch.4, p.153).

Salaman (1995, p.21) describes the tension between two methods of building a model for effective management practice. The first approach is based upon the analysis of what managers do, a descriptive approach, with a view to building a model of an ideal or creating a framework of necessary management qualities.

His second proposal is to develop 'a more conceptually inspired view of what managers are for and what their function is' (p.21). He proceeds to argue that the first method, i.e. 'what managers actually do is not an entirely sensible basis on which to build a model of what they should do...'.

Luthans *et al.* (1985) indicated that studies of the actual work of managers revealed that their work activities differed substantially from their activities as described in the management literature. Certainly, from my own and many other colleague's experiences, managers work hard and long, a finding substantiated by Mintzberg (1990, p.30). Developing this theme further, Salaman (p.22) quotes work by Martinko and Gardner (1990, p.344) who report that 'managerial work is brief, varied, fragmented, spontaneous and highly interpersonal'. When Mintzberg analysed what managers actually did, no activity patterns were evident, except one: that the work occurred in very short episodes and was highly fragmented, interrupted and brief in duration. (Certainly this view is borne out by the appendix to this chapter, which provides a recording I made of a day's various activities when I managed a counselling service.)

Salaman argues that the outcome of responding to the very many demands placed on managers may lead them to behave skilfully in ways that are inefficient and at worst, incompetent. He notes that the skills developed could thus be counter productive (p.23) and similarly, Mintzberg suggests that managers may become proficient at their superficiality (p.35).

Jordan (2003) found, during her doctoral research, that the first or primary professional training of the counselling service managers she interviewed (e.g. nurse, teacher, business person) had influenced their management styles.

Far from being systematic and reflective planners (a popular conception of proactivity), work by both Mintzberg (1990) and Stewart (1983, p.85) reveal the skilled capacity of managers to adapt and respond to a wide variety of demands (reactivity). The tension between being reactive and proactive is thus a challenging one for any manager, and ultimately may be more determined by the personality traits and preferences of the individual manager rather than the tasks presented by the post.

THE PERSONALITY OF THE MANAGER

This latter point is a central thesis of this chapter: the personality of the manager (traits, preferences, beliefs, values, philosophies, experiences, and so on) is perhaps the most significant determining feature in how that person becomes and develops as a manager. The exercise scenarios suggested earlier in the chapter might provide an insight into your thoughts and experiences of management. Similarly, attempting to respond to the list of leading questions (above) will reveal your tendencies towards taking particular perspectives and actions in contrast to a huge range of other possible response strategies.

Lago and Kitchin (1998, pp.116–122) also advocated the desirability for managers to give due attention to the effect of their personalities upon their management style and suggested, as exemplars, three different questionnaire-based tests for personal exploration. The three programmes suggested included:

1. the Myers Briggs type indicator (offering an analysis of personality preferences, based originally on Jungian ideas);
2. the Belbin self-perception team roles inventory (how one may function in group settings); and
3. a communication exercise featured in Casse (1980, pp.125–33), which reveals the particular value orientations that underpin your communication style.

CPD is a necessary adjunct to successful management practice. Each of the exercises above (and there are many more to explore) not only serve to raise awareness of your particular ways of doing things but also, crucially from a management perspective, offer data on just how different other people (and more specifically to this chapter, your work colleagues) may be in their work-based interactions and activities to yourself.

This personal and interpersonal knowledge, if it can be embraced in your interactions and tasks, will profoundly inform and hopefully enhance the efficacy of all your management activities.

EXERCISE 4

INTRODUCTION

The following exercise invites you to reflect on aspects of your personality that could well be called upon within a management role. Once such aspects are identified, then appropriate opportunities can be sought for enhancement and development.

1. Compile a list of what it is you know about you that has been derived from your training, therapy, experience, reflection, personal diary, tests, questionnaires and other relevant experiences. For example:

   - My strength within groups is as a team worker, often perceiving some of the emotional undercurrents of the group.
   - I tend to be intuitive and feeling in my responses to others.
   - I tend to focus more on social processes in communication rather than on ideas or plans.
   - I tend to be inspired by a vision of what I wish to achieve.
   - I find that confrontation is very difficult.

- I find praising a person to be very difficult.
- I am not so much interested in facts and details.

2. In recognition that this is potentially a very substantial exercise, you might wish to conduct it over a series of sessions or, indeed, compile it within a personal diary or something similar, so that it becomes a resource for personal reflection, development and potentially completing your next job application!
3. Taking one point at a time, consider what might be the further training and development tasks that you now need to engage in.

One further development of this exercise, having identified themes for development, might be to consider the following:

- What could I do today to improve this?
- What could I do this week to improve this?
- What long-term plan might I pursue to develop this?

SO WHAT ACTUALLY IS MANAGEMENT?

The word 'manage' seems to have come into the English language directly from *manegiarre* – to handle or train horses – and was quickly extended to operations of war, and from the early 16th century, to a general sense of taking control, taking charge, directing (Williams, 1983).

Cole (2004) in his book *Management Theory and Practice* helpfully offers an analysis of developments in management theory from 1910 to 2000 and proceeds to consider the historically changing definitions of management during that time. He writes:

> Early ideas about management were propounded at a time when organisations were thought of as machines requiring efficient systems to enable them to function effectively ... Later theorists modified this approach by taking account of social and environmental as well as technical factors in the workplace. Their emphasis was as much on employee satisfaction as on organisational effectiveness ... Modern approaches ... do not necessarily rule out the ideas put forward by earlier theorists, but emphasise they must be evaluated in the context of an organisation's overriding need for flexibility in responding to change in its external and internal environment, in order to meet the competing demands of all its various stakeholders (Cole, 2004, pp.5–6).

One example (and perhaps further development) of this most recent trend has been the ideas propounded by Carayol and Firth (2001) who have developed the concept of voodoo as a guiding metaphor for 'business mavericks and magicians'. Their proposals are somewhat rooted in the emergence of dot.com businesses in the 1990s and the need for managerial styles to respond to new fast business requirements.

Voodoo is described as risk embracing and courageous and requires one to be open minded and ready to accept a more subjective approach to business and life strategies driven by self-belief (Carayol and Firth, 2001). The demands made of voodoo for managers espouse 'sensible recklessness' as a reaction to the climate of 'risk-averse' businesses being threatened by their own inertia and conservatism. The book *Corporate Voodoo* inspires people to take decisive action and draws a distinction between management and leadership, where management has become embedded in older 'power' systems and leadership and participation are now encouraged amongst all those involved.

Rene Carayol, the co-author of this approach, lists, amongst his speaking themes:

- manage a little less – lead a little more;
- taking risks;
- when your heritage is not necessarily your destiny;
- continue to do what you do best – partner to achieve the rest.

Each of these themes above could constitute, in specific sets of circumstances, an operational mantra or metaphor for aspects of the management task.

In returning to our main theme, Cole (2004, p.6) notes that whilst there is no generally accepted definition of management, the classic definition is still held to be that of Henri Fayol.

> To manage is to forecast and plan, to organise, to command, to coordinate and to control (Fayol, 1949).

Inevitably, there have been many changes in emphasis and additions to the role in later definitions that include, for example the work of Mintzberg (1973) who noted from his major study of managerial work the following three roles that appeared regularly in such work:

1. The interpersonal role – embodying the notions of figurehead, leader and liaison;
2. The informational role – being a monitor, disseminator and spokesperson;
3. The decisional role – requiring entrepreneurship, disturbance handling, resource allocation and negotiation.

A decade later, Peters (1988) added:

- an obsession with responsiveness to customers;
- constant innovation;
- partnership with all in the organisation;
- leadership that embraces change and instils vision;
- control by means of simple support systems aimed at measuring the 'right stuff' for today's environment.

Some years later Stewart (1994) added further crucial concerns:

- learning what it means to be a manager in a specific context;
- learning how to improve the ability to judge others (because delegation and reliance on others is necessary);
- learning to understand more about one's own capacities and weaknesses;
- learning how to cope with stress.

In addition Stewart considers that managerial jobs are affected by the following considerations:

1. the core of the job (the personal responsibilities of the manager which cannot be delegated);
2. the constraints of the job (e.g. limited resource);
3. the choices available to the jobholder in the way in which their work is carried out.

In transposing the above perspectives that originate from the generic field of management into the perceived requirements for managers in counselling and psychotherapy agencies, Jordan (2003) offers the following attributes:

- The manager values the work with and for the particular client group involved;
- They are excellent communicators;
- They are 'visionaries';
- They are politically astute;
- They are appropriately qualified;
- They are aware of and active in the wider organisational/community milieu in which the agency exists;
- They have leadership ability;
- They have a capacity to empower others;
- They have a clear understanding of their role;
- They are hard working and resilient.

Management theory, then, has proceeded from the initial concept of managing as minding a machine to one of becoming concerned with the human processes that impact upon the work setting. This has transformed, in the early years of the 21st century, into a need to maintain responsiveness and flexibility to an ever-changing environment. This all too brief account spanning 100 years of management theory enables us both to appreciate the extraordinary range of concerns (and consequent activities) that managers have (had) to contend with and to note the continuing relevance of each of these perspectives, depending on the local circumstances and context of the organisation.

As a brief aside here, a more detailed exploration of management theories over this time span might prove useful to the newly appointed manager of a therapy agency, particularly with reference to the 'age and stage' of that agency. Hasenfeld and Schmid (1989) suggest the existence of six stages within the life cycle of a social service organisation, and each would require differing management emphases, attributes and qualities.

EXERCISE 5

INTRODUCTION

Despite the relatively short length of this chapter, the managerial issues so far considered are somewhat extensive, covering a wide spectrum of behaviours, skills and knowledge. Such a range of knowledge could prove a daunting prospect to the potential manager. The purpose of the following exercise is to counter this seeming 'mountain' of demands by reassuring you that, despite the wide range of detail covered, your own impressions so far are what are important. This chapter can always be revisited for more detail should you require.

1. Now close the book and just write down:
    (a) What you now recall are the main aspects of management that have been introduced so far in the previous section?
    (b) List some of the responses you are now having to what you have just read.
2. Now review what you first wrote in response to exercise 1 in this chapter.
3. Compare your original 'stream of consciousness' (exercise 1) with what you have just written on the contents (exercise 5, 1a) and your responses (exercise 5, 1b) to this section.
4. Can you now write a definition of what management means to you? Alternatively, within a group setting, this could be the basis for discussing this question with a view to either:
    (a) composing a group definition of management and/or
    (b) compiling a list of all the skills that are considered as useful and necessary for being a manager.

Hopefully, through having engaged in the process of these exercises, you have moved through a series of steps that have, so far, helped you to identify the following aspects of management:

- What you think of management;
- Which managers have inspired you and why;
- Managerial qualities with which you WOULD NOT wish to be associated with;
- Managerial qualities with which you WOULD wish to be associated with; and
- Dealing with some of the critical and ever-present dilemmas confronting the managerial role.

THE SPECIFIC CHALLENGE OF MANAGING COUNSELLING STAFF

'An Israeli psychologist, Boas Shamir, has shown that we ascribe to distant leaders ... characteristics such as charisma, vision, courage, passion and rhetoric. These are not necessarily the characteristics we value in our boss. Shamir found that what individuals seek in 'nearby' leaders, such as immediate line managers, includes being sociable, open and considerate of others: having a sense of humour: being intelligent: and setting high performance standards for themselves and others' (Alimo-Metcalfe *et al.*, 2002).

As has been noted earlier, there is now a wide variety of organisations offering counselling and psychotherapy. These organisations are variously dedicated to:

- specific geographical areas, for example Share Psychotherapy (in Sheffield) and the Norwich Centre;
- particular client groups (e.g. students, employees);
- the relief of suffering in those experiencing specific problems or medical conditions (e.g. addictions, aids);
- the needs of members of minority groups, etc.

These organisations also offer different therapeutic services that range from short- to long-term interventions, to working face-to-face, or via the telephone or online. The payment for such services will also differ across this spectrum, from voluntary contributions to private fees.

In part, then, it could be argued that these very different organisations will require quite different bodies of skill, knowledge and expertise of their managers relevant to the needs of that particular agency and its setting.

A counter argument to this 'specialist' view is that of a more generalised nature: i.e. that a competent manger will be able to function as a manager within a variety of organisational settings. They will have the skills necessary to harness the energies of the agency staff group, gather the information and knowledge to transpose those ideas into relevant agency policies and practices and to contribute to new developments.

Both cases are obviously true, as in yin and yang, and their 'success' or 'failure' will be somewhat dependent upon the interplay of the (new) manager's style and personality and the dynamics and personalities of the agency personnel.

Though expressed here tentatively as a hypothesis, it is considered that those who are already or who are contemplating managing a counselling service are already working within the general counselling field, most likely as counsellors and psychotherapists and probably also working within the specialist therapeutic area in which they wish to pursue a management role, e.g. student counsellors in further and higher education tending to seek management roles within student counselling services. This hypothesis, of course, is not infallible and counsellors in one sector obviously do become managers in another sector. However, within this general hypothesis, newly appointed managers already are significantly knowledgeable of the professional field, experienced in therapeutic work, cognisant of the current professional issues, academically and professionally well qualified, aware of theoretical debates and research perspectives. Managers are thus likely to be already well-qualified and experienced professionals/therapists. Where their skills and knowledge may require development, though, is within the management field.

Several 'experienced' service managers in Jordan's survey believed that the management of therapists was considerably different from other sub-groups of people since it seemed that more one-to-one attention was expected. This perspective is reflected in an (unattributed) saying which suggests that: 'Managing counsellors is like herding cats!'

Though it is acknowledged here that other categories of staff will obviously fall within the management domain of responsibility, e.g. secretarial and reception staff, cleaning staff, finance and administrative staff, committee members etc., the remaining part of this chapter will reflect on the challenges to management presented by the therapists themselves.

- Like their managers (see three paragraphs above), therapists are already highly qualified professionals.
- They may also be working currently in other environments (thus having contemporary experience of other agencies).

- Based on the 'wounded healer' hypothesis, many therapists will be extremely aware of their own backgrounds and the effects these have had upon them in their maturation.
- Therapists are used to working on their own, in challenging circumstances demanding high degrees of responsibility.
- Through their training, their therapy and their ongoing supervision therapists are continually reflecting upon their therapeutic work and the setting within which it occurs. Not only do they attempt to bring order into their understanding of personality dynamics in their clients, they inevitably will apply such understandings to colleagues and managers.

Each of the above points underlines the extraordinary potential of such a highly qualified staff group yet this very potentiality may also prove immensely problematic for the manager to optimise positively. How the staff group is related to, treated and managed (both individually and collectively) may prove key to the success of the whole organisation.

Research, comparing leadership in the UK and the US by Alimo-Metcalfe *et al*. (2002), revealed that:

1. The most important issue for managers was concern for individuals' well-being and development. (In contrast to the US where vision and charisma were cited.)
2. Managers in the UK focused more on working in close collaboration with others. They also exhibited elements of humility and even vulnerability. (Apparently this was almost absent within the US research.)
3. The research in the UK revealed that the most important pre-requisite for a leader is what they can do for their staff. (Author's note: this finding suggests a model, within the British context, of the manager as servant.) In America, the most important pre-requisite was deemed as the leader being a role model. (Similarly, the research by Jordan (2003) into the experience of University Counselling Service Managers revealed an assertion that a 'benevolent co-operative model (of management) works best and that team work was essential'. (p.42).

The 4000 respondents to the above research programme consider that leadership is about engaging others as partners in developing and achieving a shared vision and enabling staff to lead. It is also about creating a fertile, supportive environment for creative thinking and for challenging assumptions about how a service or business should be delivered. It is also about displaying much greater sensitivity to the needs of a range of internal and external stakeholders. (Within a counselling service setting these would include clients, all staff, employing bodies, management committees, the community from where patients come, the professional bodies, etc.) (Two exercises now follow.)

EXERCISE 6

INTRODUCTION

The following exercise is designed to enable you to locate one or several key metaphors or visions you have that are related to leadership and management, as it is recognised what a major part these personalised images play in relation to our behaviour in different circumstances. Such symbols and images might influence us more in our behaviours than a whole range of instruction, advice, guidance, policies and information.

1. Identify and list some metaphors or visions you have for your management/leadership tasks or role (e.g. the above research offers possibilities such as the manager as 'servant', 'role model', 'humble companion' etc.).
2. Then identify which of these might be or prove to be the most frequently employed in your managerial behaviours. (In effect, identify the metaphor that would underpin and inform your strong modus operandi in a range of situations.)
3. Now consider under what circumstances and in which conditions and with whom these personal metaphors and visions might prove limited in their application (i.e. consider the limitations, if any, to your identified themes).

The above exercise invites the possibility for locating and perhaps affirming one or several of your super ordinate (guiding) images. For some, these symbols may often be present in awareness and they can act as a yardstick against which the person evaluates his/her (managerial) behaviour.

EXERCISE 7

INTRODUCTION

In moving towards the completion of this chapter, one final element is introduced below. The issue identified in the exercise, i.e. the specific nature of the clients seen and their difficulties, can seriously impact upon staff behaviours and morale and should therefore be of great concern to the prospective manager. This area of concern is now considered through the medium of the next exercise.

1. Consider carefully the specific range of client needs and concerns brought to the service.
2. Are there any overall identifiable themes that emerge from this analysis?

3. Recognising that the counselling team (and indeed, yourself) is working with these themes continually as part of the work, what long-term effects might these have upon them?
4. What steps could you take, as manager, to address these?
5. How might these effects then impact, (however subtly or indeed outside of the awareness of the staff team) upon the dynamic processes at play between the staff and you as manger?
6. In such circumstances, what could you do?

This exercise attempts to assist you in pinpointing some of the recurring client issues in the agency as a way of understanding, through a parallel process, their potential impact upon the needs of the staff. Such sensitive knowledge will inform the manager's task in their relationships with other staff members.

CONCLUSION

Managing can be an extremely subtle, complex and indeed ill-defined task. It can also be an extremely rewarding, worthwhile endeavour to be engaged in. Whilst huge reams of research and literature exist and training courses abound, the individual manager has still to find his/her way through the specific and unique challenges of his/her particular setting.

Identifying more explicitly your 'model' of management, which hopefully will have been assisted by the exercises in this chapter, will inform and facilitate your management development and practice.

REFERENCES

Alimo-Metcalfe, B. and Alban-Metcalfe, J. (2002) The great and the good. *People Management* (10th January).

Bendix, R. (1956) *Work and Authority in Industry*. New York: Harper.

Bolton, G., Howlett, S., Lago, C. O. and Wright, J. (2004) *Writing Cures: An Introductory Handbook of Writing in Counselling and Psychotherapy*. Hove: Psychology Press.

Carayol, R. and Firth, D. (2001) *Corporate Voodoo: Principles for Business Mavericks and Magicians*. Oxford: Capstone.

Carroll, M. and Walton, M. (1997) *Handbook of Counselling in Organisations*. London: Sage.

Casse, P. (1980) *Training for the Cross Cultural Mind*. Washington, DC: Society for Intercultural Education, Training and Research.

Cole, G. A. (2004) *Management Theory and Practice*. London: Thompson Learning.

Fayol, H. (1949) *General and Industrial Management.* London: Pitman.

Handy, C. B. (1976*) Understanding Organisations.* Harmondsworth: Penguin.

Harvey-Jones, J. (1989) *Making it Happen: Reflections on Leadership.* London: Fontana.

Hasenfeld, Y. and Schmid, H. (1989) The Life Cycle of Human Service Organisations. *Administration in Social Work.* (13) 243–269.

Jordan, E. M. (2003*) The Professional Is Personal: An Evaluative Inquiry Into the "Experience" of Setting Up and Managing a University Counselling Service.* Unpublished PhD thesis: University of Middlesex in collaboration with Metanoia Institute.

Jordan, E. M. (2004) Private email to the author concerning the theme of this chapter.

Lago, C. and Kitchin, D. (1998) *The Management of Counselling and Psychotherapy Agencies.* London: Sage.

Luthans, F., Rosencratz, S. and Hennessey, H. (1985) What do Successful Managers Do? *Journal of Applied Behavioural Science,* 21 (3), 255–270.

Martinko, M. and Gardner, W. (1990) Structured Observation of Managerial Work. *Journal of Management Studies,* 27 (3), 329–355.

Mintzberg, H. (1973) *The Nature of Managerial Work.* London: Harper & Row.

Mintzberg, H. (1990) The managers job: folklore and fact. *Harvard Business Review, March–April,* 163–176.

Peters, T. (1998) *Thriving on Chaos – Handbook for a Management Revolution.* London: MacMillan.

Salaman, G. (1995) *Managing.* Buckingham: Open University Press.

Stewart, R. (1983) Managerial behaviour: how research has changed the traditional picture. In M. Earl (ed) *Perspectives on Management.* Oxford: Oxford University Press, pp.82–98.

Stewart, R. (1994) *Managing Today and Tomorrow.* London: MacMillan.

Williams, R. (1983) *Keywords: A Vocabulary of Culture and Society.* London: Fontana.

8 HOW TO REDUCE THE RISK OF COMPLAINTS AND LITIGATION

Peter Jenkins

Practitioners in the field of counselling and psychotherapy are increasingly aware of, if not actually nervous about, the prospect of becoming the subject of a hostile complaint or litigation. Levels of complaint against professionals from all walks of life, and instances of litigation by clients seeking damages for harm or stress, are evident in the increasing coverage of this topic by professional journals and in the wider media. Practitioners are widely assessed during their training on their knowledge, skills, personal development and professional practice. However, they may receive very little effective preparation for the experience of facing a complaint by an angry client, or receiving a formal letter from a solicitor announcing the beginnings of a legal action against them. These can be both professionally testing and emotionally bruising experiences, as many practitioners can testify. It is now likely that any practitioner involved in counselling practice, supervision or training, will face at least one serious complaint during their professional career. The likelihood of legal action may be less pronounced, but here, even the actual *threat* of litigation can prove to be extremely stressful for the individual or agency concerned. Once again, the level of personal distress, loss of time and financial expense are likely to be greater where the practitioner has had no prior experience of, nor adequate preparation for, this unwelcome eventuality.

This chapter sets out the main characteristics of professional complaints or litigation against practitioners, and the key steps required to minimise the risk of these occurring. Given the increasingly litigious nature of modern life, where it is no longer remarkable to sue for a spilled cup of coffee, or for the stress induced by childbirth or military service, the coverage of this topic can only be indicative of the main risks to be avoided. More detailed coverage of legal and ethical issues can be found elsewhere (Bond, 2000; Jenkins *et al.*, 2004). In addition, some forms of risk will inevitably arise largely from *client* characteristics, rather than from practitioner mistake or incompetence. For example, a client with a strongly narcissistic streak may suddenly switch from a seductive idealisation of his/her 'perfect' therapist, into vengeful denigration and pursuit of the latter, through complaints panels, or even via the courts.

UNDERSTANDING COMPLAINTS

Complaints need to be separated from legal action as a form of action against a practitioner. Complaints may be brought against an individual or an agency. A complaint can be made to:

- an individual practitioner, e.g. in private practice;
- an agency or employer providing a counselling service;
- a professional association;
- an official agency, such as the Information Commissioner or Disability Rights Commission.

A complaint may be made about an individual practitioner, for rudeness or incompetence, or to an agency, about the length of their waiting list for providing therapy, or to an official body, where an agency is alleged to be preventing client access to records, for example. Where a complaint is made to a counsellor's professional body, this will often be on the basis that the latter has breached the relevant code of ethics, for instance, by publishing a recognisable client study without consent. Where practitioners are bound by a code of ethics, then both common sense and good practice dictate that it is essential to be fully aware of, and informed about, current ethical requirements, and to comply with them (Jones *et al.*, 2000). That is, however, unless there are strong and valid reasons for having breached the code, which can be taken to a complaints panel as a legitimate defence. Ethical codes have clearly undergone an inflationary process of becoming more and more inclusive and prescriptive over the last decade. For example, what may have been assumed in the past simply to constitute good practice, as in undergoing personal therapy or regular supervision, may now carry the status of a formal requirement under a code of ethics. This may be in order to state a minimum standard of professional competence, and to make explicit what was previously understood as constituting the 'unwritten rules' of the profession. One example would be the prohibition of sexual contact with clients by the British Association for Counselling's code of ethics, which was absent prior to 1984.

LINKING ETHICS AND COMPLAINTS

There are, however, serious limitations to complaints procedures which are based on breaches of the code of ethics. As professional associations attempt to regulate their members, and to cover all possible eventualities, codes have become more and more comprehensive and prescriptive in tone, requiring frequent amendment and updating to include new possible transgressions, such as breach of confidence in the process of providing internet counselling, for example.

Some professional associations such as the British Association for Counselling and Psychotherapy (BACP) have deliberately uncoupled the code of ethics from the complaints procedure. Complaints are no longer limited solely to a breach of a specific section of a code of ethics, such as working beyond one's level of competence. Under the revised complaints procedure, complaints require evidence of either:

- professional misconduct;
- professional malpractice;
- bringing the profession into disrepute.

These more global categories have replaced the previous itemised listing of specific breaches. Practitioners who are the subject of a complaint need to justify their behaviour with reference to the values, principles and moral qualities of the ethical framework. Thus a counsellor could defend his/her decision *not* to report a teenage client's risk of self-harm to parents, on the grounds of choosing to keep faith and trust with the client, under the professional obligation of fidelity to the client. The shift for this type of ethical code has been from a rule-following approach, to one based on ethical principles (fidelity versus welfare), or on the actual outcomes achieved by the decision.

Complaints may be divided into two kinds. *Substantive complaints* are specific and capable of being resolved by referring to evidence, such as a practitioner practising without regular supervision, for example. *Non-substantive complaints*, however, revolve around a client's perception of the therapist and of their lived experience of the quality of the therapeutic work. A client may complain that the counsellor 'seemed out of his depth', or appeared to be 'cold and distant' to the client's concerns. These perceptions are extremely difficult to refute or resolve in a satisfactory manner. Firm supporting evidence is usually distinctly lacking, and much depends on subjective interpretation. Often, the complaint is the final indication of a serious breakdown in the therapeutic alliance.

WORKING TO A CODE OF ETHICS

Practitioners can try to prevent problems in the therapeutic relationship from turning into this kind of non-substantive, but still very worrying, complaint. This can be done, by addressing apparent problems of relating to, or of communicating with, the client, by offering an apology where appropriate, or by seeking to end the work and refer onto another counsellor or agency. In some cases, a client may have grossly unrealistic expectations of the therapy or of the therapist. Here, any kind of response by the practitioner is unlikely to satisfy the client, without recourse to a complaint. In the case of undergoing a non-substantive complaint, it is particularly important for the counsellor to gain access to the support of peers and colleagues. At the same time, the practitioner also needs to consider any significant insight, or learning about their personal style or professional approach, which can be derived from this often painful experience (Casemore, 2001).

Practitioners can guard themselves against the risk of a complaint by:

- being aware of and complying with professional codes of ethics;
- considering the possible ethical justifications for any divergence from specific requirements of their code of practice;
- considering the nature of supportive evidence in the event of a possible complaint (e.g. client records, agency documents, records of supervision, copies of letters to client, etc.);
- researching potential sources of support in the event of a complaint (trade union, employer's legal department if appropriate, peers, supervisor).

APPLYING ETHICAL PRINCIPLES

So far, this chapter has looked at the role of complaints, and how the risk of being the subject of a complaint can be reduced to some degree. The focus will now turn to a broader consideration of how to practice in ways which minimise the risk of complaint or litigation. This approach is derived from the set of ethical principles outlined in the BACP *Ethical Framework* (BACP, 2002). While practitioners may not subscribe to this ethical framework, or be bound by other, more prescriptive codes, these principles do provide a clear and coherent rationale for competent and non-defensive practice. The principles include:

- Autonomy: respecting the client's self-determination;
- Fidelity: keeping trust with the client;
- Beneficence: promoting the client's welfare;
- Non-maleficence: avoiding harm to the client or to third parties, such as a client's partner or parents;
- Justice: promoting equality, fairness and non-discriminatory practice;

- Self-respect: attending to self as an essential aspect of therapy, via supervision, training and continued professional development.

While these are ethical principles, drawn from a bio-medical background, they can be considered alongside the minimum requirements of legally sound practice, which will reduce the risk of hostile litigation. For example, the ethical principle of autonomy finds broadly equivalent expression in the legal concept of informed consent and in the use of an agreed contract with clients (see Box 8.1 below).

RESPECTING CLIENT AUTONOMY

Promoting client autonomy is widely accepted as one of the main aims of counselling, as currently set within a predominantly invidualistic Western culture. From a legal perspective, client autonomy can be maintained and promoted by establishing the client's informed consent to therapy, and by using a contract of agreement to record and underpin the key boundaries of therapeutic work. Negotiating and gaining client agreement to key aspects of therapy via a contract, such as the latter's goals, frequency and cost, in turn, will provide at least some evidence of the client's informed consent to therapy.

The concept of informed consent derives from medical case law, particularly in the US. Under the US legal system, and, to a lesser extent, the UK, the expectation has arisen that patients, or clients, need to be able to choose or reject proposed treatment, on the basis of having adequate information about its advantages, disadvantages and likely risks. The move towards adopting a culture of informed decision making by consumers is strongest

---

BOX 8.1 ETHICAL PRINCIPLES

ETHICAL PRINCIPLE	LEGAL CONCEPT
Autonomy	Informed consent/contract
Fidelity	Duty of confidentiality
Beneficence	Duty of care
Non-maleficence	Standard of care/duty to warn
Justice	Non-discrimination
Self-respect	Duty of reasonable care and skill

in the NHS, where the risks of medical treatment and fear of litigation are both significant factors. Adopting a stance of obtaining client informed consent to therapy can require a pre-therapy assessment process. Here, for a particular client problem such as severe anxiety, alternative approaches such as a cognitive perspective or a psychodynamic model could be outlined, together with their respective evidence bases.

This rather 'technical' approach to providing therapy will not be attractive to some practitioners, who will prefer, instead, to emphasise the need for building a strong therapeutic alliance with the client. Even here, nevertheless, it is still possible to discuss with the prospective client what the various therapy options are, such as group work as an alternative to one-to-one therapy, and to attempt to give the client a realistic understanding of what therapy entails. This might include a possible need for the client to undertake some limited 'homework' assignments, for example, if using a cognitive approach. It might also explore the likelihood that therapy may have some initially unwelcome repercussions on their family relationships, if the client becomes much more emotionally expressive or assertive as a result of the therapy.

USING CONTRACTS FOR INFORMED CONSENT

Using some form of contract or written agreement is a concrete way of registering the client's informed consent to the therapeutic process. It is also a very useful way of recording understanding and agreement on the key boundaries of therapy, in terms of dates, times, frequency, cost (if appropriate), arrangements for absence or holidays, details of recording, supervision and any limits to confidentiality which might apply. The agreement may not carry the formal status of a legal contract if there is no 'consideration' or exchange in return for the counselling received. However, the contractual document provides a useful point of reference in the case of any future disagreement over any essential aspects of therapy. This document, together with any other supporting information about the counselling service given to the client, can provide an essential tool for resolving disputes and avoiding later complaint or legal action. In essence, this process of attending to the task of gaining client informed by negotiating a working agreement helps to clarify the *mutual expectations* of client and practitioner regarding the therapy to be provided. Establishing a shared understanding of what the therapy is about is necessary both for defensive purposes, but also, and much more importantly, to provide the underpinning for a successful therapeutic alliance.

KEEPING TRUST

Client complaint or litigation is usually indicative of a serious and indeed, terminal, breakdown in trust between the two parties in therapy. Maintaining fidelity, or faith with the client, is thus both an ethical obligation and a practical step for minimising the risk of these kinds of hostile action by the client. In legal terms, maintaining fidelity with the client finds expression in the concept of the practitioner's 'fiduciary duty' towards the client. In essence, this means keeping trust with the client. A central part of carrying out this responsibility lies in the practitioner fulfilling their duty of confidence towards the client. Confidentiality is key value for practitioners, heavily emphasised in counsellor training and in codes of ethics. It lays the basis for all meaningful therapeutic work, by establishing a secure framework for the client to disclose sensitive personal material, for the purpose of carrying out therapeutic work. Client confidentiality is clearly protected by common law and statute.

Where there is a special relationship of trust, as between a therapist and client, then the former has a responsibility to keep the client's personal information confidential. This expectation can be further protected by a specific contractual agreement between client and practitioner. The *Data Protection Act* 1998 adds a further, statutory layer of protection for client confidentiality, by specifying restrictions on the disclosure of sensitive personal data. Under Article 8 of the *Human Rights Act* 1998 applying to public authorities, clients are further due the right to 'respect for privacy', if not entitled to an actual legal guarantee of privacy itself.

CONVEYING LIMITS TO CONFIDENTIALITY

While confidentiality may be a central aspect of therapy, as well as a legal and ethical obligation for the therapist, it is rarely possible for absolute confidentiality to be realistically offered to any client. Limits, or exclusions, to confidentiality, such as a duty to report suspected child abuse, or a credible threat of harm to a third party, such as a partner at risk of domestic violence, may be specified by the practitioner's contract of employment, or by a wider statutory obligation, as in the case of terrorism. Gaining client understanding of, or advance consent to, any necessary limitations of confidentiality, such as informing a client's general practitioner in the case of threatened suicide or serious self-harm, will go some way towards reducing later misunderstanding about the degree of confidentiality provided by the therapist. Information outlined by the practitioner about the role and purpose of supervision, of the nature of any proposed therapeutic recording and the client's rights of access to such records, will further clarify the client's position as an active partner in the therapy. The duty of confidentiality can also be expressed by a commitment to gain the client's prior, and appropriately informed, consent to publication for research or other professional research purposes.

While these points may not necessarily become part of a formal contractual agreement between client and practitioner, it may be helpful to cover these essential elements in a covering letter, or information leaflet, about the counselling service and the client's rights as a consumer of that service. It may seem that this attention to detail is in danger of 'swamping' the client, who may already be in a highly aroused emotional state. Yet it *is* consistent with a stance which respects the client's vulnerable and less powerful position within the therapeutic alliance.

What is crucial, rather than retreating into a defensive, and quasi-legalistic position, by sheltering behind a comprehensive but intimidating 'contract', is to establish the kind of trusting and empowering relationship with the client, where any major concerns of this kind can be honestly addressed and resolved as they arise within the therapy.

PROMOTING THE CLIENT'S WELFARE

Practitioners have an ethical responsibility to promote the client's welfare, under the principle of beneficence. In legal terms, this can be expressed as the practitioner's duty of care towards the client. Under the section of the law governing action for non-intentional harm, which derives from medical negligence law, the therapist will be held to have a positive duty of care towards the client. This entails an obligation to act in accordance with the established norms of professional practice, under the *Bolam* test established first by medical and then by later therapeutic case law. Here, failure to act in accordance with the practice of 'competent respected professional opinion' lays the therapist open to action for breach of their duty of care to the client.

FULFILLING A DUTY OF CARE

What constitutes a duty of care to the client, and how is this established by the courts? Case law suggests that the precise boundaries of a duty of care are determined by the court, as informed by relevant codes of ethics, and by the evidence of expert witnesses on what constitutes competent practice. As there may well be many different schools of thought on what competent therapy actually requires, the therapist is judged against the norms of their particular espoused model or approach. For example, a psychoanalyst who introduced 'social contact' with a client undergoing analysis would be judged as breaching the basic requirements of working with transference, as in the case of *Werner v Landau*, 1961. Alternatively, another therapist, working in a multimodal way, might claim that their adoption of 'social contact' was entirely consistent with the therapeutic stance held by the model's originator, Arnold Lazarus, and did not therefore constitute a breach with their chosen model.

Obviously, there are limits to what is ultimately acceptable to the court as competent professional practice. Recourse to credible supporting research evidence can play a key role here. Given the wide variety of therapeutic models available to practitioners, expert opinion regarding the therapist's duty of care might place very different emphasis on key aspects of professional practice. Experts could well disagree about the crucial significance for discharging key elements of the practitioner's duty of care, such as the responsibility for keeping comprehensive records, undergoing regular supervision, involvement in benign dual relationships (such as mentor and therapist) and in handling the ending of, or referral on, from therapy. Different models of therapy may also not find common ground on the need for assessment or screening of clients, the handling of interpersonal conflict within therapy or the appropriate use of massage or touch within therapy.

This diversity of perspectives on the therapist's duty of care might suggest that it is virtually impossible to know how to fulfil this professional obligation appropriately, or with any realistic degree of confidence. However, it is important, both for effective practice and for avoiding future client complaint or legal action, for the practitioner to know and work within the boundaries set by their chosen therapeutic model, and furthermore, to be able to justify their chosen form of practice by reference to credible research findings.

AVOIDING HARM

The ethical principle of beneficence has a counterpart – that of non-maleficence, or of avoiding harm to the client or to a third party. A therapist who abuses or exploits a client via intentional activity such as fraud, physical or sexual assault is, very obviously, in breach of both their ethical responsibilities and the criminal law. Other forms of harm to the client may be caused by acting negligently. A therapist might cause physical or psychological damage to the client through incompetent use of therapeutic techniques such as regression, rebirthing or via failure to make an accurate assessment of a significant risk of suicide or self-harm. This element of the therapist's practice concerns the *standard of care* expected of the practitioner. As suggested in the previous section, the precise nature of the therapist's duty of care is judged in a way which is largely relative to their chosen model of therapy. The actual *standard* of care against which they are judged will vary according to their professed level of expertise. Normally, the standard will be that applying to the ordinary practitioner. Where a therapist claims to be an expert of some kind, then the standard is raised accordingly. The implication is that a practitioner should not claim expertise which he or she cannot amply justify in terms of specialist training, experience, qualification or peer opinion. Perhaps surprisingly, the standard applied to trainees or student practitioners is *not* lowered on account of their limited experience. Based on an established legal analogy of the standard expected of a learner driver, the standard of practice expected of a student or trainee is the same as that applying to a competent practitioner holding that particular role or position.

MINIMISING HARM TO THIRD PARTIES

Practitioners can reduce the risk of complaint or legal action by avoiding inflicting harm on the client through using appropriate therapeutic techniques, and by not acting beyond their level of competence. Harm may also be allegedly caused to third parties outside of the immediate boundaries of the therapeutic alliance. In the US, successful litigation has been undertaken by third parties against therapists for the fostering of alleged 'false memories' of abuse in clients, without substantive evidence. These allegations have resulted in claims for significant emotional and financial damage by those parents accused of carrying out the alleged abuse. While similar litigation for harm to third parties has not yet been successful in the UK, therapists need to be mindful of the potential for harm to parents, partners or other parties affected by the outcomes of therapy, whether planned or unplanned. This may include an ethical duty on the therapist to warn identifiable third parties of a significant potential risk of harm, due to a credible threat of violence, or revenge, expressed by the client. The potential for complaints brought by third parties may be limited by the lack of precedent within UK case law, and also by the reluctance of certain professional associations to hear third-party complaints under existing procedures. However, both situations may possibly change at some stage in the future, so practitioners need to be cautious about the potential for harm to third parties, as well as to the immediate client, caused by their therapeutic work.

PRACTISING IN AN ANTI-DISCRIMINATORY MANNER

The ethical principle of justice requires that therapists work in a spirit of equality, fairness and sensitivity to issues of equity and access. Some codes of practice will further prioritise forms of non- or anti-discriminatory practice, which take full account of aspects of client status, experience or identity, such as gender, sexual orientation, race, ethnicity or disability, whether hidden or overt. Clients may seek to bring a complaint, or initiate a legal intervention by one of the agencies monitoring discrimination, such as the Disability Rights Commission, or the Commission for Racial Equality. Practitioners need to be as aware as possible of their own, perhaps covert, prejudices against individual clients, or members of particular client groups, and to take appropriate steps to overcome these. This might involve the therapist seeking out training on the issues relevant to groups with which they might be unfamiliar with, or for whom they lack real empathic regard. Patterns of service provision may also prompt client dissatisfaction, complaint or legal action. Untenably long waiting lists, unjustifiable client selection criteria, grossly unrepresentative counsellor staff teams or discriminatory employment practices could all fuel potential complaint or legal action under discrimination legislation, where the latter is applicable to particular counselling agencies. Policies restricting access to counselling services on the basis of age may also fall foul of laws such as the Human Rights Act 1998 applying to public authorities. One such example may be where agencies do not provide counselling to young people under 14 without proof of parental permission, thus restricting client access to the service in a way which is highly discriminatory and, arguably, untenable in law.

MAINTAINING SELF-RESPECT

The final ethical principle is probably the most contentious, suggesting as it does, a regard for the *self*, rather than an altruistic concern for the client or other parties. However, given that the practitioner relies on the self, namely their own level of knowledge, skill, experience and understanding, in order to work in the most therapeutic way possible, it becomes essential to take the necessary steps to maintain an ability to work well. Any practitioner who fails to look after his/her own personal and professional needs for any length of time runs the appreciable risk of becoming stale, tired and eventually, 'burned out' by the emotional pressures of the work. Maintaining self-respect, in a sense, becomes a *pre-condition* for fulfilling the other ethical principles over an extended period.

In practical terms, working to this ethical principle requires a continuous ability to self-monitor and 'fine tune' professional and personal responses to the needs of the client and of the wider profession. The practitioner needs to be aware of, and involved in, peer discussion and debate about current issues, to avoid the dangers of self-absorption and professional isolation. This involves a self-motivating commitment to continuing professional development, re-training, and awareness of the knowledge and research base of their own practice.

In legal terms, the ethical principle of self-respect provides a necessary foundation for the legal test of competent therapeutic work, namely that of practising with the 'reasonable care and skill', required of a professional providing a service for a fee. Effective use of supervision, peer support, personal therapy, and involvement in professional and research activities will all bring necessary forms of challenge, which are vital for stimulating fresh thinking and critical self-appraisal.

TAKING STOCK OF SUPPORT SYSTEMS

In the event of client complaint or litigation, the practitioner will need access to high levels of support. This is worth reviewing before the worst happens (see Box 8.2). Therapists may not be aware of the terms of their professional indemnity insurance cover, key telephone numbers for legal advice helplines, the extent of advice available from employing agencies or trade unions or how to gain timely access to non-technical legal guidance on essential practice issues. It can be useful to attend professional training courses on complaints systems, handling ethical dilemmas and increasing one's familiarity with legal aspects of counselling and psychotherapy.

The foregoing might suggest that the best hedge against client complaint lies in adopting a thoroughly guarded, defensive form of practice. This would be to miss the point that the best defence actually arises out of attending carefully to the *quality of the relationship with the client*. Many conflict issues occur because of a problem developing in the relationship between client and counsellor. To an extent, therapists can avoid 'glitches' in the therapeutic alliance turning into massive and irreparable problems, by attending to them as they arise. Sharing an awareness of mistakes, inattention or breaches in communication can represent a powerful means of repairing otherwise damaging ruptures to the therapeutic process (Leiper and Kent, 2001). Offering an appropriate and genuine apology, without making a formal admission of liability, may be a critical step in restoring communication and trust with the client, and thus avoiding a great deal of later conflict. In addition, recognition and sharing of errors with the client

BOX 8.2   GUIDELINES FOR PROFESSIONAL PRACTICE REGARDING COMPLAINTS AND LITIGATION

PREPARATION

- ensure clients or students have adequate information about:
  - (a) the nature of the counselling, therapeutic or training service provided;
  - (b) the codes of ethics and practice which are relevant;
  - (c) the complaints systems, both informal and formal.
- review arrangements for getting feedback on the service, whether practice or training, from clients and students, as a source of information;
- pick out potential or actual problem areas, and respond to these promptly;
- review and update documentation such as policy guidance, or handbooks for students on courses.

RESPONDING TO POTENTIAL COMPLAINT OR LITIGATION

- acknowledge the legitimacy of the complaint and of the feelings involved;
- wherever possible avoid defensive reactions to criticism and complaint;
- react speedily to set up informal channels to explore problems and negotiate solutions;
- notify and seek expert advice from employing agency, professional organisations and indemnity insurers at an early stage;
- identify and make effective use of personal support systems: undergoing a complaint can be personally challenging and draining;
- record all significant contact with clients or students where a persistent pattern of conflict, misunderstanding or complaint emerges, including phone contact, copies of letters, minutes of meetings and emails (on the assumption of potential client access under data protection law).

BOX 8.2 cont'd

RESPONDING TO ACTUAL
COMPLAINT OR LITIGATION

- contact employing agency, professional organisations and indemnity insurers immediately;
- identify potential conflicts of interest between yourself, the client and the organisation, if relevant; consider your own separate need for independent legal representation or advice;
- de-personalise the complaint: try to separate out aspects which are about practice, the service provided or the organisation, from any personal feelings of being attacked;
- distinguish carefully between an expression of concern and any formal admission of liability, which may weaken a future defence before a complaints tribunal or in a court hearing;
- encourage the client or student to bring a supporter for key meetings, also bring an independent person to chair or minute the meeting;
- record and promptly document agreed outcomes; send a letter immediately to those attending recording any decisions made;
- identify areas of practice or organisation needing change as a result of a complaint; put these into effect sooner rather than later.

Adapted from Jenkins, 1997, p.276.

---

is now widely seen by practitioners as being of potentially enormous value as a positive stimulus to the therapeutic process itself.

CONCLUSION

Practitioners face an increasing likelihood of becoming the subject of a professional complaint during their career, although the chances of hostile litigation still remain somewhat lower at present. The risks of facing complaint or legal action can be reduced, but not removed entirely, by developing a keen understanding of the dynamic links between ethical principles and the standards of competent practice expected of the ordinary practitioner. Some forms of complaint and recourse to the law will arise, not necessarily from the counsellor's practice, but from a client with an irresolvable agenda, which takes expression in persistent and vexatious litigation. However, in most situations, practitioners can reduce the risks of practising therapy in the 21st century by constantly striving to learn from experience, both their own and that of the profession to which they seek to belong.

REFERENCES

Bond, T. (2000) *Standards and Ethics for Counselling in Action*, 2nd edition. London: Sage.

British Association for Counselling and Psychotherapy (2002) *Ethical Framework for Good Practice in Counselling and Psychotherapy*. Rugby: BACP.

Casemore, R. (2001) *Surviving Complaints Against Counsellors and Psychotherapists: Towards Understanding and Healing*. Ross-on-Wye: PCCS.

Data Protection Act (1998) London: HMSO.

Human Rights Act (1998) London: HMSO.

Jenkins, P. (1997) *Counselling, Psychotherapy and the Law*. London: Sage.

Jenkins, P., Stone, J. and Keter, V. (2004) *Psychotherapy and the Law: Questions and Answers for Counsellors and Therapists*. London: Whurr.

Jones, C., Shillito-Clark, C., Syme, G., Hill, D., Casemore, R. and Murdin, L. (2000) *Questions of Ethics in Counselling and Therapy*. Buckingham: Open University Press.

Leiper, R. and Kent, R. (2002) *Working Through Setbacks in Psychotherapy: Crisis, Impasse and Relapse*. London: Sage.

9 HOW TO SET UP AND DEVELOP YOUR PRIVATE PRACTICE

Christine Wilding, Gladeana McMahon and
Stephen Palmer

INTRODUCTION

Some of you reading this chapter will have recently made a decision to enter private practice. Others may already be working in this area and be interested in developing and expanding it – and some of you may, at this stage, simply be interested in learning more about what is involved in this area of counselling and psychotherapy before you make a decision. We have intentionally written this chapter in an upbeat style so as not to discourage readers from going into private practice. However, there is a caveat: not only can private practice be rewarding, it can be demanding and challenging and warrants serious consideration before leaving the security of full-time employment.

So what *is* involved in developing a private practice, and how can you ensure that you achieve your aims? Is it really for you, and how do you visualise the reality in a few years time? Do you see yourself working full time with a flourishing and varied business, or do you see private practice as a small, part-time source of work, perhaps something that will fit around family life, or offer a little extra income to supplement the financial needs of the household?

We would like to encourage you to believe that either vision is possible. Our aim in writing this chapter is to help you focus on the most important considerations, as well as draw your attention to factors that you may have not yet taken into account. We will attempt to discuss with you the many and varied opportunities within private therapy work that will allow you to develop your practice, and we hope that the advice we will give you will be relevant to your personal ambitions, whatever they are.

We would also like to highlight at this stage that working to a high professional standard with adequate legal and security provisions in place will be just as important to a part-time counsellor seeing only occasional clients at home, as it will be for the counsellor who takes business premises and works 14 hours a day to develop a full-time, flourishing career.

IS PRIVATE PRACTICE FOR YOU?

Before making a final decision, it is worth looking at some of the basic pros and cons which may not yet have been drawn to your attention. These considerations relate less to counselling *per se*, and more to the generic business model for self-employment.

If you have previously always worked as an employee, you will have extra responsibilities now. You will not have an employer who will provide the umbrella protection of a regular salary and other benefits. You may work largely in isolation without the support of colleagues. It will be your responsibility to generate sufficient income to survive and meet your outgoings, to build and sustain a credible and acceptable professional reputation. You will need to consider the risks of personal safety. You may need to hone your skills for dealing with paper work, record keeping and accounts. You will need to keep a balance between self-development, personal health and meeting the needs of clients whilst maintaining high standards and making a reasonable living.

However, provided that you do recognise these issues, and are willing to take them on, the challenges and rewards of seeing your own business develop and flourish, the freedom of working for yourself without the pressures of office politics and other workplace problems, the ability to develop your working strategies along the lines that you feel are the best, and produce the best results, and the satisfaction of creating a business that fulfils your own dreams; these are the things that will hopefully make the sacrifices worth while.

ARE YOU READY FOR PRIVATE PRACTICE YET?

The temptation exists for 'inexperienced' counsellors to set up in private practice before they are ready for it. By 'inexperienced', we mean counsellors, psychotherapists or counselling psychologists who are not robust enough in the widest sense to handle a broad cross section of clients, who are not clinically experienced enough to deal successfully with therapeutic difficulties, and who are possibly unused to the rigours of ethical business practise.

We would suggest that, whether you are a professionally accredited, registered or a chartered practitioner or not (we appreciate that many therapists eligible for accreditation chose not to pursue this), you consider the BACP guidelines for accreditation of at least 450 hours of clinical experience as being a baseline for the work experience you will need before you start working independently. Assess the quality and type of your clinical practice in a realistic way – for example, if you have worked in a specialist environment, dealing with, for example, troubled young people, bereavement or alcoholism, this may not give you a broad enough base to take on the wider variety of client problems you may need to deal with. Whilst you might, of course, wish to set up your private practice to deal only with your speciality, your chances of finding enough clients with this one specific problem are likely to be small.

INITIAL CONSIDERATIONS?

The first consideration, once you have said, 'Yes, I am definitely doing this' is where? By this, we don't just mean, 'Shall I convert the spare bedroom or see if I can rent an office in the GP surgery?' We also mean that well-used adage, location, location, location. There is no doubt that every other issue concerning your expertise as a therapist, your business acumen and your willingness to work long and hard will fall into complete insignificance if you set up your practice in an area where you simply cannot attract clients.

However professional and well furnished your therapy room, if your clients are concerned by:

- parking difficulties;
- climbing several flights of stairs;
- the area is one they would normally avoid due to negative perceptions about possibly crime rates;
- graffiti on walls etc.,

the fact that the rent was 'a bargain' will not mitigate against the difficulty of persuading clients to visit you in this type of area or returning after the first visit.

Consider further what a reasonable area might be. It may be safe and convenient, and easy for parking but again, unless you site your premises in a high-density area, your search for clients could be unrewarding. A sparse population will not yield the numbers you may require to keep your business afloat, so moving from a city centre to an idyllic countryside environment might be a bad move to make.

SECURITY

Whilst we will presume that you know enough about the aesthetics of preparing a therapy room and to ensure that you have a basic office facility available, we would be remiss not to highlight an important issue in private practice – that of personal security. Please do consider the following issues:

- Geographical location – if your office is at home, is on the ground floor and is very obviously a part of your home, the client may perceive it as linked to other rooms and there is no sense of isolation. Taking someone up to your attic might be a different thing.
- Where do your clients come from? Limiting your clients to those who are referred from reliable sources may also minimise any difficulties. There are clients that you might be skilled and happy to see in an agency or medical setting that you would be unwise to see as a private practitioner. You will need to think about the difference between the acceptance of 'some' inherent risk and an increase in risk factors.
- Whilst being aware of the possibility of physical attack we also need to recognise the rarity of such a thing happening. In fact, we are most likely to encounter personal physical violence when we work in an office full of disparate colleagues. In the unlikely event that you are confronted by a client who seems to be becoming agitated in a way that suggests imminent violence in session. What precautions can you take, and what can you do?
  - (a) It is possible to have a 'panic button' installed in your office that is connected to your local police station.
  - (b) Where do you sit in your office? If you sit nearer the exit door than your client, this will give you an advantage if you need to leave the room quickly.
  - (c) Where you have a smallest doubt about a client in advance of a session, see if you can arrange for someone else to be on the premises if at all possible (if all else fails perhaps you could trade this with a neighbour for some babysitting time, for example).

If in doubt, you may need to consider employing a safety and health consultant to undertake a risk assessment. Finally, if you genuinely find yourself worrying about your personal safety in an office on your own, then it will probably affect the quality of your work and you may wish to think seriously about working in an independent practice.

DEVELOPING A CLIENT BASE

Once you have decided on your location, have negotiated your office space and are comfortable with regards to security, you will need to market your services.

One of the first principles of private practice is to relinquish the idea that therapy is all you will be required to do. In fact, certainly in its infancy, therapy will only be a small part of the work of establishing your practice. The key issue initially will be, 'Where do I find clients?'

Many therapists find the idea of advertising distasteful, but there are conservative forms of advertising, which most practitioners find acceptable. Consider approaching local GP surgeries and ask whether they might be willing to give your card to people (yes – don't forget to have some cards printed). Even where they employ an in-house counsellor, waiting lists for such services are often long, and many patients will be willing to go privately, if only they know where to go. Some GP surgeries even have notice boards, often commercially run by outside agencies that will charge you a fee to develop a tasteful poster for your services, and then to have it on display, perhaps with a card holder as well.

You might also consider approaching local solicitors and undertakers – businesses where the clients are going through trauma of some kind and the business in question, whilst themselves dealing only with the practical considerations, may like to recommend help for the emotional issues often involved.

'Yellow Pages' may seem a little bold for you (and security issues then become paramount) but if you look under 'Counselling and Advice' in your local directory, you will see that many therapists use this way of generating clients. Yell.Com is the internet service, and you can be entered here either as well, or alternatively.

Investing in the website listing of your professional association is likely to be money well spent. Now that counselling and psychotherapy is becoming more widely used by the general public, their awareness of the relevant professional associations is also greater. Many potential clients like the security of seeing someone who has a professional registration, and as a therapist, it can be reassuring to know that the client is taking the idea of therapy seriously enough to make such an enquiry. At the Centre for Stress Management we have noticed that most potential clients now use email to contact the Centre. They have obtained our therapist's details from websites such as those of the BPS and the BABCP. However, having your own dedicated website will provide potential clients with more details about you, as there will be room to include additional information such as your general approach to therapy. It is possible to set up and develop your own website at no financial cost by using website providers such as Freewebs (www.freewebs.com). A simple website can be set up by an absolute beginner in under 1 hour. The providers provide free and easy-to-use website templates to help you design a business-like sites. Your existing email service provider may also have a website facility.

Networking is a spin-off from advertising. Get involved with therapy groups, and agencies that deal with specialist difficulties. You could offer to give a talk to the local OCD Support Group, for example (obviously, where you have experience in that particular disorder). Even writing for a local newspaper will generate your name in print in your area.

You will eventually begin to receive 'word-of-mouth' referrals, but you will probably have an established practice before you get too many of these.

To start with then, you will need to spend a great deal of time 'on the road', and this will mean ensuring that you have already made, and had printed, professional brochures, cards, letter-heads – whatever you will personally need to ensure that you present yourself as an experienced professional, rather than a hopeful amateur.

FINANCIAL CONSIDERATIONS

The spectre of fluctuating finances and your ability to stay afloat through possible lean periods needs serious consideration. It may well be that, in order to develop your business slowly and solidly, you will continue to generate other, more regular income from either salaried counselling work or another part-time job. Unless you have sufficient funds to support you initially, or you live with someone in work who can support your first efforts financially, we do recommend that you consider starting your private practice in this way.

All businesses take time to develop, and most people starting up a business from scratch would not expect to do more than break even in the first year or two. Do take this into account.

Where making an accurate prediction of cash flow is essential to you, you should develop a business plan. A business plan is a statement of business objectives, followed by a description of how these objectives are to be achieved. Such a plan might cover a typical period of 1–3 years and is particularly applicable to small businesses and the self-employed who are starting a new business. The reason for this is that 80% of new businesses fail within the first 5 years. However, by drawing up a business plan, the typical problem of inadequate cash flow may to be spotted before the business is even started and plans made accordingly (including, of course, the possible decision of not starting the business at all).

We do not have sufficient space in this chapter to refer to business plans in more detail, and we are also mindful that, for a many practitioners, this might not be seen as an essential pre-requisite to their private practice aspirations. We will therefore refer those of you interested in knowing more to the wide variety of texts on the subject, including *Counselling in Private Practice* (McMahon, 1994) or *The Essential Skills for Setting up a Counselling and Psychotherapy Practice* (McMahon, Palmer, and Wilding, 2005) which both provide a detailed explanation of working out a business plan especially tailored to the counselling and psychotherapy profession. Some banks will also provide their new customers with business plan forms on CDs that can be completed. Another possibility is the Microsoft PowerPoint software programme which has a business plan presentation template which encourages the user to answer relevant questions during its completion.

What we would ask of you at this stage is to ensure that you will be able to exist moderately and pay your basic bills without particular reliance on therapy income for, say, the first year of your practice. This will enable you to develop your practice as you wish, and not feel pressured into taking more work than you can handle, or seeing difficult or unsuitable clients simply in order to ensure that your rent is paid. Retaining a concurrent part-time post is a safe option.

THE BUSINESS SIDE

BECOMING SELF-EMPLOYED

We will assume that you understand the principles of self-employment, that you have registered with HM Inspector of Taxes as self-employed, have set up a DDR to pay your National Insurance contributions and will be submitting an Income Tax Return by either the 30th September each year (if you want the Inland Revenue to calculate any tax for you) or 31st January each year (if you will do the calculations yourself). You can use the HM Revenue and Customs on-line service to submit your return any time up to 31st January, as the software will calculate your tax for you (for further details see www.hmrc.gov.uk). A further pointer if you are new to self-employment: where you earn £15,000 or less in any one tax year, you will not be asked to give any details of your income and outgoings beyond a total figure for each and the calculation of the difference between them (i.e. your net profit or loss).

If any of this sounds remotely daunting to you, you may be pleasantly surprised by the helpfulness of your local Tax Office. Simply call in and see them and you will have a Tax Advisor at your disposal to answer all your questions and help you on your way. Telephoning them is another option although this can be time consuming. The service is completely free, and as good as you will get from a costly accountant.

LIMITED COMPANY

Most counsellors and psychotherapists in private practice are self-employed. However, you could consider setting up a limited company which does have the benefit of limited financial liability although this does depend upon a number of factors. There are pros and cons of setting up a limited company which is a legal entity in itself – literally you would be working for your company. It would be advisable to speak to your chartered accountant or chartered tax advisor about your current situation and whether or not to become self-employed or set up a limited company as they both have different tax implications. It is worth noting that instead of going into a partnership with a colleague, a limited company or limited partnership does offer you more protection. Seek advice.

FEE LEVELS AND FEE PAYMENT

You may wonder as a practitioner moving into private practice, what level of fees to charge? The BACP publish an annual Counselling and Psychotherapy Resources Directory and you can request a copy for your area (as well as nationally, if you wish). The therapists listed will normally quote their fees or fee scales, and this will give you a better idea of what would be appropriate for you. Unless you are very anxious to build up a clientele at all costs, do not pitch your fees too low. Apart from the volume of clients you will then need to see to make a reasonable income, you will also have the difficulty of raising fees when the demand for your services becomes greater.

Review your fees annually and state this as a clear policy on the client information sheet you should give to all new clients. (This sheet should give them the practical information they need regarding your terms of working, and will act as an informal contract between you. You will be able to find further details on putting this together in one or more of our 'further reading' recommendations at the end of this chapter.) If you do not do so, it could be seen that any increase in fees changes the initial contract whereas by simply stating, 'fees are subject to annual review' you will have covered yourself should you wish to raise your fee level. It is helpful to be aware of the current charges of other therapists, if you are in a competitive environment.

Should you have difficulty with unpaid fees, and all reasonable requests for payment are ignored, going through your local Small Claims Court is a simple procedure. In all probability the mention of possible legal action may persuade your client to settle his or her account.

If you do decide to take this course of action, you will need to send the client a letter stating that if you do not receive payment by a certain date you will take legal action. Send the letter by registered post so that you have evidence of posting and if the client does not pay by the stated date all you need to do is decide whether to follow through or not. We suspect theoretical orientation will affect your view of the various options open to you. Remember you are offering a professional service and you cannot afford to have outstanding invoices left unpaid. In going to Court to settle the outstanding payment you will focus on the financial issues and not the confidential material discussed in therapy session unless your client or their representative wishes to discuss this in Court.

LEGAL REQUIREMENTS

Do make yourself familiar with the stipulations in the Data Protection Act. This was most recently updated in 1998, and checking the present regulations, as well as keeping abreast of any further changes can be done by logging on to www.dataprotection.gov.uk. The Data Protection Registrar is usually very helpful and in an attempt to make the process as simple as possible will complete your form for you so that all you have to do is check it and pay the £37 annual registration fee.

You will also need to abide by the code of ethics and practise of your professional association for document storage and confidentiality. The BACP and other professional bodies can provide you with a range of fact sheets to assist you with this.

In legal terms, professional Codes of Practice are not necessarily recognised in a court of law. Whilst they do carry some weight in some courts, it is important to ensure that your record-keeping bible is the Data Protection Act.

An important point to keep in mind is that these ethical requirements do not necessarily fully cover your legal requirements. You are under further obligation to ensure that you fulfil these as well, in case of investigation.

Whilst we do not yet have in the UK quite the culture of litigation that is prevalent in the US, the situation is changing, and you will need to ensure that you are legally protected in two ways: first, a client may decide to take you to court for some reason, and secondly, you may be asked to give evidence in a court on behalf of a client (this is not uncommon in insurance claims following car accidents, for example, where you might have been treating the client for PTSD). To cover the first eventuality, do ensure that you have adequate personal insurance cover. There are companies that specialise in insuring self-employed professionals, and it is essential that you arrange this before you see your first client. The second eventuality may result in your being asked to make case notes available to the court (Scoggins, Litton and Palmer, 1998). There has been much debate in recent years as to whether this involves therapists in violating their code of professional confidentiality. If you wish to know more about this, Peter Jenkins has written an excellent booked entitled *Legal Issues for Counselling and Psychotherapy* (2002). Also see his section in this book, Chapter 8. As a rule of thumb, expect that you will have to make your notes available if a court of law requests them.

PROFESSIONAL MEMBERSHIPS

Do ensure that you keep up your membership(s) to professional bodies. Not only will this give your clients confidence in you (and may result in a larger number of clients – some will wish to know such things before committing their time and money to you), but they will keep you in touch with up-to-date research, training courses and other professional issues that are vital if you are to keep a high level of professional competence. In addition, those that have registers that you can join.

Accreditation can offer a yardstick of competence, but requires time and effort to accomplish. You will need to weigh these two views if you have not yet taken the route to accreditation, and consider if the time and effort involved will enable you to increase and expand your practice.

CONTINUOUS PROFESSIONAL DEVELOPMENT (CPD)

This is now a 'given' for anyone belonging to any professional body. Do ensure that you complete the number of development hours required by the professional body you belong to, to ensure that your accreditations and registrations stay up to date.

More importantly, however, if you wish to develop as a therapist, you will need to constantly expand your own personal theoretical knowledge of your subject. Read, use the internet, use peer group discussions, attend courses and workshops. Develop a thirst for knowledge so that you really enjoy your on-going learning, rather than seeing it as a necessary chore.

EXTENDING SERVICES BEYOND COUNSELLING AND PSYCHOTHERAPY TO OFFER COACHING

You have probably heard about the field of coaching. If this is a service you would like to offer, you will need to consider focusing some of your CPD in this area by reading relevant coaching books/journals, attending workshops and conferences. Longer certificated courses would be advised. The skills required for coaching are similar to counselling although more goal-focused than many established therapeutic approaches. As an experienced therapist you may have a lot of skills and knowledge to bring to your coaching practice. The fee structure in life or personal coaching is similar to therapy and in some areas such as executive coaching, it is highly paid and fees of between £250 and £500 per hour are not uncommon. The book

Achieving Excellence in Your Coaching Practice: How to Run a Highly Successful Coaching Business, (McMahon, Palmer and Wilding, 2006) provides an overview to setting up a coaching practice. Some therapists use a different business website and office location for their coaching practice. If you do decide to offer coaching, then it is important to ensure that your contractually agreed coaching does not drift into therapy with a client and if you find your coaching practice addressing clinical disorders in coaching sessions it is likely you have crossed that boundary.

PRESENTATION

Dress and presentation are important. If your office is in your home, you may well see this as an opportunity to adopt a very casual dress code. Think hard about this. What image do you want to present to your clients? You may wish to dress differently according to the type of client you have. It is actually a good idea for your own dress code to reflect that of the individual client. At the very least, ensure that you look neat, clean and tidy. Research shows that clients are most comfortable where the therapist is dressed in a way that they see as appropriate to the meeting, and in line with their own dress code.

SUPERVISION AND PERSONAL THERAPY

Whilst a certain level of supervision is mandatory, do ensure that, as your practice grows, your supervision hours reflect your increased case load. BACP-accredited counsellors and chartered counselling psychologists are expected to have a minimum of one and a half hours of personal supervision per month for those months that they are seeing clients. Therapists who are not accredited would be wise to use this as a minimum yardstick for their own supervision. Do reflect yourself on your personal needs, and increase your supervision where necessary especially if you are encountering difficult cases.

There are special arguments for the use of supervision for therapists in private practice. Private practice is, in a sense, an isolated occupation. Unlike working within a counselling agency or organisation, where you will usually have constant opportunities for dialogue, support, peer supervision, theoretical discussions and an awareness of practice methods of others. You may have one-to-one and/or group supervision provided by the service whereas working alone means that, where you wish to provide yourself with such opportunities you need to be pro-active in arranging both formal and informal supervision arrangements. Do not neglect this important area of your practice.

Personal therapy is really just that. As an experienced practitioner, you will be aware of the help it can give you, and how often you need this assistance. It is not mandatory, so it is a purely personal decision. However, many therapists who found personal therapy helpful in training continue with the same therapist once they have qualified. Provided this suits you, simply continue in this way. However, there is an argument to say that, where personal therapy is also a professional development tool, changing therapists from time to time gives a broader view of different approaches from both a theoretical and personal view. You may wish to consider the benefits of this approach.

REFERRING ON

One of the basic concerns of therapists newly in private practice is how to deal with a client who, for whatever reason, seems beyond his or her level of competence. Do ensure that you have put together a list of specialist agencies and organisations who can deal with problems presented to you that are outside your experience or preferred remit. It can be helpful to at least briefly touch on the nature of a client's problem during the initial telephone conversation (where there is one), to give you an early opportunity to explain that you do not deal with such particular difficulties, but you can recommend a qualified practitioner or organisation that can.

Where you are already in the process of therapy, and a difficulty arises, make your supervisor your first port of call. You may simply be experiencing a lack of confidence in dealing with the problem that your supervisor can help you through. It may also be that the client, now that he or she feels confident and trusting in you, would prefer to continue with you even though you are not an expert in the particular area concerned (drug abuse, for example) so he or she will also contribute to the decision you finally make.

EXPANDING YOUR PRACTICE

You are more likely to flourish and do well if you expand your practice in a variety of different directions, rather than simply rely on adequate numbers of individual clients. Some of the areas that we, the authors, and other therapists known to us have developed successfully are:

- Teaching – very often, the college where you trained, and who know you, may be interested in your returning to assist with courses that they run.

Once you have some experience, you can offer your experience more widely.

- Supervision – many therapists go on to undertake supervision training a part of their CPD and then progress to supervise other therapists.
- Corporate work – many companies now like to offer stress counselling to staff members – often to pre-empt litigious staff members who may feel that their work load is unacceptably stressful.
- GP work – it may be worth enquiring whether your local surgery could use your services 1 or 2 days a week.
- Training – using your counselling skills to develop courses and workshops for other counsellors or, again, corporate settings.
- Writing – there are a variety of publications who are pleased to accept original work for publication, and, as you become more experienced, you may wish to write a book.
- Specialist 'consultancy' work – alongside, say, solicitors who may like to call on you where there are psychological issues involved in a case, and where your freelance services are a useful adjunct.

CONCLUSION

We are well aware that, in this chapter, we have touched on only some of the many areas that you will need to become familiar with as your private practice develops. However, we hope that we have at least 'pointed the way' that we have perhaps offered new information and new suggestions that you had not previously appreciated or considered and that we will have given you new directions to explore and discover more about. If you are professional and ethical, determined and business-like, confident and positive in outlook, your clients will benefit greatly from this, and your business will flourish because of reputation and your clients. In Appendix A and B, we have provided a list of useful publications and relevant organisations.

We do wish you every success as you develop this area of your work.

REFERENCES

Data Protection Act (1998) London: HMSO.

Jenkins P. (2002) *Legal Issues for Counselling and the Law*. London: Sage.

McMahon, G. (1994) Counselling in private practice. In S. Palmer and G. McMahon (eds) *Handbook of Counselling*. London: Routledge.

McMahon, G., Palmer, S. and Wilding, C. (2005) *The Essential Skills for Setting Up a Counselling and Psychotherapy Practice*. London: Routledge.

McMahon, G., Palmer, S. and Wilding, C. (2006) *Achieving Excellence in your Coaching Practice: How to Run a Highly Successful Coaching Business.* London: Routledge.

Scoggins, L., Litton, M. and Palmer, S. (1998) Confidentiality and the law. *Counselling Psychology Review*, 13(1), 6–12.

10 DEVELOPING YOUR CAREER TO WORKING WITH MULTICULTURAL AND DIVERSITY CLIENTS

Roy Moodley and Dina B. Lubin

While there has been a growing awareness of the importance of multi-cultural and diversity issues in counselling, psychology and psychotherapy since the 1960s (see, for example, Lago and Thompson, 1996; Moodley and Palmer, 2006; Palmer, 2002; Pedersen, 1999; Robinson, 2005; Sue and Sue, 1990; Vontress 1967, 1979), and many clinicians purport to practise it, very few are skilled at a level where they can feel comfortable enough to counsel clients in a multicultural and diversity context. Many therapists experience difficulties when faced with clients who are different to themselves in terms of the 'big 5' stigmatised identities (race, gender, sexual orientations, class and disability), or the 'big 7' (+ religion and age) (Moodley, 2005). The reasons for this are numerous, and not least amongst them are the lack of training opportunities for clinicians, very little or no input on graduate training programmes in counselling and far fewer ethnic minorities engage in counselling and psychotherapy; thus, clinicians are less exposed to culturally diverse clients frequently enough to increase their skills and competencies (see Moodley, 2000a and b). Moreover, multicultural counselling is perceived to be a particular therapeutic method, in the same way as the psychoanalytic, CBT and the person-centred approaches. This construction of multicultural counselling offers clinicians a false choice, that is, if they choose to work multiculturally then they are precluded from being client-centred therapists or CBT practitioners. In fact, *all* counselling is multicultural (Pedersen, 1991), clearly illustrating the point that multicultural counselling is not a specific approach of therapeutic intervention but a philosophy of practice that can easily be embedded into any one of the 400+ therapeutic approaches (Garfield and Bergin, 1994). The basis of this philosophy of practice is the therapist's awareness and consciousness of the client's narrative in the context of their culture, ethnicity, sexuality, gender, class, disability, religion and age, as well as the micro-cultural identities that clients may self-ascribe to. For example, in the category of sexual orientations, the sub-cultural categories are LGBTQ (gay, lesbian, bisexual, transgendered and queer identities), although one could argue that the concept of transgendered is appropriate to the category gender rather than sexual orientations.

The perception that multicultural and diversity counselling is a specific therapeutic approach reduces the chances that all counsellors and psychotherapists will become culturally competent in the 'big 5' stigmatised identities in therapy. Mainstream therapists seem to stay away from the race, culture, ethnicity and sexual orientations issues and let the multiculturalists deal with them, claiming a lack of training in these issues. Even if a modicum of training is offered, at best what is on offer is a programme that constitutes not more than a day's workshop within which some or all the issues of the 'big 5' tend to get discussed. This kind of training does very little to prepare counsellors, psychologists and psychotherapists to meet the mental health challenges that will face them, in a multicultural society, in the 21st century.

Four decades ago, Wrenn (1962) coined the term 'the culturally encapsulated counsellor' to critique the universal approach to mental health care of ethnic minority communities. Since then, many conceptual and theoretical meanderings have been attempted to destabilise the notion of the culturally encapsulated counselor, and to bring into consciousness the subjective ways in which clients generate meanings for their 'psychological distress'. A 'close correlation exists between a patient's cultural beliefs about his/her illness and between his/her understanding of the treatment of such distress' (Moodley, 2000c, p. 163). This equilibrium between culture, illness and cure is articulated succinctly by Good and Good when they say, 'the meaning of illness for an individual is grounded in – though not reducible to – the network of meanings an illness has in a particular culture' (Good and Good, 1982, p. 148). Clients will be able, if given the opportunity to receive different cures (for example, talking therapy and traditional healing), to systematically organise the expression of their problem into the discourse of the healer, thus 'presenting their subjective distress to each therapist appropriately ... competing and contradictory cures can be held alongside or in tandem with each other without necessarily creating conflict in the patient' (Moodley, 2000c, p. 164). This theorising reinforces the view that culture-specific meanings are still at the root of an individual's network of meanings. The cultural advocates in the multicultural counselling movement see culture as the nucleus of a client's narrative. They argue that culture is the heart and soul of all counselling relationships and therefore must be at the centre of therapy, rather than something to be considered exotic or specialised (Pedersen, 1991; Pedersen and Ivey, 1993; Speight et al., 1991). In addition, the post-structuralists' view of the client as a dynamic blend of multiple identities (Ridley, 1995), constructed through discursive practices of the social and cultural, will offer a comprehensive and sophisticated understanding of the client's subjectivity. Consequently, any form of multicultural career development, training and consciousness raising of clinicians must be at this 'heart' (of multiple identities) within which the 'network of personal meanings' of health and illness can begin to evolve.

In discussing the process of how one could develop one's career in multicultural and diversity counselling, we take as our starting point the 'big 5' stigmatised identities as the basis for any kind of counselling training and development. We explore this theme in this chapter. First, we explore the concept of multiculturalism and its various social, cultural and political meanings, the controversies and contradictions surrounding it, and its relationship to the concept of diversity. The analysis we draw from the multicultural debate is that while each modality of the 'big 5' stigmatised identities is critical to engage with, an exclusive focus on any one of these dimensions at the exclusion of one or more of the others will invariably be unethical practice. A disavowal of any one variable is the absolute denial of the client, since a client's subjectivity is constructed through the intersection of race, gender, class, sexual orientations, disability, religion and age. Second, we discuss the framework of multicultural competence explored by Sue *et al.* (1992). While we offer a critique of the framework, we have also adapted it in some way to look at the particular ways in which clinicians can benefit from its use. Finally, we conclude the chapter by discussing the various ways that clinicians can pursue training and development opportunities to update their current diversity and multicultural knowledge and skills from current conceptual and empirical research in this field. However, first we begin by locating multiculturalism and diversity in counselling.

LOCATING MULTICULTURALISM AND DIVERSITY IN COUNSELLING

The term multicultural and diversity covers a wide spectrum of meanings, ideas, ideologies and practices, many of which date to the colonial times. However, its contemporary usage, particularly in counselling, psychology and psychotherapy, is relatively new – dating back to the 1960s. In essence it is related to 'race, culture and ethnicity' and all other experiences pertaining to cultural and ethnic minorities. On the other hand, the concept of diversity in counselling and psychology appears much later in the literature, evolving as a result of the confusions and complexities surrounding the term multicultural, and the term *culture* generally. Culture itself is not specific or clearly defined, being so indeterminate that it can easily be filled in with whatever preconceptions a theorist brings to it – anything from morals, art, knowledge, belief, law, custom, music and so forth (see Halton, 1992; Taylor (1871[1920])). While there is very little agreement by the cultural commentators about the meaning of culture, there is, however, a general acceptance that culture is a process that is not static but constantly changing in time and space within a given society (Moodley and Curling, in press). However, this latter point seems to be conceptually disregarded by the more ardent members of the multicultural movement. It is this adherence to multiculture as a construct of race, culture and ethnicity without a critique on power relations and the politics of identity that makes it unfavourable as a discourse within which a client in counselling can find libratory and social justice solutions to psychological problems. Furthermore, since multiculturalism is untheorised (Willett, 1998), ideologically constituted (Bulmer and Solomos, 1996) and fails to articulate a radical approach in terms of racism, imperialism, sexism and economic oppression (Moodley, 1999b), it has not offered much in terms of clinical theorising, practice and research. The circle of neglect of any new theorising, the paucity of innovative practice and the constant recycling of the same themes in multicultural research has maintained multiculturalism's position as being narrow, fixed, essentialistic, focused on race as black, homologising ethnic groups into a single category, making it confusing. Many scholars have criticised the narrow definition of multicultural counselling in the North American context, which traditionally refers to the four major ethnic groups, viz., African-American, Asian-American, Latino/American and Native American (Pedersen, 1991; Speight *et al.*, 1991). This definition invariably excludes whites as clients from multicultural counselling, while at the same time it homologises white people by denying their various cultures, ethnicities and histories. It also denies identities that are outside the singular category of a particular colour (black, white, brown, olive), or gender, sexuality, disability and class. Hardy and Laszloffy (1992) remind us of the 'theoretical myth of sameness', which overlooks the important fact that individuals need to be understood within a broader scope than simply their race or ethnicity.

While many multiculturalists have called for a broader definition, very few scholars have argued for the inclusion of white people as clients; amongst them are Sashidharan (1986), Arredondo (1994) and Moodley, (1999a and b). Patricia Arredondo, for example, emphasises the importance of including white individuals of European descent. She says:

> Without establishing and communicating a premise that everyone is a cultural being and that cultural self-knowledge is a key to effectiveness and competency as a counselor the status quo in Multicultural Counseling will remain. It will be relegated to a corner as a specialty… (Arredondo, 1994, p. 311).

Perhaps multicultural counselling is already in its corner refusing to come out and be counted as the 'fourth force in counselling' (Pedersen, 1991). What is to be lost, and who benefits from its coming out? The emphasis on white therapist/black client as a process in multicultural counselling (which is reinforced through racist employment policies) strongly reflects and reinforces the prevailing notions that exist in our society about race, culture and illness (Moodley, 1999a and b; Sashidharan, 1986). Understood in this way, ethnic minorities can be seen as inferior, underdeveloped and deficient for being under undue stress, debilitated, apathetic, depressed, rejecting establishment values and expressing anger in unconventional ways (see Gilman, 1985).

It is critical, however, that multicultural counselling is not cornered into an ideology which espouses equality but reinforces oppressive practices. A genuine multicultural approach that accepts many alternative views (Sue *et al.*, 1998) will provide counsellors with opportunities to be more flexible with their clinical thinking, to step outside their more traditional clinically safe viewpoints and to consider the network of meanings that 'subjective distress' may hold for an individual client. As Sue *et al.* write:

> Culturally skilled counselors understand how race, culture, ethnicity, and so forth affect personality formation, vocational choices, manifestation of psychological disorders, help-seeking behavior, and the appropriateness or inappropriateness of counseling approaches. They understand and have knowledge about sociopolitical influences that impinge upon the life of racial and ethnic minorities. Immigration issues, poverty, racism, stereotyping, and powerlessness all leave major scars that may influence the counseling process (Sue, Arredondo and McDavis, 1992, p. 482).

As a result of a basic paradigm shift in recent decades in psychology away from monoculturalism towards multiculturalism, many clinicians have become more aware of the need to emphasise context, the importance of subjective meanings, language and discourse (as opposed to reductionism), complex interacting particulars (as opposed to universals) and holistic perspectives rather than narrow viewpoints and descriptors (Mahoney and Patterson, 1992; Smith, Harre and Van Langenhove, 1995).

'THE BIG 5': INTERSECTING RACE, GENDER, SEXUAL ORIENTATIONS, CLASS AND DISABILITY

The 'big 5' or the 'big 7', if we include religion and age, have now become standard ways of thinking about multicultural counselling in the context of diversity. Although there appear to be some differences, particularly in terms of whether white people are part of this process by the 'race as black, and minority ethnicity as culture' practitioners, there is now a general consensus that the 'big 5' (or 7) is now part of a critical multicultural approach to counselling in the context of diversity. There is also the tendency to replace multiculturalism in multicultural counselling with the concept of 'critical multiculturalism' or 'diversity' (Moodley, 2005). Renaming may be critical as the 'old' multicultural counselling appears to carry with it assumptions that keep it in a corner (as mentioned earlier). To move out of its corner multicultural counselling would need to shift out of its traditional borders of race, culture and ethnicity to include gender, sexual orientations, class and disability. We feel that if counsellors are not conscious of these 'other' identities in therapy, the quality of therapy becomes compromised due to the omission of critical aspects of an individual's unique identity and sense of self.

We believe that if counsellors are to practise ethically and competently, then sensitivity to all of the 'big 5' (or 7) issues are crucial. At the same time, counsellors would need to be clinically skilful as well – to be able to understand specific cultural issues without having a lens so narrow that it fails to take into account the individual within a broader scope (for example, viewing a client singularly in terms of race, i.e. a 'black man' as opposed to understanding the complexity of identity variables that go into the client's make-up, i.e. a black, gay, hearing-impaired, working-class, elderly man). The danger of inadvertently stereotyping also exists, due to presumed cultural knowledge instead of a true appreciation of the complexities of diversity (Taylor, 2000). There is also the potential for error in making the assumption that the individual's presenting issue is focused on one of these cultural identities, and subsequently ignoring or minimising the reason for which the individual has chosen to seek therapy. In working with these identities, counsellors must recognise the importance of examining the intersection and convergences between an individual's gender, racial, ethnic, class and sexual orientation identities, since no single identity takes precedence over the others in an individual's inner world (Moodley, 2003, p. 122). Moreover, these identities must be seen as fluid, shifting over time in accordance with contextual influences, such as sociopolitical realities, economic possibilities, developmental transitions, personality variables and cultural histories. At a most basic level, the therapist's own awareness and perceptions of their self as complex, multidimensional beings are critical in working across cultures. Furthermore, the cultural sensitivity, or 'cultural empathy' (Ridley and Lingle, 1996), expressed by counsellors is a key ingredient in making clinicians culturally competent (Dyche and Zayas, 2001).

There is no doubt that sensitivity towards client diversity results in better therapeutic outcomes, particularly with those groups who have experienced oppression, such as women, gay and lesbians, and ethnic minorities. Without an understanding of the unique issues faced by these groups, a clinician will be unlikely to use the most appropriate interventions for the clients, thus limiting the usefulness of the counselling experience and increasing the likelihood of premature termination. That is not to say that each individual should be 'lumped' into a category and treated in some kind of predetermined manner; however, we need to be able to consider the cultural, sociopolitical and economic contexts within which clients exist. Dyche and Zayas (2001) argue that therapists who have developed the ability to be culturally empathic are well prepared to practise psychotherapy with a diverse clientele. This entails embracing an attitude and/or skill that effectively:

> ... bridges the cultural gap between clinician and client, one that seeks to help clinicians integrate an attitude of openness, with the necessary knowledge and skill to work successfully across cultures ... and a deepening of the human empathic response to permit a sense of mutuality and understanding across the great differences in value and expectation that cross-cultural interchange often involves (Dyche and Zayas, 2001, p. 246).

In essence, it is the ability to see the world through the eyes of another, even if this view does not match ours, and to understand a client's unique self-experience while responding in a way that conveys this understanding (Ridley and Lingle, 1996). It is the ability to integrate cultural factors and the client's intersecting 'big 5' (or 7) stigmatised identities into all phases of one's clinical work, from the first session throughout the therapeutic journey, until this journey is completed. Throughout this time, clinicians would need to maintain an ongoing awareness of their clients as dynamic, complex individuals, and to acknowledge the client's cultural conceptualisations of their problems (Pedersen, 2002). For example, a young white man/woman who is involved in the 12-step programme of Alcoholics Anonymous (AA) may view their alcoholism as a disease, which is treatable through the AA fellowship and perhaps intensive inpatient treatment. However, a man/woman of a similar age bracket, perhaps a new immigrant who once lived in a Middle Eastern country, may believe that he/she has committed 'a sin, an unforgivable, moral transgression' (understood in relation to his spiritual and religious beliefs). A culturally sensitive intervention would constitute the following: taking the client's religious beliefs into account, being informed of the client's levels of acculturation, assimilation and integration in the new country, and not immediately abandon the Western belief that addiction is a disease and that treatment of this disease (whether it be a 12-step group, in patient treatment or any other type of 'program') would help the client. This course of treatment would prevent stereotyping the client into an ethnicity-focused process. To become culturally empathic, it is crucial that counsellors critically examine their own cultural biases and the cultural conditioning that they have experienced in both their professional and personal lives.

FRAMEWORK OF MULTICULTURAL AND DIVERSITY COUNSELLING COMPETENCE

The term 'multicultural competence' is one that has been widely used to describe

the ability to understand and constructively relate to the uniqueness of each client in light of the diverse cultures that influence each person's perspective. (Stuart, 2004, p. 6).

A therapist has developed this competence when he or she possess the skills necessary to work effectively and sensitively with clients from a variety of cultural and ethnic backgrounds (Holcomb-McCoy and Myers, 1999), as well as from gay, lesbian, working-class, disabled, elderly, and religious communities. Acquiring skills and competencies to work across such a diverse range of client groups (the 'big 5' stigmatised identities) seems like a daunting task. However, the first step towards cultural competence is the awareness and recognition that mental health professionals need to continually grow and further develop their professional skills, and that this needs to be a priority (Parham and Whitten, 2003). Once a clinician is motivated to know and acquire knowledge about potential clients, the skills and competence building will follow.

Much of the work around multicultural counselling competencies has been laid out extensively by Sue, Arredondo and McDavis (1992) in their widely cited document titled *Multicultural Counseling Competencies and Standards: A Call to the Profession*, which itself was a development on the seminal ideas offered a decade earlier by Sue *et al.* (1982). These competencies have become a landmark in counselling education and training as they have brought 'attention to the reality that traditional Western approaches to counselling and psychotherapy minimised the unique contributions of clients' and therapists' sociodemographic and psychodemographic characteristics to the therapy process' (Helms and Richardson, 1997, p. 69). Since its development, the multicultural counselling competency framework has undergone numerous changes and adaptations (see, for example, Arredondo *et al.*, 1996; Holcomb-McCoy, 2000; Ponterotto *et al.*, 1994; Sue *et al.*, 1998). The competency framework has had much criticism for being too complex and detailed, and for its sole focus on cultural diversity (Vontress and Jackson, 2004), resulting in further research and theorising and the development of 'more conceptually sound and clear set of principles' (Robinson, 2005, p. 25). These principles are discussed by Robinson in *The Convergence of Race, Ethnicity, and Gender: Multiple Identities in Counseling* (2005), in which she explores multicultural counselling competencies and client's multiple identities.

We have appropriated and significantly adapted the Sue *et al.* (1992) framework of multicultural counselling competencies to include the issues we raised in relation to the 'big 5' (or 7) issues of diversity. The idea of the matrix is extremely effective as a learning tool to understand the complex issues of diversity, made more interesting when it intersects the multiplicity of diversity with the multiple skills and competencies required of clinic work. The multicultural counselling competency framework is designed from a 3×3 matrix in which the characteristics of a 'culturally' skilled counsellor were cross-classified with the domains of multicultural counselling competencies (i.e. awareness, knowledge and skills) (Holcomb-McCoy, 2000, p. 85; Robinson, 2005, p. 25). Along the x-axis are:

1. awareness of assumptions, values, preconceived notions, biases and personal limitations;
2. understanding the worldview of the 'big 5' client's differences; and
3. developing appropriate intervention strategies and techniques.

Along the y-axis are the therapist's:

1. beliefs and attitudes;
2. knowledge; and
3. skills.

See Table 10.1 for details of the intersections of the three characteristics of counsellor skills and the three dimensions of multicultural competence. This is followed by a discussion on how therapists can develop competencies in these areas, including specific training strategies and interventions.

DISCUSSION

The combination of the six modalities (three dimensions of cultural competency with the three culturally skilled counsellor characteristics) makes this framework a sophisticated learning tool in counsellor training

---

BOX 10.1   INTERSECTION OF COUNSELLOR SKILLS AND DIMENSIONS OF MULTICULTURAL COMPETENCE

1. How able am I to recognise direct, indirect and non-verbal communication styles?
2. How able am I to recognise cultural and linguistic differences?
3. How sensitive am I to the myths and stereotypes of other cultures?
4. How genuinely concerned am I for the welfare of individuals from other cultures?
5. How able am I to articulate elements of my own culture?
6. How able am I to recognise relationships between and among cultural groups?

---

and education. Understanding the intersections of the characteristics and dimensions will enhance therapists' skills and competence, ensuring clinical effectiveness and producing positive outcomes in therapy. Beginning at the basic stage of the framework (i.e. therapists' awareness of their own assumptions about human behaviour, their preconceived notions, biases, values and personal limitations) towards being advocates at the public level on behalf of clients requires from therapists a commitment to the socio-political issues that gave rise to the competencies in the first place. Moreover, when each stage is appropriately complied with, the therapeutic process will result in culturally sensitive, gender harmonious and sexually unbiased therapy. In this situation clinicians are most likely to ask relevant questions, make accurate assessments, tailor their approach appropriately, be non-judgmental and not impose their beliefs and attitudes onto their clients. Pedersen (2002) developed a framework to describe the appropriate process for developing multicultural counselling competencies. This includes a needs assessment, definition of objectives and using appropriate training techniques. Pedersen proposes that clinicians begin by first assessing their current level of competency in the following areas by asking the following questions. See Box 10.1 (adapted from Pedersen, 2002, p. 9).

Experiential exercises, such as role-plays, role reversals, field placements, discussions, and direct immersion into another's culture can be very helpful to support therapists to challenge the assumptions and attitudes that may have about a particular cultural, racial, sexual or disabled group. Active participation in gay pride activities, social and political functions, community events and cultural and religious celebrations are but a few examples of ways that therapists can foster awareness, knowledge and understanding

Table 10.1 The framework of multicultural and diversity counselling competence (adapted from Sue et al, 1992)

	Awareness of assumptions, values, preconceived notions, biases and personal limitations	Understanding the world view of the 'big 5' client's differences	Developing appropriate intervention strategies and techniques
A. Beliefs and attitudes	1. Therapists are aware of how their own ethnic, gender, sexual beliefs, attitudes, experiences will influence the psychological process. 2. Therapists are aware of, and comfortable with, the differences that exist between themselves and their 'big 5' clients.	1. Therapists will value and respect differences by challenging preconceived ideas on race, gender and sexuality. 2. Therapists will contrast own beliefs and attitudes to those of the clients, in a non-judgemental way. 3. Therapists understand their own stereotypes, assumptions, racism, sexism, homophobia, religious, disability, class biases and ageism.	1. Recognise direct and indirect communication styles. 2. Being sensitive to non-verbal and para-linguistic clues. 3. Recognise linguistic and idiomatic differences related to race, gender, class, sexuality and disability. 4. Being sensitive to myths and stereotypes of the other. 5. Engage in honest self-reflection of negative and positive counter-transference reactions.
B. Knowledge	1. Therapists are aware and sensitive to their own and their clients' ethnic, cultural, gender and sexual histories. 2. Therapists are aware of the specific knowledge/s and understanding of their own race, gender, sexual orientation, class and disability experiences, and how its affects their definitions and biases of 'normality-abnormality' in clinical work. 3. Therapists have knowledge and understanding of how oppression, discrimination and stereotyping affect them personally and in their work.	1. Therapists acquire specific knowledge and information on the 'big 5' stigmatised identities. 2. Therapists understand how the 'big 5' identities may affect personality formation, vocational choices, manifestation of psychological disorders, help seeking and appropriateness of therapeutic approaches. 3. Therapists have understanding and knowledge about how the sociopolitical influences that impinge upon the lives of ethnic minorities, women, gays and lesbians, transgendered individuals, working classes, disabled people, the elderly and religious minorities.	1. Having knowledge of different therapeutic approaches suitability to clients of the 'big 5'. 2. Knowledge of how institutional barriers prevent clients from using mental health services. 3. Having knowledge of assessment instruments and use procedures and interpret findings keeping in mind the cultural and linguistic characteristics of the clients.

	4. Therapists are aware of their communication styles and its impact on the clients. 5. Therapists are aware of the limits of their competence and expertise.	4. Having knowledge about the role of the family, education, money, attitudes, values and behaviours of the clients and cultural/ethnic group they belong to. 5. Having knowledge of clients' race, ethnic, cultural, gender, sexual, class and disability histories.	
C. Skills	1. Therapists engage with learning and transformative process for themselves, so that they may become non-racist, pro-feminist, Queer affirmative, 'non-classist', 'non-disabilist' and non-ageist. 2. Therapists are aware of the role of interpreters, translators and support workers in clinical settings.	1. Therapists should familiarise themselves with current and relevant research on the 'big 5'. 2. Therapists attempt to understand the work of alternative mental health practitioners, traditional healers and indigenous healers. 3. Therapists should engage with special events, ceremonies, festivals and national celebrations related to groups and communities of the 'big 5'. 4. Therapists seek out educational, consultative and training experiences to enrich their understanding and effectiveness in working with the other.	1. Being skilled in interpreting, analysing and paying attention to verbal and non-verbal cultural ways in the transference and counter-transference responses. 2. Being skilled in the use of assessment and testing instruments. Aware of limitations related to race, gender, class, sexual orientations, disability, religion and age. 3. Being comfortable with clients seeking traditional healing. Make referrals to traditional healers if necessary. 4. Being comfortable with an interpreter or translator in the therapy room. Make referrals to bilingual therapists, if necessary. 5. Being skilled in the psycho-educational process of therapy – teaching clients to negotiate therapy goals, expectations, legal rights and counselling approaches. Engage in advocacy work on client's behalf.

of the other cultures, genders, sexualities, social classes, disabilities and ages. Knowledge and information helps 'clarify the alternatives and reduce the ambiguity of any given situation' (Pedersen, 2002, p. 9). d'Ardenne and Mahtani (1989, for example, have observed 'that counsellors working across cultures flounder when they fail to take into consideration a wide range of knowledge that is culturally significant to their clients' (p. 15). One way to avoid floundering is for therapists to ask the following questions. See Box 10.2 (adapted from Pedersen, 2002, p. 9):

The answers to these questions invariably lead to other questions or quest for knowledge. See Box 10.3 (adapted from Pedersen, 2002, p. 10).

Clinicians can meet these objectives through educational experiences (such as guided self-study via the internet or library research), audiovisual material and familiarisation with the latest research findings regarding

---

BOX 10.2

1. How well do I know the histories of cultures other than my own?
2. How well do I know about the resources available for teaching and learning in other cultures?
3. How well do I understand the way that my own culture is perceived by people in other cultures?
4. How much professional expertise do I have which is relevant to people of other cultures?
5. How much of the information that I have will be useful to people of other cultures?

BOX 10.3

1. Knowing about social services and how they are delivered in other cultures.
2. Knowing about culture shock and acculturative stress.
3. Knowing how members of other cultures interpret their own rules, customs and laws.
4. Knowing the patterns of non-verbal communication in other cultural groups.
5. Knowing how the similarities and differences between cultures are patterned.

BOX 10.4

1. How able am I to use the teaching and learning techniques of other cultures?
2. How able am I to establish empathic rapport with individuals from other cultures?
3. How able am I to analyse feedback accurately within the context of other cultures?
4. How able am I to develop new ideas in the contexts of other cultures?
5. How aware am I of the institutional barriers that may prevent minorities from accessing mental health services?

---

mental health, current legislation and new medical and/or treatment advances. Learning in this way will develop skills and competencies to work in multicultural and diversity settings. However, an unskilled and incompetent therapist will be exposed to both the social and the psychic environments – of themselves and their client – resulting in them making clinical miss judgements that may result in the clients' pre-mature termination. Moreover, they may carry out inappropriate interventions, work oppressively and have unsatisfactory outcomes in the therapy. Therapists need to assess themselves by asking the following questions found in Box 10.4 (adapted from Pedersen, 2002, p. 10).

It is not enough simply to read about the other or learn vicariously through other clinicians – therapists must spend time getting to know their clients and get an appreciation for what it is like to be in their clients' shoes and view the world through their clients' eyes. Sometimes a consultation with a professional with specific expertise is appropriate, even perhaps a traditional healer or spiritual leader (see Moodley and West, 2005).

TRAINING PARADIGMS TO SERVE THE UNDERSERVED

The responsibility for ongoing continuing education should be a requirement of the work setting as well as a requirement of therapists' professional development. Publications, such as The American Psychological Association's *Guidelines on Multicultural Education, Training, Research, Practice, and Organizational Change for Psychologists* (2003), while outlining principles relating to training clinicians in multicultural counselling, offers only limited use if it is not integrated into a more extensive training programme.

This should be one that incorporates an experiential component that exposes the clinician to actual case scenarios and hands-on situations while respecting the underlying foundation on which the guidelines are based. For example, psychology interns at the University of Colorado Health Sciences Centre are gaining experience in diversity through 'learning sign language to counselling refugees to spending two weeks conducting mental health screenings on an American Indian reservation' as a way to serve the underserved (Dittmann, 2004, p. 72).

Many of the concerns around 'ethics' arise from the increasing awareness that professionals who are not properly trained in this area potentially cause harm to their clients, since they unwittingly impose values of a so-called dominant culture, and do not approach therapy with the openness and flexibility that is so crucial when therapists work with those who are culturally different (Pedersen and Marsella, 1982). Training of clinicians on a more institutional level is also a key aspect of building multicultural competence. If therapists work in an environment where cultural diversity is rarely or never addressed, then therapists ignore a fundamental component of human relationships, reinforcing the philosophy that 'if we don't talk about it, it doesn't exist'.

Learning to identify, acknowledge and work within the reality of diversity makes clinicians amenable to critically examining their cultural biases instead of behaving as if they do not exist. In-service trainings, seminars, workshops, retreats and any number of continuing education opportunities can be invaluable at both professional and personal levels. Ultimately, if a clinician is in a work setting where diversity is acknowledged – and even celebrated – it encourages an open, accepting attitude towards clients. Sometimes even a small gesture, such as the placing of a rainbow sticker on one's office door conveys a 'gay-positive' message amongst therapists and clients alike. Advances in information technology, such as email and the internet, are also useful tools that provide us with a whole world in which to gather information and communicate with others. Once having all this cross-cultural information, learning and knowledge, a question arises: 'What do we do with it?' According to Harper and McFadden the,

> counseling professionals must stop to think about culture and counseling in a divergent, creative, practical, real-life, real-time, and futuristic way ... this means addressing the controversial issues that face (us) ..., for example, terrorism, racism, religious conflict, racial and ethnic violence, ... human injustice, AIDS and other diseases, the human impact of globalization and natural disasters, and alcohol and other drug addiction (Harper and McFadden, 2003, p. 388).

What a daunting task for the counselling professional ... and who is to care for the therapist? Ongoing group and individual supervision may be the very best approach to self-care, prevent internalisation of the negative impact of the therapist's external world, ameliorate clinicians' cultural sensitivity, monitor countertransference responses and encourage discussion of client vignettes. In analysing specific cases with supervisors and fellow clinicians, it is often much easier to identify problem areas such as judgemental attitudes, biases and stereotyping, all of which can result in a failed rapport between clinician and client. Finally, any form of involvement, engagement, training and learning in a multicultural and diversity context ought to be about having fun, enjoyment, pleasure, joissance and the joy of being different with the difference of the other.

CONCLUSION

In this chapter, we have discussed the various ways in which therapists could develop their career in counselling in a multicultural and diversity context. We have explored the ideas and current thinking in multicultural coun-selling, i.e. first, to replace multiculturalism in multicultural counselling and second, to integrate or converge the 'big 5' (or 7) stigmatised identities (race, gender, class, sexual orientation, disability, religion and age). Clearly, our current understanding of multiculturalism is limited and riddled with the complexities and confusions of the 'big 5' (or 7), resulting in the evolution of diversity as a term to embrace the integration of the 'big 5' (or 7) issues. Clearly, it is impossible to acquire all the cultural knowledge and philosophies, know the history, literature, arts and religious writings of the numerous ethnic minority groups that live in the West, let alone the other requirements for cultural competency of the 'big 5' (or 7). It may be impossible for any one therapist to be fully acquainted with the changing, flexible and dynamic worldviews of all these multicultural and diversity identities. As we have emphasised in this chapter, the multicultural and diversity competency framework is the cornerstone that governs the relationship in the therapy room. Thus, if a therapist is 'working with' a deaf client who also happens to be black, gay and working class, a critical multicultural and diversity competency framework will let the client 'be' (become) in therapy, through the client's own 'network of meanings' in a context of civil(ian) rights, cultural rights and human rights.

REFERENCES

American Psychological Association (2003) Guidelines on multicultural education, training, research, practice, and organizational change for psychologists. *American Psychologist*, 58(5), 377–402.

Arredondo, P. (1994) Multicultural training: a response. *The Counseling Psychologist*, 22, 304–314.

Arredondo, P., Toporek, R., Brown, S. P., Jones, J., Locke, D. C., Sanchez, J. and Stadler, H. (1996) Operationalization of the multicultural counseling competencies. *Journal of Multicultural Counseling and Development*, 24, 42–78.

Atkinson, D., Morten, G. and Sue, D. W. (1993) *Counseling American Minorities: A Cross-Cultural Perspective*. Dubuque, IA: Brown.

Bulmer, S. and Solomos, J. (1996) Introduction: race, ethnicity and the curriculum. *Ethnic and Racial Studies*, 19, 777–788.

d'Ardenne, P. and Mahtani, A. (1989) *Transcultural Counselling in Action*. London: Sage.

Dittmann, M. (2004) Training to serve the underserved. *APA, Monitor on Psychology*, November, 72–75.

Dyche, L. and Zayas, L. H. (2001) Cross-cultural empathy and training the contemporary psychotherapist. *Clinical Social Work Journal*, 29(3), 245–258.

Garfield, S. L. and Bergin, A. E. (1994) Introduction and historical overview. In A. E. Bergin and S. L. Garfield (eds) *Handbook of Psychotherapy and Behavior Change*. Chichester: Wiley, pp. 3–18.

Gilman, S. (1985) *Difference and Pathology: Stereotypes of Sexuality, Race and Madness*. Ithaca, NY: Cornell University Press.

Good, B. J. and Good, M. -J. D. (1982) Towards a meaning centred analysis of popular illness categories: "fright-illness" and "heat distress" on Iran. In A. J. Marsella and G. M. White (eds) *Cultural Conceptions of Mental Health and Therapy*. Drodrecht: Reidel, pp.141–166.

Halton, E. (1992) The cultic roots of culture. In R. Munch and N. J. Smelser (eds) *Theory of Culture*. Berkeley/Los Angeles: University of California Press, pp. 29–63.

Hardy, K. V. and Laszloffy, T. A. (1992) Training racially sensitive family therapists: context, content, and contact. *Family in Society*, 73(6), 364–370.

Harper, F. D. and McFadden, J. (2003) Conclusions, trends, issues, and recommendations. In F. D. Harper and J. McFadden (eds) *Culture and Counseling: New Approaches*. Boston: Allyn & Bacon, pp. 379–393.

Helms, J. and Richardson, T. Q. (1997) How 'Multiculturalism' obscures race and culture as differential aspects of counseling competency. In D. B. Pope-Davis and H. L. K. Coleman (eds) *Multicultural Counseling Competencies*. Thousand Oaks, CA: Sage, pp. 60–79.

Holcomb-McCoy, C. C. (2000). Multicultural counseling competencies: an exploratory factor analysis. *Journal of Multicultural Counseling and Development*, 28, 83–97.

Holcomb-McCoy, C. C. and Myers, J. E. (1999) Multicultural competence and counselor training: a national survey. *Journal of Counseling and Development*, 77(3), 294–302.

Lago, C. and Thompson, J. (1996) *Race, Culture and Counselling*. Buckingham: Open University Press.

Mahoney, M. J. and Patterson, K. M. (1992) Changing theories of changes: recent developments in counseling. In S. D. Brown and R. W. Lent (eds) *Handbook of Counseling and Psychology* (2nd edn.). New York: Wiley, pp. 665–689.

Moodley, R. (1999a) Challenges and transformation: counselling in a multi-cultural context. *International Journal for the Advancement of Counselling*, 21(2), 139–152.

Moodley, R. (1999b) Psychotherapy with ethnic minorities: a critical review. *Changes, International Journal of Psychology and Psychotherapy*, 17(2), 109–125.

Moodley, R. (2000a) Counselling and psychotherapy in a multicultural context: some training issues, part 1. *Counselling. Journal of the British Association for Counselling and Psychotherapy*, 11(3), 154–157.

Moodley, R. (2000b) Counselling and psychotherapy in a multicultural context: some training issues, part 2. *Counselling. Journal of the British Association for Counselling and Psychotherapy*, 11(4), 221–224.

Moodley, R. (2000c) Representation of subjective distress in black and ethnic minority patients: constructing a research agenda. *Counselling Psychology Quarterly*, 13(2), 159–174.

Moodley, R. (2003) Double, triple and multiple jeopardy. In C. Lago and B. Smith (eds) *Anti-Oppressive Practice in Counselling*. London: Sage, pp. 121–134.

Moodley, R. (2005) Diversity matrix revisited: criss-crossing multiple identities in clinical practice. Keynote paper at *'Multicultural and Counseling' Symposium*. Ithaca, NY: Cornell University.

Moodley, R. and West, W. (eds) (2005) *Integrating Traditional Healing Practices into Counseling and Psychotherapy*. Thousand Oaks, CA: Sage.

Moodley, R. and Curling, D. (2006) Race, culture, multiculturalism. In Yo Jackson (ed.) *Multicultural Psychology Encyclopedia*. Thousand Oaks, CA: Sage.

Moodley, R. and Palmer, S. (eds) (2006) *Race, Culture and Psychotherapy: Critical Perspectives in Multicultural Practice*. London: Sage.

Oropeza, B. A. C., Fitzgibbon, M. and Baron, A., Jr. (1991) Managing mental health crises of foreign college students. *Journal of Counseling and Development*, 69, 280–284.

Palmer, S. (ed) (2002) *Multicultural Counselling. A Reader*. London: Sage.

Parham, T. A. and Whitten, L. (2003) Teaching multicultural competencies in continuing education for psychologists. In D. B. Pope-Davis, H. L. K. Coleman, W. M. Liu and R. L. Toporek (eds) *Handbook of Multicultural Competencies*. Thousand Oaks, CA: Sage, pp. 562–574.

Pedersen, P. B. (1991) Multiculturalism as a generic approach to counseling. *Journal of Counseling and Development*, 70, 6–12.

Pedersen, P. B. (1999) *Hidden Messages in Culture-Centered Counseling: A Triad Training Model.* Thousand Oaks, CA: Sage.

Pedersen, P. B. (2002) Ethics, competence, and other professional issues. In P. B. Pedersen, J. G. Draguns, W. J. Lonner and J. E. Trimble (eds) *Counseling Across Cultures* (5th edn.). Thousand Oaks, CA: Sage, pp. 3–26.

Pedersen, P. B. and Ivey, A. (1993) *Culture-Centered Counseling and Interviewing Skills.* Westport, CT: Praeger.

Pedersen, P. B. and Marsella, A. J. (1982) The ethical crisis for cross-cultural counseling and therapy. *Professional Psychology*, 13, 492–500.

Ponterotto, J. G., Rieger, B. P., Barrett, A. and Sparks, R. (1994) Assessing multicultural counseling competence: a review of instrumentation. *Journal of Counseling and Development*, 72, 316–322.

Ridley, C. R. (1995) *Overcoming Unintentional Racism in Counseling and Therapy: A Practitioner's Guide to Intentional Intervention.* Thousand Oaks, CA: Sage.

Ridley, C. R. and Lingle, D. W. (1996) Cultural empathy in multicultural counseling: a multidimensional process model. In P. B. Pedersen, J. G. Draguns, W. J. Lonner and J. E. Trimble (eds) *Counseling Across Cultures* (4th edn.), Thousand Oaks, CA: Sage, pp. 21–46.

Ridley, C. R., Li, L. C. and Hill, C. L. (1998) Multicultural assessment: reexamination, reconceptualization and practical application. *The Counseling Psychologist*, 26, 827–910.

Robinson, T. L. (2005) *The Convergence of Race, Ethnicity, and Gender: Multiple Identities in Counseling* (2nd edn.) New Jersey: Pearson.

Sashidharan, S. (1986) Ideology and politics in transcultural psychiatry. In J. L. Cox (ed.) *Transcultural Psychiatry.* London: Croom Helm, pp. 158–178.

Smith, J. A., Harre, R. and VanLangenhove, L. (1995) *Rethinking Psychology.* London: Sage.

Speight, S. L., Myers, L. J., Cox, C. I. and Highlen, P. S. (1991) A redefinition of multicultural counseling. *Journal of Counseling and Development*, 70, 29–36.

Stuart, R. B. (2004) Twelve practical suggestions for achieving multicultural competence. *Professional Psychology: Research and Practice*, 35(1), 3–9.

Sue, D. W., Bernier, J. E., Daran, A., Feinberg, L., Pedersen, P., Smith, C. T. and Vasquez-Nuttale, G. (1982) Cross-cultural counseling competencies. *Counseling Psychologist*, 19, 45–52.

Sue, D. W. and Sue, D. (1990) *Counseling the Culturally Different* (2nd edn.). New York: Wiley.

Sue, D. W., Arredondo, P. and McDavis, R. J. (1992) Multicultural counseling competencies and standards: a call to the profession. *Journal of Counseling and Development*, 70, 477–486.

Sue, D. W., Carter, R. T., Casas, J. M., Fouad, N. A., Ivey, A. E., Jensen, M., LaFromboise, T. D., Manese, J. E., Ponterotto, J. G. and Vasquez-Nuttall, E. (1998) *Multicultural Counseling Competencies: Individual and Organizational Development*. Thousand Oaks, CA: Sage.

Taylor, R. L. (2000) Diversity within African American families. In D. H. Demo, K. R. Allen and M. A. Fine (eds) *Handbook of Family Diversity*. London: Oxford University Press, pp. 232–251.

Taylor, E. B. (1871[1920]) *Primitive Culture: Research into the Development of Mythology, Philosophy, Religion, Art, Custom*. London: Murray, reprint 1920.

Vontress, C. E. (1967) The culturally different. *Employment Services Review*, 4(10), 35–36.

Vontress, C. E. (1979) Cross-counseling: an existential approach. *Personnel and Guidance*, 58, 117–122.

Vontress, C. E. and Jackson, M. L. (2004) Reactions to the multicultural counseling competencies debate. *Journal of Mental Health Counseling*, 26(1), 74–80.

Willett, C. (1998) *Theorizing Multiculturalism*. Massachusetts: Blackwell.

Wrenn, C. G. (1962) The culturally encapsulated counselor. *Harvard Educational Review*, 32, 444–449.

11 HOW TO DEVELOP YOUR RESEARCH INTERESTS

Annette Fillery-Travis and David A. Lane

We qualify as counsellors, psychotherapists or chartered clinical or counselling psychologists and develop our expertise as therapists, with our primary interest being client benefit. We are also part of a profession which prizes its scientific credentials and the evidence base to our work. Yet, do we continue to regard evidence as central to our therapeutic practice or do we become embedded in a particular theoretical stance, ignoring contrary evidence? Do we, in practice, even eschew research altogether?

As a profession we argue that we need to re-examine our roles and activities given the emerging identities of ourselves and those we work with and the demand for evidence-based practice (Drabick and Goldfried, 2000). As we have seen in the earlier chapter on continuing professional development (CPD), every practitioner will now engage with research either as a consumer, a participant or as a researcher themselves. This chapter is based on an assumption that we do continue to prize research and seek to inform our practice by undertaking our own research. However it will not be a treatise on how to undertake academic research nor will we repeat all the excellent textbooks available on methodologies and approaches. Instead we will look at issues for practitioners as they undertake research within their own practice. This is an equally rigorous and robust process but one which serves the needs and aspirations of the practitioner more fully.

Before we being to develop a roadmap of how practitioners can approach research we will look at the underpinning debate around the scientist-practitioner model and the research paradigms available to us.

WHY DO RESEARCH?

The scientist-practitioner model is one of a practitioner working scientifically, using validated methods of assessment and treatment where they exist and where not, applying scientific principles to the individual case. This implies a mutual exchange between academic research in the field and professional practice. However there is a view that science has failed to inform practice. There has been a ranging debate on the principal reasons for this but effectively it is one of scale. The scientist is concerned with the rigorously and objectively generic whilst the practitioner is dealing with the individual within their practice. Thus the perception is of each looking to different horizons and using different skill sets to get there.

However it is clear that separate camps for research and practice are no longer tenable. Dawes (1994) identifies that it is an element of professional responsibility for the practitioner to activity seek out research evidence to inform their work and not to rely instead on the dubious validity of professional experience. Thus it is not surprising that as the field of professional psychology grows, the newer professional entities such as coaching psychologists, for example, are choosing the scientist-practitioner model as a basis of practice. Stoltenberg, Pace and Kashubeck-West (2000) claim that the model provides a framework through which important scholarly and practice-based advances can continue to occur. They argue that psychologists cannot be competent in the delivery of their practice unless they know how to evaluate it. Conducting one's own research is an essential precursor to understanding and utilising the published research literature in an informed way.

In a similar vein, Belar and Perry (1992) propose that the scientist-practitioner model provides an invaluable framework for theory building whereby, through a systematic approach to enquiry, random observations can be shaped into hypotheses that can presage the development of new theories and interventions which have substantive implications for professional practice. They argue that the influence of science is not always instantaneous but does shape how psychologists work.

Thus the scientist-practitioner model can be seen as integrating the three complementary roles of practitioner, consumer of research and producer of research (Crane and McArthur Hafen, 2002). As Lane and Corrie (2006) argue, this is not the same as the evidence-based practitioner, whose role is one of implementing specific interventions and consuming research to stay up to date. The scientist practitioner is more participatory and is concerned with integrating both the consumption and production of research in practice with a distinct professional identity.

That participation also informs the model of science which is appropriate for practice-led enquiry. For example, counselling psychology has actively promoted alternatives to the narrow definitions of science. Van Duerzen-Smith (1990) suggests that psychology has traditionally organised itself around discovering objective facts rather than exploring what it means to be human, with all the dilemmas and choices that this entails. For her, psychology needs to embrace more fully its artistic and dialogic dimensions over and above its preoccupation with what she sees as overly narrow scientific principles. As a discipline strongly connected with humanistic values and principles, counselling psychology argues for a scientist-practitioner model that is practice led, phenomenologically focused, respectful of diversity and interested in the uncovering of subjective truths (Woolfe and Dryden, 1996).

In summary it is now regarded as good practice for practitioners to be engaged in research and audit – evaluation, research, development or more generally enquiry. Through this engagement the practitioner can access and integrate knowledge from their clinical practice with that from research to achieve a real sustainability of practice where they are able to function within diverse environments and handle significant ambiguity.

But is there anything unique about practitioner research or is it simply a scaled-down version of academic research? You, as a practitioner, will be bringing your practice to the research so the generic model of 'research' as meaning a sterile, objective and disconnected activity, undertaken as separate from practice, is not appropriate. The practitioner researcher (or what Lane and Corrie, 2006, term the modern scientist-practitioner) is in the thick of it getting their hands dirty. The model of science which will be used will be very different and it is this which we will consider next.

WHAT'S DIFFERENT ABOUT PRACTITIONER RESEARCH?

Research has traditionally been associated with a type of knowledge production known as mode 1. It was epitomised by a researcher working within a single discipline looking at an issue isolated from its economic, social and political context. Often nicknamed 'curiosity-led research' this type of research did not have to relate directly to practice in the belief that through 'development' work a use might evolve for it in the future. Nowadays there is a universal requirement to identify a return on investment and research has not been immune to this driver. The consequence has been a move to mode 2 working, where the potential application of the research to practice is considered at the very start of the work. These 'real-world' questions will often require transdisciplinary working with others and will need to take into account a range of stakeholders (Gibbons *et al.*, 1994). Practitioner research is by definition 'issue-led research' and as such sits very neatly as a mode 2 type of activity. Indeed McLeod (1994) defines practitioner research as 'research carried out by practitioners for the purpose of advancing their own practice'.

There are two important elements to this definition:

1. The activity is controlled by the practitioner and the research is conducted by them with their own constructs.
2. The researcher is explicit about its purpose, i.e. the research is embedded within practice addressing an issue of practice.

There are certain general characteristics of practitioner research (Shaw, 2003):

- The research questions, aims and outcomes are determined by the practitioners themselves.
- The research is usually designed to have a benefit or an impact which is immediate and direct.
- It focuses on the professional's own practice and/or that of his or her immediate peers.
- It is small scale and short term.
- Usually it will be self-contained, and not part of a larger research programme.
- Data collection and management is typically carried out as a lone activity.
- It is one kind of 'own account research'.
- The focus is not restricted. While it will commonly be evaluative, it may be descriptive, developmental or analytical.

When you are considering your own research it is clear that the overall size and content of the research has to be appropriate to you as the practitioner, i.e. something which can be undertaken and managed whilst working in practice. It is one of the main challenges for any practitioner researcher to keep the scale of their enquiry appropriate to their time and resources.

STRIVING FOR INTEGRITY IN THE RESEARCH PROCESS

It is when you research that you are effectively putting your theoretical basis forward and deciding to review it. This makes it, in effect, a deeply personal experience and reflexivity becomes an important consideration for the would-be researcher.

Within the positivistic tradition which dominated quantitative research for so long researchers strove for detached indifference to their research. This is a paradigm which sits well within mode 1 working but as our previous discussion illustrates it does not sit well with mode 2.

The researcher and the practitioner are two modes of working which cannot be completely separated – your beliefs, values and knowledge about your practice will influence how you view events and your role. If we take a constructionist or critical realist view of knowledge (as we discuss later), i.e. we believe that knowledge is relative to the perspective from which it is viewed, then it is clear that the researcher practitioner must take his or her 'view' into account when considering the research.

RESEARCH PARADIGMS –
IDENTIFYING YOUR WORLD VIEW

The 'view' of the researcher will influence everything from the choice of research question to the methodology employed to explore it. It is effectively the paradigm under which the research activity will take place. In a real sense this research paradigm will determine the whole framework of the research.

We will take a short exploration of paradigms here with particular reference to the practitioner researcher. A first point of reference for this exploration is to identify the type of research which you are considering.

Is it based upon:

- developing a broad knowledge base that is (hypothetically) universal and generalisable;
- optimising effective practice through 'standardising' aspects of technical delivery (such as developing treatment manuals); and
- justifying the use of a particular practice by demonstrating its effectiveness.

Such issues are underpinned by a view that reality (truth) exists independently of us. Researchers are required to apply the right process and the answers will be revealed. Thus they are empirically bounded relying upon two assumptions. The first is that scientific observation is neutral. The second is that knowledge of the world becomes more robust according to the extent to which scientists agree and are able to generalise their findings.

While it is often assumed that this is the 'best' way to do research, it can be problematic because the phenomena of interest to us are frequently dilemmas, values, choices and relationships. This approach also fails to take account of the realities of practice, where innovations and improvisations are common. Although favoured academically it may be less well suited to the client practice level. For the practitioner, the pursuit of truth is less informative than the pursuit of knowledge that is practical.

An alternative to the empirical approach to research and one that is now frequently used is the idea of evidence-based practice, or the 'what works school', which is founded on the concept of falsification. In its more recent variants (Lakatos, 1970) it is concerned with processes that answer such questions as:

- What are the relative merits of each competing theory in the context of a given enquiry (in terms of the extent to which they are falsifiable)?

- What are my own criteria of falsifiability (that is, what are my own individual theoretical preferences and at what point would I be prepared to reject them)?
- What are the criteria against which I assess the validity of my hunches, intuition and spontaneous actions?
- What are the factors (personal assumptions, people, situations and work contexts) that have led me to reject certain ideas in favour of others?

It is useful, for example, in exploring the assumptions that underpin a particular service provision (for example, the use of a cognitive-behavioural approach to the treatment of depression in a clinical setting) where we can explore the strengths and limitation of the theory to the setting.

What is appealing about this approach for the practitioner researcher is that it creates a place for intuition, creativity and improvisation and provides a framework for their systematic use. Within this framework any theory can be admitted to conjecturing, as long as the circumstances in which we would be prepared to relinquish it are clearly specified. It places a priority on:

1. working with the best theories available (rather than aiming to uncover universal or generalisable findings);
2. ensuring best practice by working towards continual refinement of existing theories; and
3. continually refining theory through generating conjectures that can be shaped into falsifiable hypotheses for rigorous testing.

However, in a critique of empiricist approaches to research Thomas Kuhn (1970) argued that while this all seems very rational, in reality scientists, just like practitioners, look for evidence which confirms, not disputes, their hypothesis. We are disinclined to test and reject favoured ideas (paradigms) in the way that the falsification position suggests.

In the light of a Kuhnian story about science, we would be concerned in shaping our research agenda with questions such as:

- In which paradigm(s) was I trained?
- Which paradigms are most influential in my practice now? How have I got here?
- To what 'community of scientists' (in a broad sense) do I currently belong?
- What types of reasoning, formulation, creativity and intervention does this paradigm encourage and discourage? Most particularly:
  - given that different paradigms emphasise different questions, how would the nature of my research enquiries change if I switched paradigm?

This helps us to guard against using research to perpetuate an existing frame of practice.

In an even more fundamental critique, the concept of an objective reality to be uncovered through research is rejected within this paradigm. If we were to argue that there is no such thing as an objective reality then we must remain sceptical about any form of knowledge that purports to uncover it. This position, advocated by social constructionism, is a radical philosophical challenge to the empiricist worldview and to research based upon it (see Burr, 1995; Gergen, 1985, 1992 for an overview).

From this perspective we might argue that:

1. All knowledge is historically, culturally and socially embedded;
2. What we regard as truth or reality is, in fact, the product of on-going social exchanges through which meanings are communicated, negotiated and co-constructed; and
3. Different types of social exchange predispose us towards certain types of action over others (Burr, 1995).

Implicit in this worldview is the belief that there are no 'facts' which exist apart from our constructions of them; truth becomes relative, and no single perspective (including a scientific one) can have greater validity than any other.

If we were to adopt this view we would seek a research process that would help us develop:

- A fuller appreciation of how social and political discourses lead us to regard certain types of knowledge as more rigorous than others.
- Greater understanding of how we have been enabled and constrained in our work by the dominant (empiricist) discourse about science.
- A more detailed understanding of how we innovate and intervene through gathering practitioners' 'common sense' accounts.
- Knowledge of 'common assumptions' about professional practice that guide our actions.

This approach places a premium on our reflexivity which includes self-criticism and this alerts us to the human subjective processes involved in undertaking research; that is, knowledge is relative to their own perspective (Edwards and Potter, 1992; Potter and Wetheral, 1987).

An alternative critique has been posed by Roy Bhaskar (1975, 1979) and Manicas and Secord (1983) and has led to a story about science termed 'critical realism'.

Like social constructionism, critical realism recognises that knowledge is a product of historical and social processes and that discourse plays a central role in shaping human reality. However, critical realism (as opposed to the naïve realism of the empiricist worldview) proposes that our experience of the world is based on the interaction of many systems including those that exist independently of our discursive constructions of them. In other words, there is a social reality which exists independently of discourse. This world comprises substantive underlying structures against which any socially constructed reality must be negotiated.

If there are realities which exist apart from socially embedded discourse, and which shape our experiences and actions, then we need a way to investigate them. This transforms the task of science into one of inventing theories that aim to represent the world. As Manicas and Secord suggest,

> Sciences generate their own rational criteria in terms of which theory is accepted or rejected and can be deemed to be rational because there is a world that exists independently of our ability to know it (1983, p. 401).

In addition to the issues raised by social constructionism, questions through which we critique our practice and our research upon it would include:

- As agents of change, how do we go about engineering desirable outcomes in our work?
- What tools, strategies and interventions do we need to achieve them?
- What are the external factors that we need to take into account to maximise the chances of engineering a preferred outcome (including any practical constraints of time, money or context)?
- What are the ways in which different types of professional intervention enable or constrain the self-interventions of our clients?

Adopting this perspective would lead to research processes which would have the potential to fundamentally change the nature of our practice.

The research paradigm you choose will be the one which is more congruent with your beliefs, values and practice; therefore, it is not so much a choice as a recognition of the 'view' that you are bringing to your research. However, once identified, it will provide a framework for the entire activity. Such a framework can be particularly useful for when we research we are stepping into the unknown, asking a question which has not been answered before. There may be an expected view of what answers the research will uncover but it will not be certain. Some practitioners find this exciting but all will appreciate that sitting with this level of uncertainty can be challenging.

It is at this point that having a road map for the process of practitioner research can hold the ambiguity at bay and we will consider this next. Such a road map can provide structure for your research by identifying how research happens and what are the essential elements are and when they should be addressed. Some practitioners may feel that this is too constricting but that would be too limited a view. Such a road map should not constrain choice of methodology, analysis or approach – it should facilitate fuller exploration of these by providing a design for the overall activity.

A ROAD MAP FOR RESEARCH

In thinking about research, we have found it helpful to organise our reasoning skills around three domains. These reflect the creation of understanding in clinical practice (Lane and Corrie, 2006) but as applied to research of practice. We would see these as relevant to psychological practice across all areas of application. These are:

- purpose;
- perspective; and
- process.

PURPOSE – WHAT DO YOU WANT TO ACHIEVE, WHO FOR AND WHY?

He who stands on tiptoe does not stand firm. (Lao-Tzu; 500 BCE translation 1989).

In undertaking any psychological enquiry, it is vital to be clear about its fundamental purpose. The shape that your enquiry subsequently takes and the stories you tell about that enquiry will follow on from here. Therefore, the starting point is a shared learning journey between you and the stakeholders for your research and begins as you define the purpose of your work together. This gives rise to the following questions:

- What are you setting out to achieve (you might call this outputs, results, processes of change, relationship or journey.)? How do you explain this; what is the story you seek to tell that gives rise to the research?
- Is that story seeking to demonstrate a relationship between events (traditionally to prove or disprove a relationship) or is the story about exploring a relationship, one of understanding or action?
- What is the value of the research to the stakeholder? What is their purpose in engaging in this encounter with you, here and now? What do you need to do to make it possible for stakeholders to tell their story, to feel heard in the research?
- What type of client purpose is served by your research?
- What boundaries do you place on the purpose of the research that would not be consistent with a practitioner researcher stance?

There is one essential task in this section but it will take a significant part of your time as a researcher to achieve it and that task is developing your research question.

DEVELOP YOUR RESEARCH QUESTION

The research question is the hub and anchor of all of the activity within the research. It informs what methodology is appropriate and what data should be collected. You will actively return to it repeatedly throughout the research to check that the research is on the right track. A poorly defined question will spread confusion and leave you lost within the activity.

The research question will again be:

- Informed by the researcher's paradigm as identified above.
- Explicitly informed by the practice of the practitioner. A characteristic of work-based research in general and practitioner research specifically is that it will draw out the knowledge that is tacit within your practice and make it explicit.
- Must be an area you are passionate about. It will represent significant investment in time and resources you will need this passion to sustain you.
- It must be tractable, i.e. it can be answered by research.
- Not so broad that it will take a lifetime to answer it.
- But of sufficient depth to warrant research.
- Tempered by identification of the constraints you are working under in terms of 'bounded rationality'. A researcher practitioner will often have to be content with the sufficient in terms of a research element instead of the optimum.
- Inclusive of stakeholders views.

The question must be specific, concise and well defined so that all participants and stakeholders are agreed upon it. This is often not a trivial task. An example may be of help here.

If one was to ask:

Does coaching improve the performance of executives?

Then, assuming we are agreed on what constitutes coaching, there are still two words which have a variety meanings depending upon your perspective – these are 'improve' and 'performance'.

From the perspective of an HR professional who is a stakeholder 'improved performance' may mean increase in scores on 360 degree feedback. For the manager of the coachee it may mean 10% increase in sales. While from the viewpoint of the coach it may be perceived satisfaction from the coachee that they have addressed certain issues which were designed to improve performance.

Obviously the question needs to be more specific and the terms 'success' and 'performance' need to be strictly defined for the research.

Whilst reflecting upon the research question it is also necessary to find out about the issue you are interested in. Researchers will often either assume no one has ever asked their question before and miss valuable information or assume that their question has already been answered and perpetuate a false premise. The researcher should always carry out some desk work to find out about their issue – what have others identified; do they share similar views upon the subject of the enquiry? What is already known? Does it speak to my question? Does it inform my question? This 'literature review' will be a piece of desk research in its own right. But whilst reading, and critically analysing what is read, you will find your research question will evolve and develop to become honed and fit for purpose. A word of caution at this point is that many researchers find it difficult to hone down the question as they discover many tantalising side issues and alternative viewpoints. It can seem overwhelming! It is at this point that critical friends become important.

RECRUIT CRITICAL FRIENDS WHO WILL PROVIDE THE 'GRIT FOR THE OYSTER'

Within academic research the researcher will spend a significant time in critical analysis of their research plans with colleagues and collaborators producing a planning document or research proposal detailing exactly what the enquiry is about, why it is important, how it is to be conducted etc. Within the proactive practice context there is a tendency to side track this process and the research then suffers from not having a thorough grounding. Critical friends or collaborators are essential for the development of a robust research plan. They will remind you of your limitations and identify when you are being waylaid by interesting side lines away from your research question.

ENGAGEMENT WITH OTHER STAKEHOLDERS IS ALSO CRITICAL AT THIS STAGE

The research may be undertaken purely for interest by the practitioner but there will always be other stakeholders who will have an interest in the activity. Clear identification of stakeholders and their particular needs will enhance and develop the form of the research. They will bring other perspectives to the research and we will deal with these explicitly when we discuss ethics in the next section.

PERSPECTIVE – HOW YOU ARE GOING TO DO IT AND WHY?

We have identified that the way you will have framed your research question will be heavily influenced by your own beliefs in respect to your practice and what your dominant research paradigm is. This influence will carry through to your choice of route for getting the information to address your inquiry – your research methodology. There are a great many texts looking at research methodologies in the social sciences and we list a number of texts which are helpful to the practitioner below. These books provide a thorough listing of the available methodologies and the corresponding approaches and techniques. Several approaches, such as action research and soft systems methodology, are well suited for the 'insider' researcher who is fully aware of his or her organisation or practice issues. The insider knowledge of the research practitioner can place him or her at an advantage over the external researcher. But as identified before the researcher must also guide against subjectivity working against their inquiry.

It seems a truism to say the choice of research approach is dependent upon the question but novice researchers often find the choice difficult as they are still 'looking for the right answer'. If the research question is specific and well constructed then the approach will often follow:

Going back to our earlier example:

It is clear that with the HR professional and the manager as stakeholders a quasi-experimental design can be used in which a group of executives are coached and their 360 assessments or sales figures compared before and after coaching. There will be a large number of variables to be considered such as length of coaching and the coaching process but a literature review may identify the relative ranking of these variables and their corresponding influence thus allow them to be controlled.

With the coach the inquiry has more depth. The emphasis is on the coachee's perception of what has happened to them. In this inquiry a case study, focus group or survey can all be brought to bear depending upon the context and access to the individuals.

It is often the case with practitioner research that multiple tools will be used within the inquiry. For example you may want to use a questionnaire to obtain a viewpoint from a relatively large sample of people and then interview a sub-set of this sample to explore the information in more depth. At the same time you will be looking into the literature on the subject to see if any other researcher has found similar findings which can inform your study. This planned use of multiple techniques is an example of triangulation and enhances the validity of your findings. You are, in fact, seeking as many perspectives on the issue under investigation as possible and identifying any commonality. In other inquiries the researcher may not be interested in the commonality of experience but just that of the individual so will only conduct in-depth case studies.

We have already explored how the perspective of the researcher can determine the dominant research paradigm but there are also the other participants within the research to consider. Your stakeholders or research subjects (clients) also bring perspectives of their own which will inform your work together and which must, therefore, be given equal consideration in the inquiry that follows. Engaging with these perspectives gives rise to questions such as:

- On what sort of research journey are you and your client engaged?
- Some journeys proscribe certain routes (perspectives or methodologies). How do you ensure coherence between your and your client's journey?
- What are the values, beliefs, knowledge and competences that you each bring to the encounter?
- What do you do to ensure that the client is able to explore the values, beliefs, knowledge and competence within the research encounter?

Working with and honouring these alternative perspectives is the realm of research ethics – an essential element of the whole practice of research. There are a range of ethical guidelines available to researcher practitioners (for example BPS) and the reader is strongly recommended to review their own professional bodies guidelines. Obviously clinical research is bounded by the local board of ethics and each of these boards will have lists of contacts with whom you can discuss your study if appropriate. For social science research the ethical procedure may be less onerous but this can not be done as a 'tick box' form to be completed and then forgotten. The potential for doing harm within an inquiry through omission or commission is very real. The researcher is in a position of power and as such must take responsibility for their actions as within any psychological interaction. You must leave the lightest of foot prints within the world of the client or participant.

PROCESS – THE RESEARCH ACTIVITY ITSELF

In effect the research activity starts at the point where you first consider the structuring of your research question. It is therefore pivotally important that a research diary is kept from that point to capture the work that is done as it is done. An analogy is with the lab book of the clinical or natural scientist – the place where all the work on data collection, interpretation and analysis is stored.

Research is by its very nature problematic and unpredictable. This can be difficult to handle within a research environment but as a practitioner researcher you may not have the flexibility to respond as you may wish. Issues such as resource management may intercede and stop the full fulfilment of your research aims. Bounded rationality is a concept which warns us that as researchers we will, at times, need to be content with the sufficient and not the optimum which we originally designed. If faced with a substantial rethink then use of critical friends and any external stakeholders can again be pivotal at the redesign stage.

There will be a time when your research activity has provided you with data which you can then analyse and interpret. At this point it is useful to consider the following:

> Data are not information. Information is data endowed with relevance and purpose. Knowledge is information endowed with application. Wisdom is knowledge endowed with age and experience (Davenport, 2002, p. 10).

Therefore although as researchers we may be shy of disseminating our results it is only through sharing our experience and the outputs that our data becomes knowledge.

If knowledge is information endowed with application, our concern as practitioners might lie with the forms of knowledge we are trying to describe. Recently it has been argued that we can view knowledge as being of four main types (Scott *et al.*, 2004):

- Type 1: **Disciplinary knowledge**. Scientific description is seen as the superior form of knowledge and the only possible way of seeing the world. The practice setting may be a source of data but knowledge is valued for its own sake not for its application. This type of knowledge rarely forms part of practitioner-based research.
- Type 2: **Technical rationality**. The practitioners are required to divest themselves of their practice knowledge in favour of knowledge that transcends their local and particular knowledge. This framework supports the idea of evidence-based practice in that the concern is not to understand the political, ethical or consequential contexts for work but rather 'what works'. The emphasis is on efficiency not knowledge for its own sake. This does form the type of research which is asked of practitioners particularly in relation to evaluating therapies.
- Type 3: **Dispositional and transdisciplinary knowledge**. This is based on the assumption that knowledge is non-predictable, non-determinist and contextualised. Practice is a deliberative action concerned with making appropriate decisions about practical problems in specific situations. The emphasis is on knowledge developed by the individual through reflection

on practice. This is often favoured by practitioners and can lead to much improved local services as it address local issues.

- Type 4: **Critical knowledge.** This is based on the critique of existing forms of knowledge. Its purpose is explicitly political and the emphasis is on change. Individuals are seen to be positioned within discursive and institutional structures which influence how they understand themselves and others. Critiques of that understanding are encouraged and there is an attempt to undermine the conventional knowledge discourses with which both scientists and practitioners work. This is rarely attempted but can form a serious basis for critiquing our endeavours; unfortunately, such critiques often appear from service users or outside the profession rather than from within it.

Type 1 is seen as lying within the domain of the academic/university-based researcher, but the other types may represent a contribution to knowledge from practice, i.e. how you can achieve impact for your research. Achieving impact in the world takes place through workshops, reports to sponsors, conferences, community of practice, changes to practice and policy and yes though publishing and that is the subject of the next chapter!

GOING FORWARD

There is the potential for the university-based world of science and the work-based world of applied practice to collaborate, thus breaking down the science-practice divide. Universities are now acknowledging that knowledge is produced not only by them but by the world of practice and they have a role in recognising and accrediting that knowledge. Garnett (2004) has identified key contributions that university/work-based partnerships can make to building intellectual capital within work-based projects, including exploring the nature and implications of the apparent lineage between work-based learning, knowledge creation, organisational decision making and bounded rationality.

The partnership between the work place (practice) and the university (science) provides a powerful resource to overcome the research-practice divide. Thus practitioner-led research can be about impact not simply about originality. It has value in its own right not as a poor relation to academically driven research.

REFERENCES

Belar, C. D. and Perry, N. W. (1992) National conference on scientist-practitioner education and training for professional practice of psychology. *American Psychologist*, 47, 71–75.

Bhaskar, R. (1975) *A Realist Theory of Science*. Leeds: Leeds Books.

Bhaskar, R. (1979) *The Possibility of Naturalism. A Philosophical Critique of the Contemporary Human Sciences*. Atlantic highlands, NJ: Humanities Press.

Burr, V. (1995) *An Introduction to Social Constructionism*. London: Routledge.

Crane, D. R. and Hafen, M. (2002) Meeting the needs of evidence-based practice in family therapy: developing the scientist-practitioner model. *Journal of Family Therapy*, 24, 113–124.

Davenport. K. (2002) Northeast Iowa Regional Library System, in a letter printed in the May 1, 2002. *Library Journal*, 127(8).

Dawes, R. M. (1994) *House of Cards. Psychology and Psychotherapy Built on Myth*. New York: The Free Press.

Drabick, D. A. G. and Goldfried, M. R. (2000) Training the scientist-practitioner for the 21st century. Putting the bloom back on the rose. *Journal of Clinical Psychology*, 56(3), 327–340.

Edwards, D. and Potter, J. (1992) *Discursive Psychology*. London: Sage.

Garnett, J. (2004) *The Potential of University Work Based Learning to Contribute to the Intellectual Capital of Organisations*. London: National Centre for Work Based Learning Partnerships, Middlesex University.

Gergen, K. (1985) The social constructionist movement in modern psychology. *American Psychologist*, 40, 266–275.

Gergen, K. (1992) Toward a post-modern psychology. In S. Kvale (ed.) *Psychology and Postmodernism*. Beverley Hills, CA: Sage.

Gibbons, M., Limoges, C., Nowotny, H., Schwartzmann, S., Scott, P. and Trow, M. (1994) *The New Production of Knowledge: The Dynamics of Science and Research in Contemporary Societies*. London: Sage.

Kuhn, T. S. (1970) *The Structure of Scientific Revolutions*. Chicago: University of Chicago Press.

Lakatos, I. (1970) Falsification and the methodology of scientific research. In I. Lakatos and A. Musgrave (eds), *Criticism and the Growth of Knowledge*, Cambridge: Cambridge University Press.

Lane, D. A. and Corrie, S. (2006) *The Modern Scientist Practitioner: A Guide to Practice in Psychology*. London: Routledge.

Lao-Tzu (1989) *Tao Te Ching*. Translated by Stephen Mitchell (1989) London: Macmillan.

Manicas, P. T. and Secord, P. F. (1983) Implications for psychology of the new philosophy of science. *American Psychologist*, 38, 399–413.

McLeod, J. (1994) *Doing Counselling Research*. London: Sage.

Potter, J. and Wetherell, M. (1987) *Discourse and Social Psychology: Beyond Attitudes and Behaviour*. London: Sage.

Scott, D., Brown, A. J., Lunt, I. and Thorne, L. (2004) *Professional Doctorates: Integrating Academic and Professional Knowledge*. Bucks: Open University Press.

Shaw, I. (2003) Qualitative research and outcomes in health, social work and education. *Qualitative Research*, 3(1), 57–77.

Stoltenberg, C. D., Pace, T. M. and Kashubeck-West, S. (2000) *Counselling Psychology and the Scientist-Practitioner Model: An Identity and Logical Match, Not an Option.* (on CD).

van Duerzen-Smith, E. (1990) Philosophical underpinnings of counselling psychology. *Counselling Psychology Review*, 5(2), 8–12.

Woolfe, R. and Dryden, W. (1996) *Handbook of Counselling Psychology*. London: Sage.

USEFUL TEXTS FOR RESEARCH METHODS

Bell, J. (1999) *Doing Your Research Project* (3rd edn). Milton Keynes: Open University Press. (ISBN 0-335-20388-4) (approx. £12).

Blaxter, L., Hughes, C. and Tight, M. (1996) *How to Research*. Milton Keynes: Open University Press. (ISBN 0-335-19452-4) (approx. £12).

Gill, J. and Johnson, P. (1997) *Research Methods for Managers* (2nd edn). London: Paul Chapman Publishing Ltd. (ISBN 185396350X).

Marshall, P. (1997) *Research Methods: How to Design and Conduct a Successful Project*. Plymouth: How to Books Ltd.

USEFUL TEXTS FOR PRACTITIONER RESEARCH FRAMEWORKS

Choo, C. (1998) *The Knowing Organization*. New York: Oxford University Press.

Edwards, D. and Potter, J. (1992) *Discursive Psychology*. London: Sage.

Gill, R. (1998) *Modes of Arguing: Theoretical Positioning*. London: Sage.

Glaser, B. G. and Strauss, A. L. (1967) *The Discovery of Grounded Theory: Strategies for Qualitative Research*. Chicago: Aldine.

Potter, J. and Wetherell, M. (1987) *Discourse and Social Psychology: Beyond Attitudes and Behaviour*. London: Sage.

Robson, R. (1993) *Real World Research*. Oxford: Blackwell Publishers. (ISBN-0-631-17689-6).

Schensul, J. J. and Schensul, S. L. (1992) Collaborative research: methods of enquiry for social change. In M. D. Lecompte, W. L. Millroy and J. Preissle (eds) *Handbook of Qualitative Research in Education*. New York: Academic Press, pp. 161–199.

Zuber-Skerritt, O. (1996) *New Directions in Action Research*. London: Falmer Press (ISBN 0 7507 0880).

12   HOW TO WRITE FOR PUBLICATION

David Winter and Del Loewenthal

One of the principal features of research, as for example indicated in its definition by the British National Health Service (NHS), is that its findings are planned to be open to critical examination and accessible to all who could benefit from them, or open to 'public dissemination'. Publication of research results is one of the main ways, albeit not the only way, by which this may be achieved.

More selfishly, one often hears the maxim 'publish or perish', since one's publications are often a major consideration in selection for jobs or in recommendations for promotion, particularly in the academic field. In addition, it is possible to obtain a PhD on the basis of one's published work. Publications are also increasingly a factor by which not only individuals, but also institutions are judged. For example, university departments in the UK are periodically subjected to a research assessment exercise (RAE), which results in their being assigned a rating largely on the basis of publications by their staff. The rating received, as well as indicating the prestige of the department, determines the level of funding which it receives. The NHS is moving towards a similar system.

Such pressures have often led to 'salami' publishing, in which a researcher squeezes as many papers as possible, often each with minimal content, out of a study. In view of this, the emphasis, at least in the university RAE, has shifted from the quantity to the quality of the publications produced by a department. Yet, despite all this, the publication of research can importantly lead to more effective practice and better decision making. Such published research may of course focus on aspects of the process or outcome of psychotherapy or counselling and theoretical or methodological issues.

WHAT HAS BEEN PUBLISHED ON PUBLISHING?

In reviewing the mainly psychological literature on writing for publication, many papers were found to be based on the author's personal experiences rather than empirical research. Nevertheless, we consider it important to start with what has gone through the relative rigours of different publication processes as a basis for our own suggestions (which are also not always empirically based).

DIVERSE PERSPECTIVES

Dorn *et al.* (1986) typically show the diverse perspectives that are offered regarding the prospect of getting published. They include:

- combining cognitive, affective and behavioural domains;
- an exploration of writing as personal reflection;
- writing as an act of persuasion;
- a perception of writing as rhythm.

BARRIERS AND RESOURCES

In a survey of practitioners who have published, Staudt *et al.* (2003) view writing for publication as part of professional practice. They examined:

- What facilitates practitioners writing for publication;
- What barriers they experience.

In a survey of those publishing their first article, Dies (1993) offers a similar approach regarding:

- difficult obstacles encountered;
- types of resources found most helpful.

THE BOOK

For those wishing to write a book, Ogren (1998) in a heuristic study on the role of creativity in the publication process concludes that the elements of the writing for publication process should be undertaken in the following order:

- researching the market;
- writing the proposal;
- writing the query letter;
- writing the sample chapters;
- identifying potential publishers.

Ogren also stresses that sufficient time must be devoted to the writing and publication process, and that the most crucial challenge lies in incorporating creativity, organisation and business sense.

PERSONAL IDENTITY

Clarkson (2000) explores the question 'whose idea is it anyway?' This may for some be an important obstacle/barrier as Casanave and Vandrick (2003) explore in terms of 'scholarly identity construction'. They examine the practical, political and personal issues involved in:

- concerns faced by newcomers;
- interactions between authors, editors and membership reviewers;
- the construction of personal identity through writing.

THE JOURNAL ARTICLE

For those wishing to publish in journals it is suggested that it is important to explore the criteria used for accepting journal manuscripts (Weiss, 1989). Cottone and Wolf (1984) provide a summary of the publication manual of the American Psychological Association. However, it is worth noting that Ono *et al.* (1996), in examining these guidelines, recommend:

- Report participant participation if individual differences are the primary concern of the study.
- Ignore the requirement of reporting the statistical significance level.
- Do not be overly concerned with the word count.

Thus it would appear that all the criteria are not always met and that they can be interpreted differently.

OBTAINING CONSENT

Ethical dilemmas in terms of writing for publication focus primarily on obtaining consent. Patterson (1999) usefully explores how securing consent for publication generates further complex questions:

- A need that is unrelated to the client/patient is brought into the consulting room (and many analysts are uneasy about asking).
- The response is coloured by vicissitudes of the transferential relationship thus compromising a possibility of informed or meaningful consent.
- Reading the article is likely to affect the client/patient's view of treatment in unpredictable ways.
- With or without consent attempts to safeguard confidentiality usually through disguising the client/patient, delaying submission and publishing

in journals not thought to be widely read by the public can still pose uncomfortable questions.

Whilst Patterson is exploring psychoanalytic therapy (as is Rodriguez, 1992) these issues would appear to be of importance for therapeutic work in general.

CLARITY, STYLE, CONTENT: DIFFERENCE AND DISAPPOINTMENT

The further general area involves those studies (for example Piercy, 1996) of clarity, style and content as components of good writing. Matteson (1989) further suggests describing the standard organisation of a professional paper in common rather than scientific language as a way to make writing for publication both easier and better. Also as a further aid to clarity and getting published, Vacha-Haase *et al.* (2001) stress the importance of thoughtful recording of statistical results.

It would thus appear that the skills required for counsellors and psychotherapists and others in related professions have some similarities with, but are different to, those required in writing masters and doctoral dissertations (Calvert, 1991).

Finally in concluding this literature review, a word of warning from Crombach (1992) when you have successfully published and this is subsequently frequently cited, Crombach suggests that, unfortunately, a large citation count does not imply that an article's intended message has been widely understood or appreciated!

STEPS IN PRODUCING A PUBLICATION

If, for whatever reason, you decide to attempt to publish, you embark on an often lengthy process involving a number of questions, decisions and hurdles. We shall now consider how these might be negotiated.

MESSAGE OF THE PUBLICATION

One of the first questions that you will need to consider is what it is that you want to communicate in the publication. Your research may well have touched upon several themes and issues, and you should decide which of these will be the primary focus of your publication. The next decision is likely to be what type of publication might best enable you to say what you want. The option that you are most likely to pursue, and which will be the principal focus of this chapter, is a journal paper.

WRITING A JOURNAL PAPER

CHOICE OF JOURNAL

The first decision that you will need to make is to which journal you wish to submit the paper. The considerations which will enter into this decision will include the nature of the intended audience for your paper, the usual subject matter of the journal concerned, and its prestige. In relation to the first question, you will need to decide, for example, whether you primarily wish the paper to be read by other researchers within your specialist field or by a wider audience of clinicians, and also how international is your preferred readership.

In relation to the subject matter of the journal, you may do well to consider whether it has any particular theoretical or methodological bias, whether it primarily publishes reports of empirical investigations, or whether it is open to publishing more theoretical papers, literature reviews or case reports. It is likely to help your decision process if you look through back copies of the journal. You may also find that a journal is planning a special issue in your area of research, in which case you may wish to submit your paper for this issue. In regard to the journal's prestige, this may be judged by its 'citation index', providing an indication of the frequency with which papers from the journal are cited in other publications, and its 'impact factor' according to the Institute for Scientific Information. A website listing these indices is http://wok.mimas.ac.uk.

AUTHORSHIP

If your research has been collaborative, you will next need to make decisions about the authorship of the paper. If these issues are not addressed early in the process of preparing a publication, unfortunate misunderstandings may ensue. Firstly, there is the difficult question of who is listed as an author as opposed, for example, to merely receiving an acknowledgement in the paper. In the past, there was sometimes a tendency for lists of authors to be over-inclusive so that if you were concerned about publishing or perishing you might be able to get your name on a paper, albeit as 61st author, by, for example, licking the stamps on envelopes to research participants. Nowadays, however, guidelines are more stringent and authorship is reserved for those who have made a significant contribution to a particular study (International Committee of Medical Journal Editors, 1988). As stated in the *Publication Manual of the American Psychological Association* (1994),

Authorship is reserved for persons who receive primary credit and hold primary responsibility for a published work. Authorship encompasses, therefore, not only those who do the actual writing but also those who have made substantial scientific contributions to a study. Substantial professional contributions may include formulating the problem or hypothesis, structuring the experimental design, organizing and conducting the statistical analysis, interpreting the results, or writing a major portion of the paper. Those who so contribute are listed in the byline. Lesser contributions, which do not constitute authorship, may be acknowledged in a note. These contributions may include such supportive functions as designing or building the apparatus, suggesting or advising about the statistical analysis, collecting or entering the data, modifying or structuring a computer program, and recruiting participants or obtaining animals. Conducting routine observations or diagnoses for use in studies does not constitute authorship. Combination of these (and other) tasks, however, may justify authorship.

The second authorship consideration is the order in which authors' names appear on the paper. Alphabetical order may sometimes be used as a way of avoiding decisions about prioritisation, but while this is good for people whose name commences with the letter 'A' it is less so for those named 'Loewenthal' never mind 'Winter'. The more common solution is for the first author to be the person who made the major contribution to the paper, perhaps by writing it or being responsible for the idea on which the paper is based. Decisions may also need to be made about designation of responsibilities amongst the authors, for example for writing different sections of the paper. If this is done, it may need to be agreed that the first author is responsible for editing the various contributions in order, for example, to ensure consistency of style.

INTELLECTUAL PROPERTY

A related issue which it would be as well to address at this stage concerns the ownership of your study. For example, are all of the authors free to write reports on aspects of the study, perhaps for publication elsewhere, and if so what will be the authorship of these reports, and do all the authors have a right of veto on the paper? A major relevant consideration is that a condition for submission of a paper to most journals is that the work has not been published elsewhere. If you are writing a major journal paper but in the meantime one of your co-authors writes a report on the study and submits it for publication in another journal, this may jeopardise the publication of your first paper. One of the authors of this chapter discovered that this had occurred only when contacted by the copy editor of the second journal to check his contact details!

There may also be other intellectual property issues which you will need to address with your employer before embarking on preparing a publication. For example, although this is unlikely in the field of counselling and psychotherapy, is the publication likely to jeopardise any possibility of the patenting of an invention by your research team?

JOURNAL STYLE

Having decided on your preferred journal, your next step should be to obtain a copy of the journal's notes for contributors, which are usually printed inside the back cover or the journal web page. This will give you information on such matters as the maximum length of your paper, its structure, and the way in which the references should be presented. The notes will often refer to a more detailed style guide to which the journal adheres, and of which you would also be strongly advised to obtain a copy. For example, most American, and several British, psychological publications adhere to the guidelines presented in the *Publication Manual of the American Psychological Association*.

PREPARING TO WRITE

You should now be ready to write. To do this effectively, it will usually be necessary to give yourself protected space and time: good writing is rarely produced in a setting in which you are constantly interrupted. On the other hand, it is all too easy to prevaricate and to wait for ideal conditions in which to write, which is as likely to happen as if you were waiting for divine inspiration. Our suggestion would be to force yourself to break through the inertia, to sit at the computer and to start writing, remembering that in the word processing era there is no reason at all to expect perfection at the first attempt. It may also be necessary to set yourself deadlines. Once you do start writing, you (and your family and friends) may well find that you gather a momentum and that you become increasingly immersed in what you are writing and may find it hard to tear yourself away from it.

STRUCTURE OF THE PAPER

Before embarking on the paper itself, it is usually best to write an outline, setting out how you anticipate the paper will be structured in terms of headings, subheadings and the material which you are likely to consider under each of these. In an empirical paper, the main headings will generally be abstract, introduction, method, results and discussion. Let us consider each of these sections in turn, although you may not necessarily write them in this order.

The abstract is likely to be one of the last sections of the paper which you write but is perhaps the most important since, unfortunate though this may be, it will be the only part of the paper that many people will read. In many instances it will be only the abstract that is fully searchable on the publisher web page and it will be this section that could draw the reader in especially on pay-per-view websites and should be written with this in mind. It should be written as if it will be read by the non-specialist, and it should indicate all of the major ideas and findings presented in the paper while keeping strictly to the journal's word limit.

The introduction should explain concisely why you carried out the study and why you did so in the particular way which you chose. It should refer to the major relevant literature but should not aim to review in detail every study in the field. It may well end by listing the hypotheses which your study investigated. You should find that you will already have written much of this section of the paper, as well as much of the method section, in the protocol of the study which you prepared, for example, for your application for ethical approval.

The method section will generally have subheadings, for example for subsections describing the participants and the measures used in the study. It should include sufficient detail to allow the study to be replicated. For example, it is not sufficient to say that your participants were 40 schizophrenics and 40 clients with anxiety disorders, since you will need to provide details of how the participants were recruited, how their diagnoses were arrived at, what diagnostic subgroups they fell into, what treatment they were receiving, what was the duration of their symptoms and their demographic breakdown. If your measures include some which you have designed yourself, you will need to include details of their psychometric properties and a few sample items. If your study involves the use of raters, their inter-rater reliability will need to be reported. If it is a randomised controlled trial, it is likely to have to be presented according to 'CONSORT' standards (Moher *et al.*, 2001), which may be found on a website entitled www.consort-statment.org.

The results section should include not only the results of your statistical tests but also descriptive statistics, for example measures of the central tendency and variation on the variables which you have studied in each group of participants. Reports of statistical tests should not just present p values but should give the values of the statistics from which they are derived, and any other information (e.g. confidence intervals) which the journal requires. They should also indicate whether one or two tailed tests were used. If you include tables and figures, they should all be referred to in the text but should be fully comprehensible without any reference to the text and should not simply repeat information which is presented in the text. Although it may give you great satisfaction to produce elaborate figures from your new graphics package, you should remember that journal editors do not like too many tables or figures since they are expensive to reproduce and take up considerable space. Also check the publication details of your chosen journal – if your chosen journal is only published in black and white, colour figures will need to be redrawn or will lose their effect in greyscale so this should be borne in mind. Journal editors have sometimes appeared to be prejudiced against reporting the results of qualitative research, partly because they have not known by what criteria to assess such research. Qualitative researchers have therefore taken the initiative to produce such guidelines (Elliott *et al.*, 1999), which you would be well advised to read before preparing a qualitative paper.

The discussion should not just restate your results but should discuss them. It should not be over-speculative and should not waste space in, for example, discussing the possible implications of a difference between groups which has fallen just short of statistical significance. It should acknowledge the limitations of the study and, for example, if you have failed to obtain significant results should consider whether your sample sizes were adequate to provide sufficient power for your statistical tests. Although a lack of significant findings should not be a reason for non-publication of a paper, it is unfortunately the case that there is a publication bias against non-significant findings. This, incidentally, means that reviews of the literature which report a few significant findings in a particular area may provide inappropriate conclusions if there are so many unpublished non-significant findings that the significant findings may have been obtained only by chance. If you do obtain non-significant findings, and these cannot merely be explained by lack of statistical power, it is therefore as important to attempt to publish them as it is to attempt to publish significant findings.

The references should be complete and presented accurately in accordance with the style adopted by the particular journal. This can now be facilitated by the use of reference manager software. It is worth making a precise record of every reference that you come across while the study is in progress since it can be very tedious when you are writing the paper to have to search out information on references which you have not fully recorded previously. For example, you should bear in mind that many journals, when you refer to a book chapter, will require you to indicate the page numbers of that chapter. Also, when you give a quote in the text, you will be required to give the page number of the quote.

Finally, you should give careful thought to the title of the paper. This should combine being concise with accurately reflecting the contents of the paper. If, in addition, it is able to catch the reader's attention, this is a useful bonus.

Your paper is likely to go through several drafts before it is ready to be submitted for publication, but when you have produced your final draft do read it through very carefully and try to persuade someone else to do so as well.

SUBMISSION

When you are satisfied with what you have produced, you may then submit it and sit back for a few months to await the verdict. For most respectable journals, the process which will be followed is that the paper will be sent out for peer review by two or three referees, who may be experts on different areas of relevance to it. For example, one reviewer may be very familiar with your particular field of research while another may be an expert on statistics. Although the review process will generally be blind, in that the authors' names will be removed from the paper before it is sent to referees, it is sometimes all too easy for a referee to pick up clues as to the identity of a paper's authors. If half of the reference list consists of publications by a particular individual, you can make a fair guess that the individual is one of the authors of the paper. The referee will be given a certain length of time, generally a month, to return their review, which generally, as well as a detailed report on the paper, will include ratings on various dimensions as well as an overall recommendation.

The questions which the referees are likely to attempt to answer in reviewing a paper are as follows:

> Is the topic appropriate for the journal to which the manuscript is submitted?
> Is the introduction clear and complete?
> Does the statement of purpose adequately and logically orient the reader?
> Is the literature adequately reviewed?
> Are the citations appropriate and complete?
> Is the research question clearly identified, and is the hypothesis explicit?
> Are the conceptualisation and rationale perfectly clear?
> Is the method adequately described? In other words, can the study be replicated from the description provided in the paper?
> If observers were used to assess variables, is the interobserver reliability reported?
> Are the techniques of data analysis appropriate, and is the analysis clear? Are the assumptions underlying the statistical procedures clearly met by the data to which they are applied?
> Are the results and conclusions unambiguous, valid, and meaningful?
> Is the discussion thorough? Does it stick to the point and confine itself to what can be concluded from the significant findings of the study?
> Is the paper concise?
> Is the manuscript prepared according to the style guide?
> (Bartol, 1981)

It is worth remembering when preparing your paper that referees are not paid for the service which they provide, that they will be likely to be preparing their review on top of their normal work duties, which normally means in the evenings or weekends, and that a careful review is likely to take at least half a day of the reviewer's time. Many is the time when each of the authors of this chapter has, for example, sat on a hotel balcony on holiday trying to review a paper and wondering why we are doing this, and such reactions are particularly likely if a paper has been carelessly prepared.

While occasionally one reads a gem of a paper, which is clearly a major contribution to knowledge and a privilege to review, an unfortunate number of submitted papers are extremely sloppy stylistically, if not also in their content. Papers are often submitted with no attention at all to the journal's style guide, giving the impression that the author is too arrogant to bother themself with such trivialities, or they may be littered with misspellings or grammatical errors. While this may not necessarily mean that there is not something of value hidden beneath a shoddy presentation, the reviewer may not have the patience to find this. Papers are also often written which are full of repetition and verbiage and which say in 20 pages what might be said in two pages. To write a short paper is generally a much harder task than to write a long one: as George Bernard Shaw once wrote, borrowing from a 17th century letter by Pascal (2004), 'I am sorry this letter is so long, I did not have the time to write a shorter one'.

Papers may also be submitted which assume that the reader is as familiar with the area as is the author and which therefore do not bother to explain the concepts and procedures employed. An irritating variation on this theme is the paper which is littered with abbreviations, often with no explanation of what they mean. A paper which states that it is examining whether CBT, CAT or PCP is the most appropriate treatment for OCD is unlikely to be received sympathetically by a reviewer. Finally, one occasionally receives a paper in which the author has clearly not checked the content: for example, one of us recently reviewed a paper in which the author discussed and provided a convincing rationale for a difference between two groups on a particular measure but failed to notice that the difference which he in fact found was in completely the opposite direction to the one which he was discussing!

Figure 12.1 presents some dos and don'ts in writing a paper if it is to stand a fair chance of acceptance.

THE EDITOR'S VERDICT

When the editor receives the referees' reports, you will be sent these together with the editor's decision. This will be either that the paper is accepted without alteration, that it is accepted subject to various amendments, that it requires extensive revision and will then have to be sent out to review again, that it can be resubmitted as a one- or two-page brief report, or that it is rejected. If it is felt to be more appropriate for another journal, the editor may suggest some alternatives. Some editors, with clear ideas of what constitutes a good paper, may convey this in their letter of disposition. As stated by one editor,

> A paper is a communication of facts and ideas, not of feeling. It is to help the reader's intellectual functions, not to generate emotions or provide mystical insights. It is philosophy rather than literature or art. Therefore, to do its work

Figure 12.1   Dos and don'ts in writing a paper

DOS
- select the most appropriate journal;
- make explicit agreements with your colleagues about authorship;
- set deadlines;
- adhere slavishly to the journal's notes to contributors and style guide;
- write grammatically;
- avoid abbreviations – but if you have to use them, define them;
- assume a relatively naïve reader and put yourself in their shoes;
- give sufficient details of the method for the study to be replicated;
- make sure that you've chosen the correct statistical tests;
- provide necessary detail in the Results section (e.g. measures of central tendency and variation);
- discuss the limitations of the study;
- double check that your conclusions are justified by the results;
- cite references appropriately;
- read (and ask a colleague to read) the paper before submission;
- if English is not your first language, ask a colleague for whom it is to read the paper;
- read your proofs carefully.

DON'TS
- prevaricate;
- submit a paper the contents of which you've already submitted elsewhere;
- produce five papers on the basis of a study which has considered the correlation between two variables;
- include irrelevant material;
- say in ten sentences what you could say in one;
- assume that the editor and referees will find the study as fascinating as you do;
- be tempted to use your new graphics package when you've already presented the same information in a table;
- present material in the introduction which should be in the method, in the results which should be in the discussion, etc.
- be over-speculative;
- regard rejection or suggested amendment as a narcissistic blow – and another opportunity to prevaricate;
- submit the paper to another journal without modifying it accordingly.

efficiently, it must have clarity of thought, simple expression and a logical sequence in its presentation, and avoid repetition and fine phrases. A paper is about something, it has a subject and a point of view. That subject may be the answer to a question, and experiments or clinical observations may be made to find the answer, or it may be an hypothesis or the critique of an idea or a method. The summary of the paper should indicate what the essential subject and aim of the paper is, and whatever it is the author must make sure that he keeps to the point of his subject and does not wander off reporting irrelevant data or speculation ... The Editor views everything in three ways. He is part administrator, part reader's friend, and part poet (Crammer, 1978).

You may well feel, after writing a paper on a study in which you have been immersed for many years, that you have produced a fascinating and ground-breaking contribution to the literature. It may then come as a major narcissistic blow when you open the editor's letter and find that he or she does not share this view. However, you should remember that most prestigious journals have a high rejection rate (for example, a median rate of about 70 per cent for British Psychological Society journals). It is most unlikely that your paper will be accepted outright and therefore you should feel that you have done well if it is accepted subject to amendments. We would suggest, therefore, that if this is the verdict you should forget any indignation which you may feel about the referees' comments and at the earliest opportunity you should start work on making the amendments. If there is inertia in starting work on your paper in the first place, there is often even more inertia in going back to something which you have written and reworking it.

If the verdict is major revision and resubmission, you may wish to decide whether you prefer to submit the paper to an alternative journal in the hope that they will accept it with less revision. However, if you do decide to revise, you should take seriously all the points raised by the reviewers. In your letter accompanying the resubmitted paper, you should indicate how each of these points has been addressed. If you strongly disagree with any of these points and decide not to amend the paper accordingly, you should indicate in your letter the reasons for your disagreement. Reviewers, just like authors, can occasionally be careless and it is not unknown for a reviewer's criticism to be based on a misreading of the paper.

If the paper has been rejected, you will need to consider whether the reviewers have identified fatal flaws in it, for example in the design of your study. If they have not, you may decide to submit it to another journal but if you do so be sure to present it in a form appropriate to that journal's style rather than just sending it off without any amendment.

After your paper has been accepted, there will be a delay of up to a year before it is published. During this time, you will receive the proofs. Do check these carefully, and reckon on this taking several hours. To do so use standard symbols for correcting proofs, and do not use this as an opportunity to make late changes to the paper. The paper will have been read by a copy editor, who may occasionally have changed your wording in the interests of what they consider greater clarity or better grammar. You need to remember, though, that copy editors are unlikely to be familiar with your area of research and so you should check carefully that the changes which they have made have not altered the sense of your paper.

OTHER PUBLICATION OUTLETS

BOOK

If you have a lot to say, are in no great rush to say it, and are looking to fill up your evenings and weekends for the next few years, you might consider writing a book. In this case, your first step will be to write a proposal indicating why the book is necessary and outlining its content, including the proposed list of chapters and, ideally, one or two sample chapters. You would then select a publisher on the basis of such factors as their prestige, whether they have a publication record in the area concerned, and their current publication policy. To give one example, Wiley used to publish a large number of paperbacks in the field of psychology and psychotherapy with an intended market of students, academics and clinicians. However, its policy has recently changed, and it is now primarily interested in the publication of large handbooks aimed at the library market.

Having sent your proposal to a publisher, you can then sit back and wait, often for a very considerable time, while the proposal is sent out to reviewers and their reports considered by the editorial board. Most likely they will reject it, in which case you will need to start the whole process again with another publisher. During this period, it may help you to persevere if you remember how many famous books initially received a string of rejection notices from publishers.

EDITED BOOK

One variation on the book theme is to edit a book. This may be a particularly attractive option if you know a number of colleagues who are working in a certain field and might be inveigled into writing chapters. However, it can be very frustrating, and can lead to the end of some perfect friendships, if your potential contributors do not come up with the goods by their deadline or if what they produce simply is not good enough.

BOOK CHAPTER

Another option, and one for which you are likely to receive invitations when your own work becomes more widely known, is to write chapters for other people's edited books. It is also relatively common, particularly in these days of desktop publishing, for the organisers of professional conferences to produce books of selected papers from their conferences. However, it is worth remembering that the readership for such books is often not very extensive.

NEWSLETTER ARTICLE

Your work can also be published in a newsletter, for example of a professional society or a special interest group in your field. With this option, however, it will be unlikely to reach a wider readership.

INTERNET OPTIONS

The internet has opened up a range of new options for the dissemination of one's work, including ejournals. While such options do guarantee a wide potential readership, they are not yet recognised by research assessment exercises.

PUBLICATION

Maybe 2 years after you started writing it and as many as 5 years after you embarked on your project, your paper will appear in print, you will receive a set of offprints if it is a journal paper, and you will be likely to start receiving correspondence from interested readers. You should then discover that it has been worth the effort, and you may even find yourself getting addicted to the whole process.

REFERENCES

American Psychological Association (1994) *Publication Manual of the American Psychological Association.* Washington, DC: American Psychological Association.

Bartol, K. M. (1981) Survey results from editorial board members: lethal and nonlethal errors. Paper presented at meeting of American Psychological Association, Los Angeles.

Calvert, P. (1991) Writing skills. In G. Allan and C. Skinner (eds) *Handbook for Research Students in the Social Sciences.* Oxford, England: Falmer Press/Taylor & Francis, pp. 96–106.

Casanave, C. and Vandrick, S. (2003) *Writing for Scholarly Publication: Behind the Scenes in Language Education.* Mahway, NJ: Lawrence Erlbaum Associates.

Cottone, R. and Wolf, A. (1984) Writing for publication: a summary of the publication manual of the American Psychological Association, Third Edition. *Journal of Applied Rehabilitation Counseling*, Spr, 15 (1), 5–8.

Clarkson, P. (2000) *Ethics: Working with Ethical and Moral Dilemmas in Psychotherapy.* London: Whurr Publishers.

Crammer, J. L. (1978) How to get your paper published. *Bulletin of the Royal College of Psychiatrists*, 2, 112–113.

Crombach, L. (1992) Four psychological bulletin articles in perspective. *Psychological Bulletin*, Nov, 112 (3), 389–392.

Dorn, F., Kerr, B., Miller, M. and Watkins, C. (1986) Breaking into print: guidelines for mental health counsellors. *American Mental Health Counselors Association Journal*, July; 8 (3), 122–131.

Dies, R. (1993) Writing for publication: overcoming common obstacles. *International Journal of Group Psychotherapy*, Apr; 43 (2), 243–249.

Elliott, R., Fischer, C. T. and Rennie, D. L. (1999) Evolving guidelines for publication of qualitative research studies in psychology and related fields. *British Journal of Clinical Psychology*, 38, 215–30.

International Committee of Medical Journal Editors (1988). Uniform requirements for manuscripts submitted to biomedical journals. *British Medical Journal*, 296, 401–405.

Mattesson, M. (1989) Preparing a manuscript for publication. *Occupational Therapy in Mental Health*, Win; 7 (4), 69–79.

Moher, D., Schulz, K. F. and Altman, D. G. (2001) The CONSORT statement: revised recommendations for improving the quality of reports of parallel group randomized trials. *Annals of Internal Medicine*, 134, 657–662.

Ogren, H. (1998) From creative idea to creative product: a heuristically oriented case study. *Dissertation Abstracts International: Section B: The Sciences and Engineering*, May; 58 (11-B), 6253.

Ono, H., Phillips, K. and Leneman, M. (1996) Content of an abstract: de jure and de facto. *American Psychologist*, Dec; 51 (12), 1388–1340.

Pascal, D. (2004) *The Provincial Letters*. Whitefish, Montana: Kessinger.

Patterson, A. (1999) The publication of case studies and confidentiality – an ethical predicament. *Psychiatric Bulletin*, Sep; 23 (9), 562–562.

Piercy, F., Sprenkle, D. and Daniel, S. (1996) Teaching professional writing to family therapists: three approaches. *Journal of Marital and Family Therapy*, Apr; 22 (2), 163–179.

Rodoriguez, L. (1992) Incomoda el inconcienete?/Is the unconscious disturbing?, *Revisita Uruguaya de Psicoanalisis*, 76, 171–177.

Stuadt, M., Dulmus C. and Bennett, G. (2003) Facilitating writing by practitioners: survey of practitioners who have published. *Social Work*, Jan; 48 (1), 75–83.

Vacha-Haase, T. (2001) Statistical significance should not be considered one of life's guarantees: Effect sizes are needed. *Educational Psychological Measurement*, Apr; 61 (2), 219–224.

Weiss, L. (1989) *The Health Professionals Guide to Writing for Publication*. Springfield, IL: Charles C. Thomas.

13   STRESS AND BURNOUT

Kasia Szymanska

As therapists we deal with other people's stress on a regular basis. This includes student stress, supervisee stress, client stress and peer stress. While our training and experience has equipped us with the skills and tools to support others, to be successful in our work we need to practise what we preach, be our own 'stress managers', and apply the techniques we so readily dispense to others and the qualities we value such as empathy and nurturance to our own problems, whether they are professional, personal or a combination of both.

So, as therapists how do we deal with our own stresses? In my experience therapists can tend to push aside their own stress, postpone dealing with it or disregard it altogether. Paradoxically we embrace client fallibility whilst overlooking or disregarding our own fallibility, the clients' mental health problems always come first! The reasons why therapists need to maintain a demeanour of psychological robustness are complex and rooted in cultural assumptions, individual personality traits and an intrinsic need to retain professional respect and integrity. However, these reasons do not protect us from stress; we need to develop a healthy attitude to self-care in order to manage our work in ethical and safe manner which benefits clients, colleagues and students.

In this chapter I will address the issue of therapist stress and burnout from both a cognitive behavioural and multimodal perspective with a greater emphasis on the stresses of client work. First, I will focus on the signs of stress and burnout, second the common factors that can contribute to both before going onto focus on strategies to reduce stress.

WHAT IS STRESS AND BURNOUT?

There are many definitions of stress, for example, Lazarus and Folkman (1984) state that, 'Stress results from an imbalance between demands and resources', while Gregson and Looker (1996) provide a more comprehensive definition which takes into account physiological and behavioural responses and their interface with the environment. They write that stress

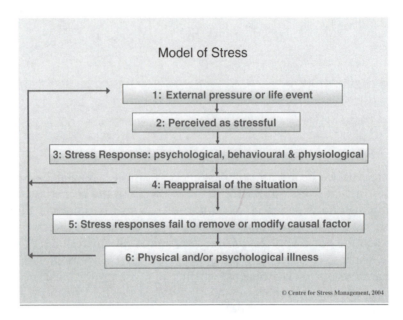

Figure 13.1   Model of stress ((© Palmer and Strickland, 1996) Published with the kind permission of Stephen Palmer and Linda Strickland)

is, 'a whole-body-and-mind interactive response to a demand or a pressure (stressor)'.

An instructive staged model highlighting the process of stress acquisition encompassing Gregson's and Looker's definition is shown in Figure 13.1 (adapted from Palmer and Strickland, 1996). For example, a therapist who is a self-employed seeing clients and working as trainer from home needs a new computer (Stage 1, external pressure). On the basis that he is building up his private practice and training portfolio and as yet has not got any surplus cash to pay for the computer he perceives finding and buying a computer as an expensive and stressful experience (Stage 2). As the therapist tries to manage without a computer (going to the internet café to type up letters, notes and training material) he experiences moderate symptoms of stress (Stage 3). These symptoms include irritability, poor concentration, tension headaches and negative thinking, 'this is so unfair, why me'. In his endeavour to find a solution he agrees to take on more training work, to speed up the process, unfortunately this extra work requires more effort than anticipated, typing handouts and photocopying in combination with seeing clients leaves the therapist overworked and having to cancel some clients to make time for the deployment of the training (Stages 4 and 5), which ultimately leads to tiredness, poor sleeping and flu and an increase

Figure 13.2   Symptoms of stress (adapted from Cooper and Palmer, 2000)

PSYCHOLOGICAL
- Anxiety;
- Anger;
- Poor concentration;
- Low self-esteem;
- Depression;
- Guilt and shame;
- Mood swings.

BEHAVIOURAL
- Procrastination;
- Increase in alcohol and caffeine consumption;
- Disturbed sleeping patterns;
- Irritability;
- Poor time management;
- Increased absenteeism;
- Over-eating;
- Passive or aggressive behaviour.

PHYSIOLOGICAL
- Tension headaches and muscle tension;
- Palpitations;
- Skin complaints;
- Indigestion;
- Increase in illnesses;
- Racing heart;
- Asthma;
- Diarrhoea;
- Insomnia.

in negative thinking, 'How could I have being so stupid?', 'How can I treat clients when I can't even manage my own life?' (Stage 6) and a cycle of stress.

Some of the inherent symptoms of stress are outlined in Figure 13.2, and grouped under three headings psychological, behavioural and physiological symptoms. In addition, below are some signs you may recognise which are often associated with increased stress levels:

- increase in cynicism;
- psychological detachment;
- increase in self-doubt;
- perceiving you are a fraud and will be 'found out';

- shame;
- avoidance of clients, trainees and colleagues;
- omnipresent anxiety;
- blurred boundaries;
- over-empathising with client symptoms which mirror your own;
- denying you have a problem.

The end result of protracted stress is known as burnout. Kotler and Hazler (1997) aptly refer to it as 'rustout'. It is physical and psychological exhaustion, with four additional symptoms:

1. cognitive, affective, behavioural and physical distress;
2. decreased effectiveness;
3. reduction in motivation; and
4. dysfunctional behaviours and attitudes in the workplace.

Unlike other disorders it tends to be work related and more common in individuals with high expectations (Schaufeli, 1999). Furthermore Garden (1991) found that it was more common in 'feeling types' as opposed to 'thinking types', the latter being a prevalent characteristic of the therapeutic profession.

CAUSES OF STRESS LEADING TO BURNOUT

Some of the more common variables contributing to stress are described below:

1. (a) Organisational stressors within clinical settings. When Norcross and Guy (1989) conducted a small survey among seven 'master clinicians' pertaining to sources of stress in psychotherapy work, they identified ten stressors, the key stressors being time pressures, organisational politics, excessive workload and professional conflicts. Other stressors include responsibility for their clients' lives, too much paperwork, the monotony of the job and the struggle to manage their own emotions.
   (b) Organisational stressors within academic settings. The difficulties in academia include managing relationships with students, preparation of course material dealing with differences that arise with colleagues, developing and accrediting new courses, overcoming poor resources, e.g. a lack of video equipment and trying to keep on top of marking.
2. Managing difficult interactions with clients. These include working with clients who are actively suicidal and often clients with personality

issues such as borderline personality disorder traits, who can at times prove to be more demanding in the therapeutic relationship.

3. Dealing with personal issues. Significant stressors or stressors occurring over a prolonged period of time, such as relationship problems, illness and bereavement issues, can undermine therapeutic effectiveness. In addition knowing when to stop counselling and manage personal problems can be a pressure in itself.

4. Self-expectations. As therapists we can often place unrealistic demands on ourselves such as, 'I must be of help to all my clients', 'This client should be better by now' and 'I mustn't make any mistakes'.

5. Managing self-employment. Being self-employed can contribute feelings of being unsupported, a sense of isolation and strong economic concerns and ultimately impact on family life.

6. The processes of transference and counter transference. A classic example of transference is the client's infatuation with the practitioner and Leahy (2001) lists some common counter transference issues such as feeling uncomfortable if the client is sexually attractive, going over the therapeutic hour, problems in asking for money and managing polices and failing to take a full sexual history.

7. Knowing how to respond to the knowledge that other therapists maybe working in an unethical manner with their clients.

8. Coping with the same psychological problems that clients present with, e.g. depression and anorexia.

9. Managing dual roles, for example, in a rural area a therapist providing therapy for clients and working as policemen in the same area.

10. Managing multifaceted roles. A large number of therapists work in a variety of settings; while this can be deemed as good experience, it can also contribute to an increase in stress levels, having to juggle different roles and dealing with the stresses fundamental to every post.

The above list is by no means exhaustive and outlines only some of the more common variables associated with therapist stress. It is important to remember that it is a combination of variables that can lead to stress and over an extended period to feelings of tiredness, irritability, a lack of compassion, a sense of cynicism, feelings of helplessness and apathy.

STRATEGIES TO REDUCE STRESS

A proactive approach to stress is the only route to managing pressures. Therefore some suggestions for dealing with stressors are outlined below.

A SEVEN-STEP PROBLEM-SOLVING MODEL

Problem solving is widely applied within the cognitive behavioural arena. It is an empowering, researched staged model, which provides a structured and systematic pro forma to managing difficulties efficiently. The stages are desribed below.

STAGE 1: IDENTIFY THE PROBLEM

This stage quite simply involves clearly defining the problem which needs to be resolved.

STAGE 2: SELECT THE GOAL(S)

At this point use the acronym SMART to aid goal setting. Goals need to be Specific, Measurable, Achievable, Realistic and Time bound.

STAGE 3: EXPLORE OPTIONS

This involves brainstorming all the options on paper. The key here is to use your imagination to generate options whilst suspending judgement.

STAGE 4: CONSIDER THE CONSEQUENCES OF THE OPTIONS

At this stage, go through your list and discard unviable options, then consider which of the options left you could use to make a decision. Often if the decision is difficult, writing down the advantages and disadvantages of the options can be illuminating.

STAGE 5: MAKE A DECISION

At this stage make a decision using the options outlined.

STAGE 6: AGREE SPECIFIC ACTIONS

In this penultimate stage is it important to ensure all actions are explicit and to consider if there are any psychological blocks to undertaking the actions.

STAGE 7: EVALUATE ACTIONS

Evaluation can be scheduled for a specific date.

The above process can be undertaken on your own, however it may be helpful to do this in supervision or with a colleague who can offer support.

TRANSLATING SELF-DEFEATING THOUGHTS INTO SELF-HELPING THOUGHTS, WHICH SERVE TO EMPOWER OUR WORK AS OPPOSED TO HINDERING PROGRESS

As therapists we are not exempt from self-defeating thinking which heightens stress levels. Recognising our own capacity for self-defeating thinking in different scenarios and accompanying shifts in affect and possible physiological responses is the first step in the cognitive behavioural process used to evaluate and respond to self defeating thinking. Undertaking a cognitive behavioural evaluation of our own thinking is a healthy and effective way of managing stress and preventing burnout.

The first step is to identify and write down key self-defeating thoughts which can lead to emotional distress, such as:

- I must help all my clients, if I don't this means I'm failing as a therapist.
- I have to be respected by all my peers.
- I must give a perfect presentation to the students; otherwise they will think I'm not good at my job.
- If I don't perform well, then my contract will be cut.
- I must be there for my clients, at all times.
- If I don't get any more work, I'll be ruined financially, it will be awful.

Having written down the thoughts the next step is to evaluate the thoughts using Socratic questioning. For example, if you look at the first thought on the list, 'I must help all my clients, if you don't this means I'm failing as a therapist. Ask yourself the following questions:

- Where does it get me to think this way? (nowhere only stressed)
- Where is the evidence that I must help *all* my clients?

If you strongly believe that you must help all your clients, use the survey method, speak to at least five or more colleagues and ask them if they also hold the same belief. Do they believe that if they don't help all their clients they are failing?

Ask yourself what other factors contribute to client progress? For example what part does client motivation play? Make a list of the advantages and disadvantages of holding onto this belief. If, for example, your client was lawyer who also believed that he must win all his cases and help all his clients, how would you respond to him? Having weakened your conviction in the thought, write down a realistic/self-helping response, such as, ' I would like to help all my clients but that is impossible for lots of reasons and that certainly doesn't suggest 'I'm failing only that I'm human like all my colleagues'.

Other disputing strategies used in the Rational Emotive Behavioural arena (Neenan and Dryden, 2000) can also be helpful, these include logical, empirical and pragmatic disputing. Below is an example of strategies applied to the second self-defeating thought, 'I must be respected by my peers':

- Logical disputing: How does it logically follow that although you want to be respected by all your peers, you must be?
- Empirical disputing: Where is the evidence that the world must meet all your demands?
- Pragmatic disputing: Is this belief indispensable in your life? Will this belief help you reach your goal?

The key to this process of cognitive restructuring is practise, whenever you recognise a self-defeating thought write it down, dispute it and then write a response to it.

ESTABLISH A PROFESSIONAL SUPPORT NETWORK

We all need support, so talking to colleagues who are also working in the same field provides an opportunity for sharing personal and professional concerns, achievements, new developments and processing experiences. This is often easily achieved if we meet colleagues in our own work settings or at conferences and workshops or live within commuting distance from fellow professionals, however it is much harder for therapists working in isolated parts of the country or living abroad who are physically unable to meet colleagues on a regular basis. The answer here lies in telephone or email support, while therapists may miss the element of face-to-face discussion, the opportunity for sharing remains intact. Personally I have found that the support I get from my colleagues is invaluable and equally as important as formal supervision.

ENSURE YOU RECEIVE REGULAR SUPERVISION

Supervision is an integral part of working with clients, and a necessary yet often overlooked part of working in other arenas such as academia. However, finding a supervisor to oversee your client work can be an onerous task, the supervisor needs to be within commuting distance, preferably their theoretical orientation needs to match your own and if you are working with a specific population, your supervisor needs to have the training and experience to provide you with appropriate support. In addition, as many practitioners working within organisations (e.g. the NHS) are now assigned a supervisor who may also be their line manager, the issue of dual relationships may influence the supervisory relationship. A survey of cognitive behavioural psychotherapy supervision practices conducted by Townend, Iannetta and Freeston (2002) found that of the 170 therapists who returned their questionnaires, 57 had a dual-role relationship with their supervisors. Of these, ten respondents indicated that the relationship impacted on their ability to discuss their clinical performance or clinical problems with their supervisor. Clearly not feeling safe enough to discuss client or personal issues in the session can contribute to isolation and stress, if possible supervisees in this position may benefit from discussing these issues with peers or even finding additional external supervision.

Another adjunct to one-to-one work is peer supervision groups (internal to organisations or external), although these groups can have their own problems. Being honest about your personal problems and how they impact on your work can be hard when your peers are also your work colleagues, likewise expressing doubts about your own competency as practitioner can feel unsafe. Another option is suggested by Kottler and Hazler (1997) who suggest one-to-one peer supervision with a trusted partner to discuss not only client work but also other professional and personal issues such as managing counter transference issues in the supervisory relationship. They emphasise the following points:

1. Provide a factual outline of client case that is causing you the most problems.
2. State the client's behaviours that are causing you the most stress, e.g. not attending regularly and demanding psychological insight at the end of every session.
3. Describe how you feel as result of being with this client.
4. Ask for constructive feedback from your partner, taking into account your reaction to this client to assess why your progress with this client has been difficult.
5. Make a list of the strategies that you used unsuccessfully with this client.
6. Agree not to use any of the strategies that you have tried which have been unsuccessful.
7. Make a list of strategies, together with your partner, that you can use and put them into practice.

One area where supervision is often overlooked or discounted due to time constraints is within academic settings. In this setting it is not so much supervision as an opportunity to proactively manage difficulties as they arise, share opinions, get feedback and benefit from peer experience that is required.

DEVELOP YOUR OWN STRESS MANAGEMENT PLAN

Developing your own personalised stress management plan is a key factor in the management of personal stress and prevention of burnout. It is both motivational and therapeutic. A helpful pro forma is Lazarus's (1989) BASIC I.D. structure (see Palmer and Dryden, 1995, or Palmer, Cooper and Thomas, 2003, for in-depth application to stress counselling and management). Lazarus concluded that our personalities are composed of seven modalities, behaviour, affect, sensations, imagery, cognitions, interpersonal relationships and drugs/biology. The first letter from each of these modalities forms the acronym BASIC I.D., which can be utilised by practitioners to assess sources of stress and develop strategies to target it. Table 13.1 provides an example of how a practitioner could use the BASIC I.D. to manage stress resulting from overwork.

Table 13.1 Modality Profile

Modality	Modality problems	Proposed intervention	Review of interventions
Behaviour	Increase in client load leading to greater alcohol consumption.	Reduce to two pub measures of wine every other day.	Review at the end of the month.
		Reduce client load by two people starting from next month.	Review in 2 months.
Affect	Tiredness and apathy towards work.	Challenge self-defeating cognitions leading to apathy.	Review at the end of the month.
Sensations	Tension in my back. Poor concentration.	Massage once a month.	Review in 3 months.
		Meditate for 3 mins every other day.	Review at the end of the month.
Imagery	Body tension.	Use relaxation imagery every third day.	Review at the end of the month.
Cognitions	Write down unhelpful thoughts.	Challenge unhelpful thought.	Review at the end of the month.
Interpersonal	Little contact with other therapists.	Arrange telephone contact once every 2 weeks and meet up once a month.	Review in 2 months.
Drugs/biology	Poor circulation.	Start swimming once a week.	Review at the end of the month.

CONCLUSION

Stress is an inevitable yet unwanted component of all professions; the therapeutic arena is no exception. To discount our own stress is naïve, contrary to personal growth and potentially damaging to clients and our working relationship with colleagues. We must maintain a 'hands-on' approach to our own stress; embrace the challenge of stress in order to provide a professional service to clients, students alike.

REFERENCES

Cooper, C. L. and Palmer, S. (2000) *Conquer Your Stress*. London: CIPD.

Gregson, O. and Looker, T. (1996) The biological basis of stress management. In S. Palmer and W. Dryden (eds) *Stress Management and Counselling*. London: Casell.

Garden, A. M. (1991) The purpose of burnout: a Jungian interpretation. *Journal of Social Behavior and Personality*, 6, 73–93.

Kotler, J. A. and Hazler, R. J. (1997) *What You Never Learned in Graduate School: A Survival Guide for Therapists*. New York: Norton.

Lazarus, A. A. (1989) *The Practice of Multimodal Therapy: Systematic, Comprehensive, and Effective Psychotherapy*. Balitmore: John Hopkins University Press.

Lazarus, R. and Folkman, S. (1984) *Stress, Appraisal and Coping*. New York: Springer.

Leahy, R. L. (2001) *Overcoming Resistance in Cognitive Therapy*. New York: Guilford Press.

Neenan, M. and Dryden, W. (2000) *Essential Rational Emotive Behaviour Therapy*. London: Whurr.

Norcross, J. C. and Guy, J. D. (1989) Ten therapists: the process of becoming and being. In W. Dryden and L. Spurling (eds) *On Becoming a Psychotherapist*. London: Routledge.

Palmer, S. and Strickland, L. (1996) *Stress Management: A Quick Guide*. Dunstable: Folens.

Palmer, S. and Dryden, W. (1995) *Counselling for Stress Problems*. London: Sage.

Palmer, S., Cooper, C. and Thomas, K. (2003) *Creating a Balance: Managing Stress*. London: British Library.

Schaufeli, W. (1999) Burnout. In J. Firth-Cozens and R. L. Payne (eds) *Stress in Health Professionals*. Chichester: Wiley.

Townend, M., Iannetta, L. and Freeston, M. H. (2002) Clinical supervision in practice: a survey of UK cognitive behavioural psychotherapists accredited by the BABCP. *Behavioural and Cognitive Psychotherapy*, 30, 485–500.

APPENDIX A: SUGGESTED FURTHER READING

LEGAL AND ETHICAL ISSUES

Bond, T. (2000) *Standards and Ethics for Counselling in Action*, Sage Publications: London.

British Association for Counselling and Psychotherapy, *Ethical Framework for Good Practice in Counselling and Psychotherapy*, British Association for Counselling and Psychotherapy: Warwickshire.

Clayton, P. (2001) *Law for the Small Business*, Business Enterprise Guides, Kogan Page: London.

Jenkins, P. (1997) *Counselling, Psychotherapy and the Law*, Sage Publications: London.

Jenkins, P. (2002) *Legal Issues in Counselling and Psychotherapy*, Sage Publications: London.

SUPERVISION

Carroll, M. (1996) *Counselling Supervision: Theory, Skills and Practice*, Cassell: London.

Inskipp, F. and Procter, B. (1994) *Making the Most of Supervision*, Cascade Publications: Twickenham.

PROFESSIONAL ISSUES

Bongar, B., Berman, A., Maris, R., Silverman, M., Harris, E. and Packman, W. (1998) *Risk Management with Suicidal Patients*, The Guilford Press: New York.

Daines, B., Gask, L. and Usherwood, T. (1997) *Medical and Psychiatric Issues for Counsellors*, Sage Publications: London.

Palmer, S. and McMahon, G. (1997) *Client Assessment*, Sage Publications: London.

Sills, C. (1997) *Contracts in Counselling*, Sage Publications: London.

Wilkins, P. (1997) *Personal and Professional Development for Counsellors*, Sage Publications: London.

PRIVATE PRACTICE

Clark, J. (2002) *Freelance Counselling and Psychotherapy*, Brunner-Routledge: London.

McMahon, G., Palmer, S. and Wilding, C. (2005) *The Essential Skills for Setting Up a Counselling and Psychotherapy Practice*, Routledge: London.

BUSINESS ISSUES

Harold, S. A. (2002) *Marketing for Complementary Therapists*, How to Books: Oxford.

APPENDIX B: USEFUL ORGANISATIONS

OFFICIAL ORGANISATIONS

Data Protection Registrar
Wycliffe House
Water Lane
Wilmslow
Cheshire
SK9 5AF
01625 545 745 (enquiries)
01625 535 711 (admin)
www.dataprotection.gov.uk

INSURANCE COMPANIES

Howden Professionals
1200 Centuary Way
Thorpe Park Business Park
Colton
Leeds
LS15 8ZA
0113 251 5011
www.howdenpro.com

Towergate Professional Risks
Towergate House
Five Airport West
Lancaster Way
Yeadon, Leeds
West Yorkshire
LS19 7ZA
0113 294 4000
www.towergateprofessionalrisks.co.uk/

PROFESSIONAL ORGANISATIONS

Association for Coaching
66 Church Road
London
W7 1LB
www.associationforcoaching.com

British Association for Counselling and Psychotherapy (BACP)
1 Regent Place
Rugby
Warwickshire
CV21 2PJ
0870 443 5252
www.bacp.co.uk

British Psychological Society (BPS)
St Andrew's House
48 Princess Road East
Leicester
LE1 7DR
01162 549 568
www.bps.org.uk

Institution of Occupational Safety and Health
Membership Department
The Grange
Highfield Drive
Wigston
Leicestershire
LE18 1NN, UK
www.iosh.co.uk/

United Kingdom Council for Psychotherapy (UKCP)
2nd Floor Edward House
2 Wakley Street
London EC1V 7LT
020 7014 9955
www.psychotherapy.org.uk

Confederation of Scottish Counselling Agencies (COSCA)
18 Viewfield Street

Stirling
FK8 1UA
www.cosca.org.uk/

Irish Association for Counselling and Therapy (IACT)
8 Cumberland Street
Dun Laoghaire
Co. Dublin
Eire
www.irish-counselling.ie/

TRAINING IN COACHING

Centre for Coaching
Broadway House
3 High Street
Bromley
BR1 1LF
Tel: +44 (0) 20 8228 1185
http://www.centreforcoaching.com

INDEX